re:viewing egypt

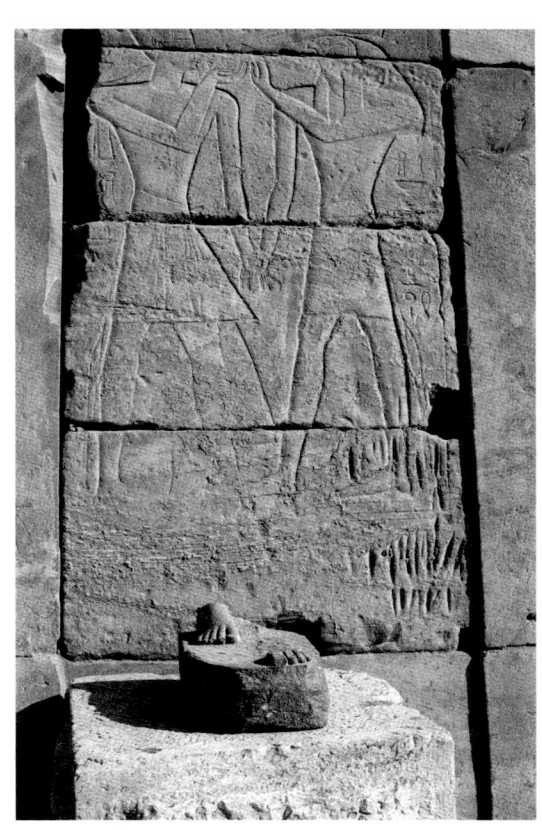

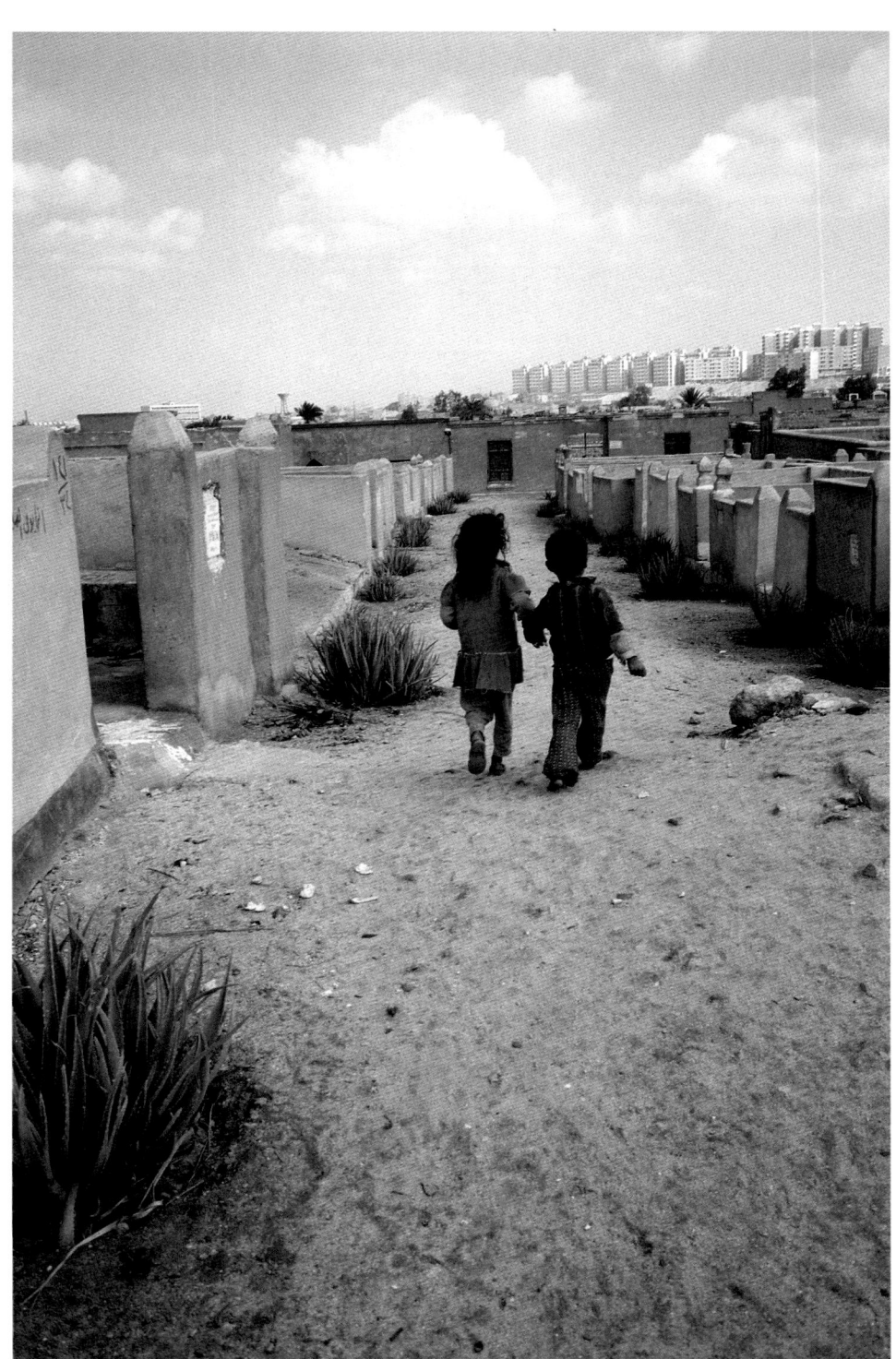

re:viewing egypt
IMAGE AND ECHO

Photographs by
Xavier Roy

Text by
Gamal al-Ghitani

Translated by
Humphrey Davies

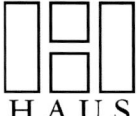

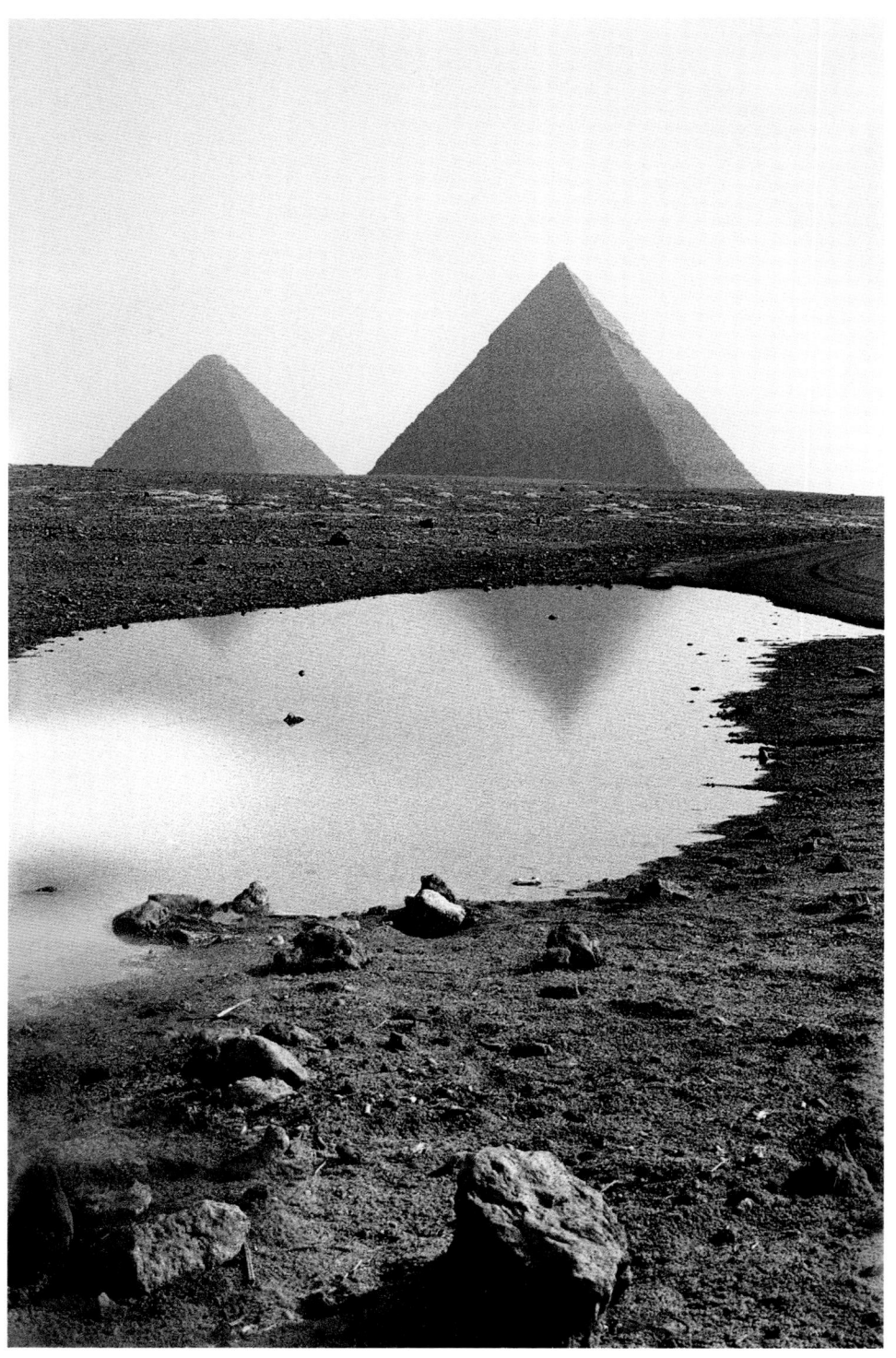

the duality of existence
origin and shadow

Gamal al-Ghitani

Shadow and origin, origin and shadow.
Two eyes, two openings in the nose.
Two hands, two feet.
Earth, water. Male, female. Sky, earth.

A name is uttered. There can be no signifying original without a name, and a name without original referent is nothing but motes of dust. This is the essence of the spirit of Egypt that Xavier Roy has captured, an essence he has come to know as it exists in its current vessels, which is to say, at the time of his visit. During his limited time in the country, using his piercing vision, he has penetrated to what is infinite in the Egyptian reality. In the deep vision are numerous elements, of which the most important is duality. Each element has a dual existence, even after its evanescence. A person dies. The body breaks down into its elements but may continue to seek existence through its name. This brings to mind one of the puzzling questions regarding Egypt's popular heritage, namely, which is the origin? The shadow or the original? Egyptians today practice many of the particularities of everyday life precisely as their ancient ancestors did.

The Egyptians devised the concept of eternity as a counter to the Nothing and considered the name an equivalent of existence, one that extended beyond it. Through the lens of his camera, the eyes of Xavier Roy have seen the invisible, observed the hidden, and the penetrating quality of his gaze takes me back to moments of my boyhood, of my days in Upper Egypt and Gamaliya.

The bright forenoon of my childhood in Cairo's ancient heart. I sit on the roof beside my mother. It is winter. We seek the warmth of the distant sun, whose rays come through the gaps in the clouds, form a pyramid, and descend in clearly visible angled lines toward the earth. A pyramid of light, falling from the high empty spaces. The Egyptian created its physical equivalent, a pyramid of stone ascending from earth to sky. Which then is the origin? The eternal light or the stone? Night or day? Where did this inspired shape come from? From the triangle? From that opening in the clouds? Or from the ascent of the stone toward the highest point, where pinnacle and void exist together, where temporal existence evanesces and what remains begins? I try to imagine that pyramid of light through the eyes of an ancient Egyptian on a bank of the Nile, the Nile which Xavier Roy has grasped is the spring and the origin. In the past, the city was less crowded than it is now. The sky was closer. In the autumn, in winter, colors flooded the sky. The shadows on the ground, on the sparkling Nile, took on new shapes, and the pyramids of light penetrated the gaps in the clouds. The pyramid, that inspired form, is the abridgment of abridgment.

which egypt?

The discovery of agriculture provided the opportunity for profound, calm contemplation, and from this profound contemplation the spiritual formation of humankind, the coming to maturity of a fundamental view of life, all of whose subsequent manifestations in the form of beliefs I consider to be no more than copies taken from the original, began, as humans, contemplating, waiting for their crops to grow, or for the first drop in the river's flood, grasped the connection between their limited existence and infinity, the vast universe, the endless sky, the movement of the celestial bodies—the link between all these and the life of a single human being, bracketed as it is by birth and death. It is the same course as that run by the sun, the source of heat and light, the same course run by the river into which the first drop of water falls, heralding the flood that, little by little, will arrive, not coming to take them unawares, not arriving at one go, but beginning as a drop of water, that same drop with which begin river, sea, and all the oceans of the world.

It is gradation. It is unhurried change. And with the gradation there is ascent, an ascent that reflects itself in building. The 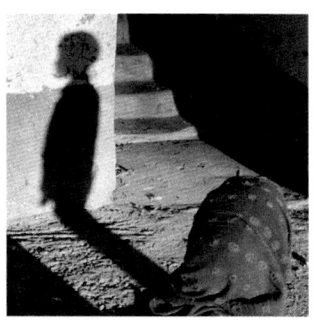 pyramid rises higher, little by little. It starts on the surface of the earth. Then the gradual movement progresses toward the point at which all angles meet, and every element. At its culmination, the building is complete, the form complete. It is also the void, the end. At the summit of the pyramid is that point where nothing brings all things into being, precisely as the first drop of water contains the entire river, the whole flood. Without the drop there would be no river, no sea, and without it there would be no point.

It is gradation. Humankind observes it in the rising—unhurried at first, then faster—of the sun, which seems so settled at its starting point on the horizon that at first one might think it would remain there forever. The movement of the shadow, however, gives notice of the movement of the universe. From this came the idea of the obelisk. It is a gesture in stone to what lies above, to the center. The sky is circular, and every circle has a center. The circle is the most precise expression of the universe because it is a perfect form, with neither beginning nor end, one that may be entered from any point. Thus beginning and end become complicit with each other, for any point may be both the circle's beginning and its end. It is life. It is time. Arrival and departure occur at one and the same moment. The circle is a symbol of both the beginning and the end, one numbered among the ancient Egyptian symbols, in their language, in the components of the alphabet, on the facades of the temples. From it sprout the two beating wings, around it are two hands, which are the driving force, the hidden source of the movement behind the course of the celestial bodies. The circle is a basic element in Egyptian decoration, whether Coptic, Islamic, or Jewish. In the mosques built in Egypt by the Mamluks, and especially those in which the culture has returned, with the restoration of stability and creativity, to its distant roots, I behold the sun, depicted in the same color of red granite. The source of origin is the same, the rock and the stone are the very same rock and stone. At one period, the symbol shows its true face, at another it is transformed into a code. The circle looks down at me from the dome of Sultan Hasan (thirteenth century CE). In the school and *khanqah* of Barquq, in mosques, *kuttab*s, and temples we find the circle and its allusions to the universe.

The obelisk points toward the center, the center of the circle, to the hidden driving forces. It is the architectural and artistic point of reference for the steeple of the church and the minaret of the mosque. In its upward trajectory it is transformed into a little pyramid that also ends in a point. All things proceed toward nothingness, to the eternal, only to return once more. Sunrise, sunset, flood that begins with a drop and ends in drought.

The flowing gradation that bears witness to movement, to the surplus that will turn into dearth, is one of the most important features of the Egyptian view of life. Architecture has no equal as a repository for memory. At the beginning, it is the response to the factors of climate and environment. Later, the spiritual and intellectual view of life adds its insights. No Egyptian temple can be approached suddenly. It must be approached via a slow rise on broad, barely noticed, steps or a paved way that ascends toward the entrance. This is what we find at the temple of Seti I at Abydos, the temple of Deir al-Bahari, at the temple of Seti I at Luxor, and at the temple of Ramesses II. All the temples are based on gradation. Gradation in the way that leads up to them, in the awe-inspiring, towering entrance that leads to a spacious hall whose roof is pierced by openings that link earth and sky, link the limited, the enframed, to the infinite, and, at the same time, act as skylights. The next hall is narrower and darker, only the elite may enter it—and so it continues until we enter the Holy of Holies, where the statue of the god is to be found and which only the chief priest and the king may enter. The Holy of Holies became in the church the altar, in the synagogue the ark, in the mosque the prayer niche. Such too is the case with the pyramids, in that no matter how large or massive they may be, they narrow as they grow taller and end at a point. The temple, likewise, in its expansive spread over the earth, proceeds in stages that culminate at the Holy of Holies. Even the decorative elements follow the principle of gradation. The lotus flowers in the first courtyard are open, in the middle hall their petals draw closer to one another, and finally, when we reach the final stage, we find that they are tightly closed.

Nothing is born complete and nothing comes into existence of a sudden. There has to be preparation. There has to be a signal. Does not the light arise indistinctly at its point of origin, before the sun's disc appears? Does not a little of it remain after the sun has set? There is gradation in the life of man, in his steps, in time. Existence proceeds in stages, is a journey. The beginning is from nothing and the end is at the point where nothing is. The pyramid form is expressive of this view of life. It is the construct that starts from a broad base and is oriented to the four directions. Then, in its sloping ascent, it diminishes until the entire form ends at that point where all things disappear and all begin. Gradation and duality. Nothing exists without its opposite, its antithesis. These two observations are the fruit of contemplation—the 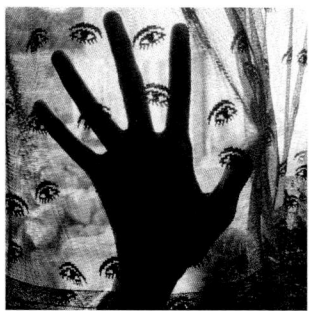 longest and deepest process of contemplation, perhaps, in the journey of humankind.

Among these dualities are the twin processes of demolition and construction. This is why the Egyptians started building. The awareness that, in keeping with the movement of the universe, things cease to exist is hard to accept. Each extinction, however, generates its opposite and creates something new. Thus they rejected the idea of death, rejected the idea of eternal annihilation, and instead conceived the idea of the voyage of the sun, from setting to rebirth. They conceived the idea of the dead existing in another world, one to be regarded as an extension of tangible existence. In so doing, the Egyptians, out of love for and attachment to this world, invented the next. What preoccupied them was how to survive in nonexistence. The methods they adopted were numerous, foremost among them building, the building of a tomb containing the symbols of existence and the items of daily life that would be linked to both the cardinal and the intermediate points of the compass. The tomb was a way station between two worlds, between two existences. Thus the Egyptian was, and still is, more concerned with his eternal resting place than with the house he occupies in this lower world. Tombs still have their special places in the cities, always on the margins, a parallel text. I have often contemplated the tombs of the Copts, of the Muslims, of the Jews, with their allotted space and number, in Cairo and in Alexandria—the calm, the careful planning of the streets. Some of these mausolea are treasures of architecture. Observe the care given to the writing of the name, preceded by the title of, and sometimes by the position previously occupied by, the departed. There is a silent communion between those who still strive in this lower world and the departed, some of the latter writing quite openly on their tombs that they seek from the living their prayers for mercy on their souls, that they should think well of them, and that they should take them as lessons to be learned from, for they themselves are destined for the same resting place. I contemplate what is written on the grave markers within the tombs—verses from the Noble Qur'an, the Bible—and that diversity in shape among the markers, some of which, such as those of the tombs in the cemetery of Zawyat Sultan on the east bank of the Nile in the province of Minya, look like works of modern art—half-domes that follow one another like the waves of a frozen sea. Similar are the tombs in the desert of Hiww, close to Qena and Luxor. From ancient times until now, and despite the change of religion and language, the main preoccupations of the Egyptians have been to find an eternal resting place for their bodies and to be remembered after their departure.

In the Mamluk age, the sultan, the moment he assumed power, would commence the construction of a mosque. In reality, he was building a tomb, for the mosque would include his shrine, and beneath his shrine would lie his grave. The ancient Egyptian concern for survival in the face of extinction imposed itself on these rulers of foreign origins, who, it must be remembered, came to Egypt as children and absorbed its culture and view of life.

After Gamal Abd al-Nasser's death in 1970 the Egyptians discovered that he had been preoccupied with building himself a final resting place and had been contributing to a savings cooperative, from whose funds the mosque in which he now lies was built. President Anwar Sadat was preoccupied with building himself a tomb in the village of Mit Abu-l Kom, though he did not live long enough to do so, being assassinated in 1981.

Rulers and princes built mosques in order to lie among the living in a place filled with the odor of sanctity, so that they might add a further legitimacy to their memory, and so that their names might remain on people's lips.

Who created the name? Did the name precede the appearance of writing? Was it created in parallel to the latter or shortly thereafter? Or was it extremely ancient? Let us imagine a world without names. Could it have existed in the form that we know? The name is a codification, a summarization, of the actual. Its continuing existence means the continuing existence of its owner, even if he is no longer alive and striving. I pause in bewilderment, overwhelmed with questions before the meaning of the name, its status, and its signification.

the name is existence

In the legend of the goddess Isis—the first mother, the wife, the sister, the companion, the incarnation of the very essence of femininity and its abundance—in that story fashioned from the soul of the Nile Valley and the contemplation of its origins in the universe and the cosmos, a unique scene occurs.

King Ra, before his assumption into the eternal as a god, had many names, including a hidden name within which resided the secret of his power. Isis the beautiful, with her charm and coquetry, sought to discover the hidden name by a stratagem. One of the stories that has come down to us, written in hieroglyphic, records some of the details of the dialogue that took place between them, after he had been bitten by a snake.

Isis says to Ra, "Reveal to me your name, my holy father, for one may live through that."

Then she says to him, "If you reveal it to me, the name will come out, for he whose name is mentioned lives."

The God Ra, however, refuses to speak it. Yet, even though he has been bitten and is severely hurt, the poison is coursing through his body, and he feels the fire burning his insides, he utters the following words: "It would be good that you should listen to me, my daughter Isis, that my name may be capable of coming from my body to your body. The mightiest of the priests among the gods has concealed it, so that it may take ample space in the boat of eternity."

Ra dies, without speaking his name, which remains hidden, unknown. Now, among the Muslim mystics, there is what is known as "the Mightiest Name of God." In Muslim belief, God has ninety-nine names, each the anti-thesis of the other ("the Compassionate," "the Tyrannical"), but there is one name that is mightier than all. Any who acquires or has knowledge of it attains powers that lie beyond those of humankind—not power as envisaged by the traditional, coercive concept, but gnosis, the penetrating vision. In the biographies and anthologies that recount the lives of the Righteous Friends of God, it is mentioned that some of those who attain high spiritual rank are informed of the Mightiest Name of God. Among these was Dhu-l-Nun al-Akhmimi, of Nubian origin but born in the city of Akhmim, in Upper Egypt. The historical sources say that he was the founder of "the Sciences of the People," that is, Sufism. What most attracts my attention, however, is a certain expression that occurs in all the sources on Sufism—namely, that "he had knowledge of the bird script" (the ancient Egyptian language, and the hieratic script in particular, being known to the Arabs as "bird script" by reason of the frequent repetition therein of pictures of birds). Does this mean that Dhu-l-Nun was skilled at reading the ancient Egyptian language? It is certain that, as late as the end of the eighteenth century CE, some Egyptians in Upper Egypt spoke Coptic, the final stage of ancient Egyptian, which became a religious language used in the prayers in the churches, and that during the past four decades there has been a movement to revive it. Had Dhu-l-Nun, in the eight century CE, mastered the ancient Egyptian script? Had others done so?

The continuation of existence is implicit in the survival of the name, in its repetition. The name is a synonym of existence, is parallel to it, indeed goes beyond it, for its owner ceases to exist physically while the name sometimes remains, via offspring, buildings, the creation of a work of art, good deeds, or fond memories.

To aspire to immortality, to survival after death, is a human trait. It is to take action against obliteration, against that sempiternal force that rolls on forever, that erases every living thing. In confronting this force, the Egyptians fashioned written characters, an architecture created from emptiness, from the air that we breathe, from time that elapses and returns. The words thus created were the building blocks for names, ideas, and meanings, the characters symbols parallel to existence, the writing a way of fixing it, of transporting it from one time to another, of extending existence to the utmost limit of time, where it will exist only when uttered.

All this took place in the unimaginably distant past. To get an idea of how long ago, we have to realize that the time separating King Mina, who united Upper and Lower Egypt, to the birth of the Lord Christ is twice that which separates us today, in the sixth year after the start of the third millennium according to the Christian reckoning, from the latter.

The Egyptian takes care to incise his name in stone, on his eternal resting place, or through some trace that he leaves. His existence lies in his name. Indeed, the name has significations and powers that transcend the visible. When I was a child, I would sometimes fall ill, or one of my siblings would. My mother, who was born in southern Egypt and lived there throughout her youth and until she married and moved to Cairo, believed in the power of the name. Every step she took had to be accompanied by the mention of the name of God, and, the Egyptians especially, and Muslims in general, along with Copts, do likewise before eating, before leaving the house, before sleeping, and on waking. If someone addresses another directly, he will say to his interlocutor, "Very well. Say His name first," meaning he should say, "In the Name of God" first. If he enters a place, usually he will pronounce the name of God to expel the evil forces. My mother would place her hand on my forehead and repeat the name of God, saying, "God's name upon you and upon your brother who is better than you," meaning here the "spiritual twin," in reference to an ancient Egyptian belief according to which each of us has an unseen spiritual twin who lives in an invisible world, and that whatever befalls a person in the visible world befalls this twin in the invisible.

Belief in the name as a locus of revenge is ancient and persists to this day. If a mother sees that her child is sick, she will believe that someone has cast the evil eye on him or her. This too is an ancient Egyptian belief according to which a look may bring harm to the one looked upon. This is known as *hasad*, or envy. When this occurs, the mother will fetch a piece of alum and place it on a metal sheet over a low flame, causing it to assume a number of shapes as it melts. At this moment, the mother looks hard and, if she sees features that she recognizes will say, with confidence, "It's the mother of So-and-so," thus discovering the identity of the person who is the source of the envy, usually a woman. She then starts the actions that will put an end to the envy and initiate the cure by bringing a piece of paper, fashioning from it something resembling the human form (the "doll"), and a sharp needle, with which she pierces the figure's eyes, repeating, "In the eye of the mother of So-and-so."

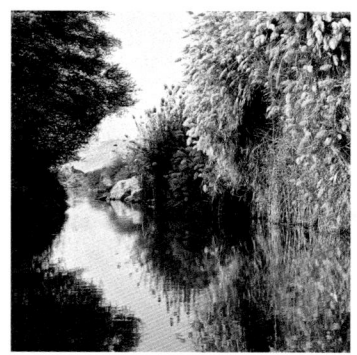

She mentions the woman's name several times, while at the same time pointing the needle at the eye sockets. In many ancient tombs of the era following the conversion of the Egyptians to Christianity, we see faces whose eyes and noses have been disfigured in the way I have mentioned, in accordance with the ancient belief that to disfigure the drawing where the eyes are means to afflict the person with blindness, while the destruction of the nose means to deny him or her life itself, that is to say, to destroy it utterly, in existence and nonexistence.

In popular belief, the possibility of affecting a particular person by the use of magic continues to this day and such magic is known as *'amal* ('action' or 'work'). In all such cases, a knowledge of the name of the person intended is, of course, essential, and yet more important is a knowledge of the name of the mother, specifically. In Upper Egypt, to mention a mother's name was considered shameful, and if a man wished to mention his wife, he would refer to her as "Mother of So-and-so," mentioning the name of his eldest son. The concept of the concealment of the name remains well-grounded within us as Egyptians. I remember that I used to have to fill out an entry visa form from one of the foreign embassies and was taken by surprise to find a line on which it was requested that I write the name of my mother, God rest her soul. Inwardly I rebelled and I was able to do so only with distaste, and under compunction.

To conceal the name is to cast protection over it. A significant incident from the history of ancient Egypt is that which befell the brilliant architect Senmut, designer of the temple of Deir al-Bahari and lover of Queen Hatshepsut. Senmut, like all Egyptians, was preoccupied with the immortalization of his name, and being highly intelligent, realized, when at the peak of his influence over the queen—over, that is to say, the political power—that his name would become a target for his enemies after his death and that they would do their best to erase it, just as Queen Hatshepsut had erased the name of her brother whose power she had usurped. He therefore resorted to a stratagem to ensure the survival of his name, or, to put it differently, the survival of his existence, inscribing it on the back of the doors of the temple where those opening the door would not see it, because it would be on the inside. In his tomb, he wrote it once, then covered it with paint and wrote it again on top of the paint, then covered the second layer with a third. Things turned out as he had expected, the name being erased from the final layer; it remained however, on the second and third. This is why we know it and why I can, today, mention it and write it down. Has not his intention thus been realized? Does not the repetition of the names of those who departed thousands of years ago mean that they are still among us, in some form? Is not the name the epitome of the existence of the individual, whether in life or in death?

In the belief of the ancient Egyptians, Ptah's was the mouth that pronounced the names of all things, and in so doing brought them into being and ended the time of nothingness, when one name had yet to be pronounced. That is to say, Ptah uttered the names of all that might potentially exist and the things, as a result, appeared.

When a child is born, it must be given a name. The name does not spring from within its bearer, it acquires it and, simply by virtue of the fact that it is described by it, a textual resonance comes about between the name and the thing named. I imagine that, were my name to be different, I would be a different person. The individual cannot exist without a name and the name endows the individual with identity. Thus, to avoid the possibility of being renamed in the afterlife, the Egyptians tried, by various methods, to guarantee that their names would survive in the world of nonexistence. When the kings and nobles mentioned their names, they surrounded them by cartouches to ensure their protection. The civil servants prayed before the statue of the king, glorifying his name. On the body of the chariot of Thutmose IV, we find the enemy depicted as falling beneath a raised scepter, which is held, not by the king, but by his name. Thus the name of the king, or the god, was transformed into a source of special power that sorcerers could use. The name of the god Amun, for example, was also that of an efficacious potion used to render crocodiles weak and powerless. The spells that use the name are innumerable and we can see them in the amulets that certain men of religion (Muslims and Copts) prepare to protect the child from envy or to treat it for sickness through the power of the name.

When I was a child, my father and mother would warn me against dark places, in

Juhayna, my birthplace, or in the old city of Cairo, and especially against deserted dwellings. These were haunted by afreets, by evil spirits, and if one had to approach them or pass by them, one had to say the name of God, either out loud or to one's self. The

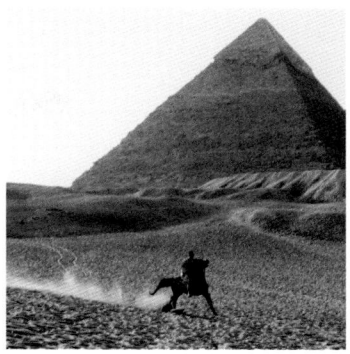

name of God prevented the appearance of the unknown creatures who wished to do us harm. Here we can clearly see the influence of ancient Egypt—the faith in the Mightiest Name of God, the Hidden Name. It may be that to utter the word *Allah* is to allude to the Hidden Name that none but a tiny number among the perfected, the righteous, have knowledge of.

I still remember a moment that affected me greatly when I was a child. My younger brother, God rest his soul, was sick. When he failed to recover despite the doctors' prescriptions, my father carried him to a well-known sheikh. The sheikh examined my brother, looking long into his face. He asked for the names of his parents. When giving the name of my mother, which was required in order to make the amulet, my father bent over and whispered. After the sheikh had read some spells and smoothed my brother's fevered brow with his hand, he said in a firm voice, "If Friday's sun rises upon him, he will be cured, with God's permission."

Then he placed around his neck a necklace bearing the amulet, which was inscribed with strange names and letters and shapes. We waited, and before the first thread of light of the Friday's dawn appeared, young Muhammad departed for eternity. Something of his features remains with me, as does a profound impression of those moments that I spent in the mystery-filled room of the sheikh, and I have a question to which till this day I have never been able to find the answer: why did my father whisper, when the only people in the room were the sheikh, himself, and his two children?

The name—its meaning and what it represents—will remain the most significant feature of ancient Egyptian thought and belief. The name is only a kind of shadow of ephemeral, material existence. This is what the Egyptians discovered during their great intellectual and spiritual adventure, and this is what brought about their faith in the Creator, in what lies behind the visible world. It is this hidden relationship that Xavier Roy has observed with his piercing eye, a relationship that is so hard to observe other than through the agency of those endowed with special insight, of whom, there can be no doubt, he is one.

To my wife Sophie and my daughters Pauline and Aurélie

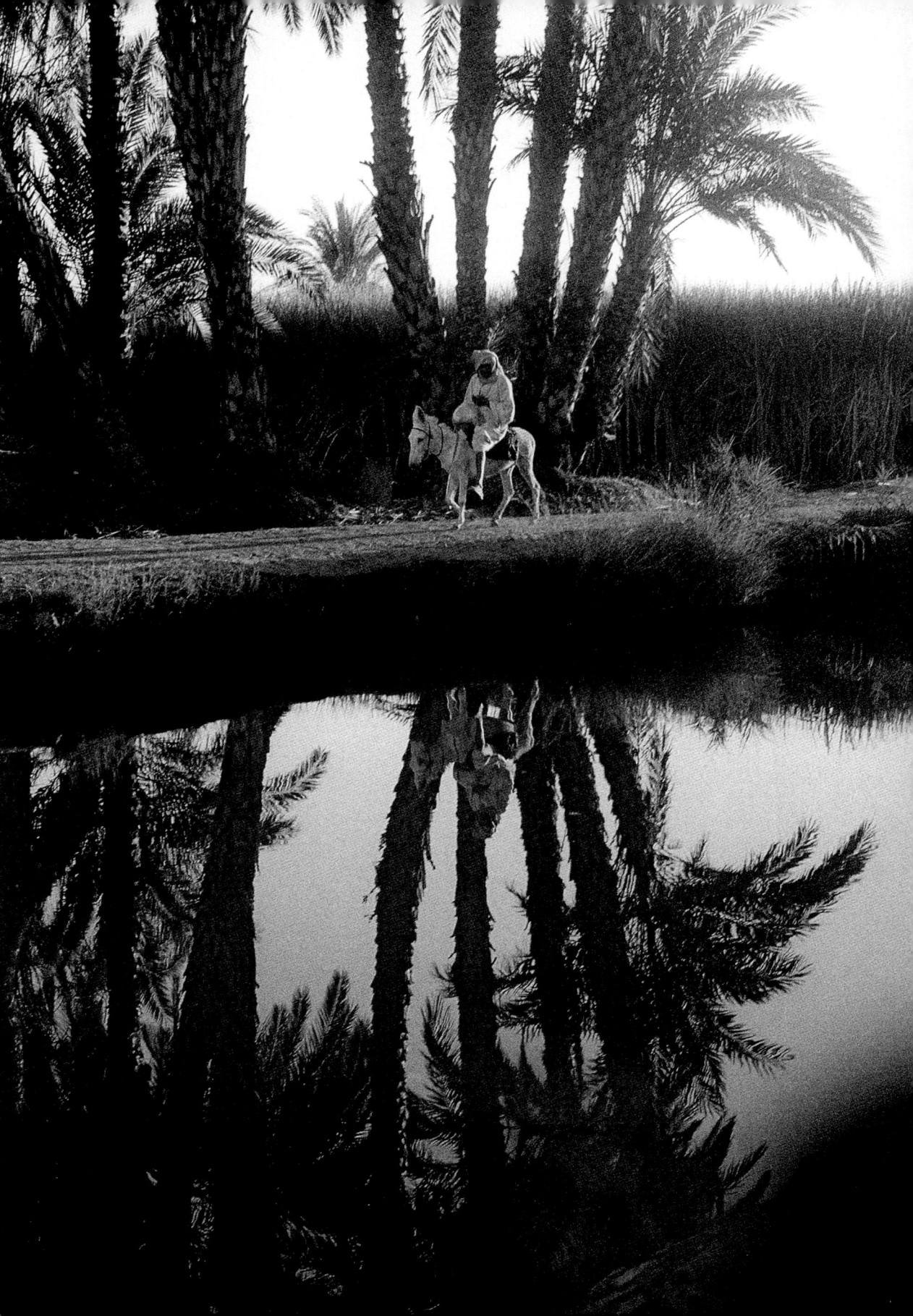

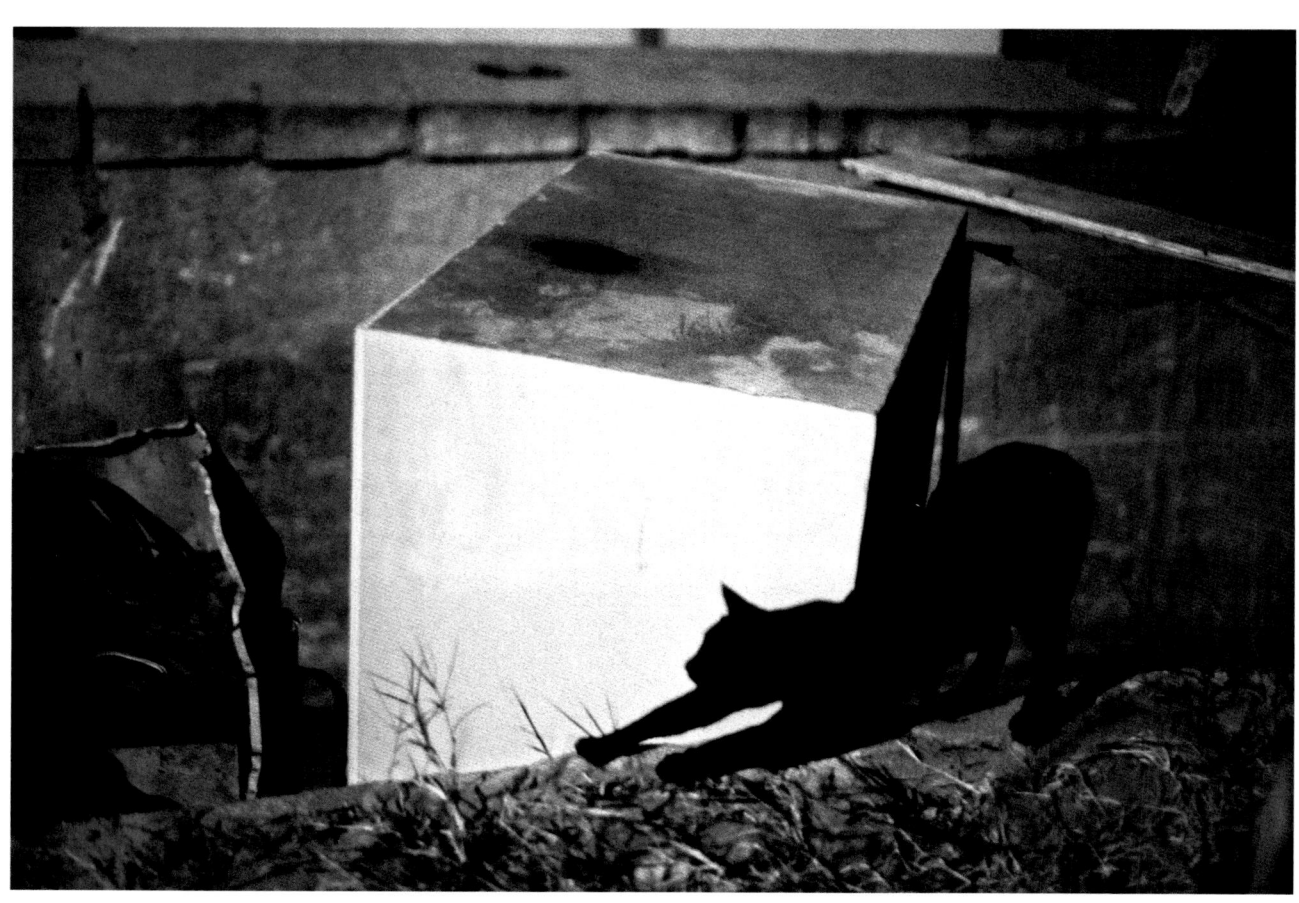

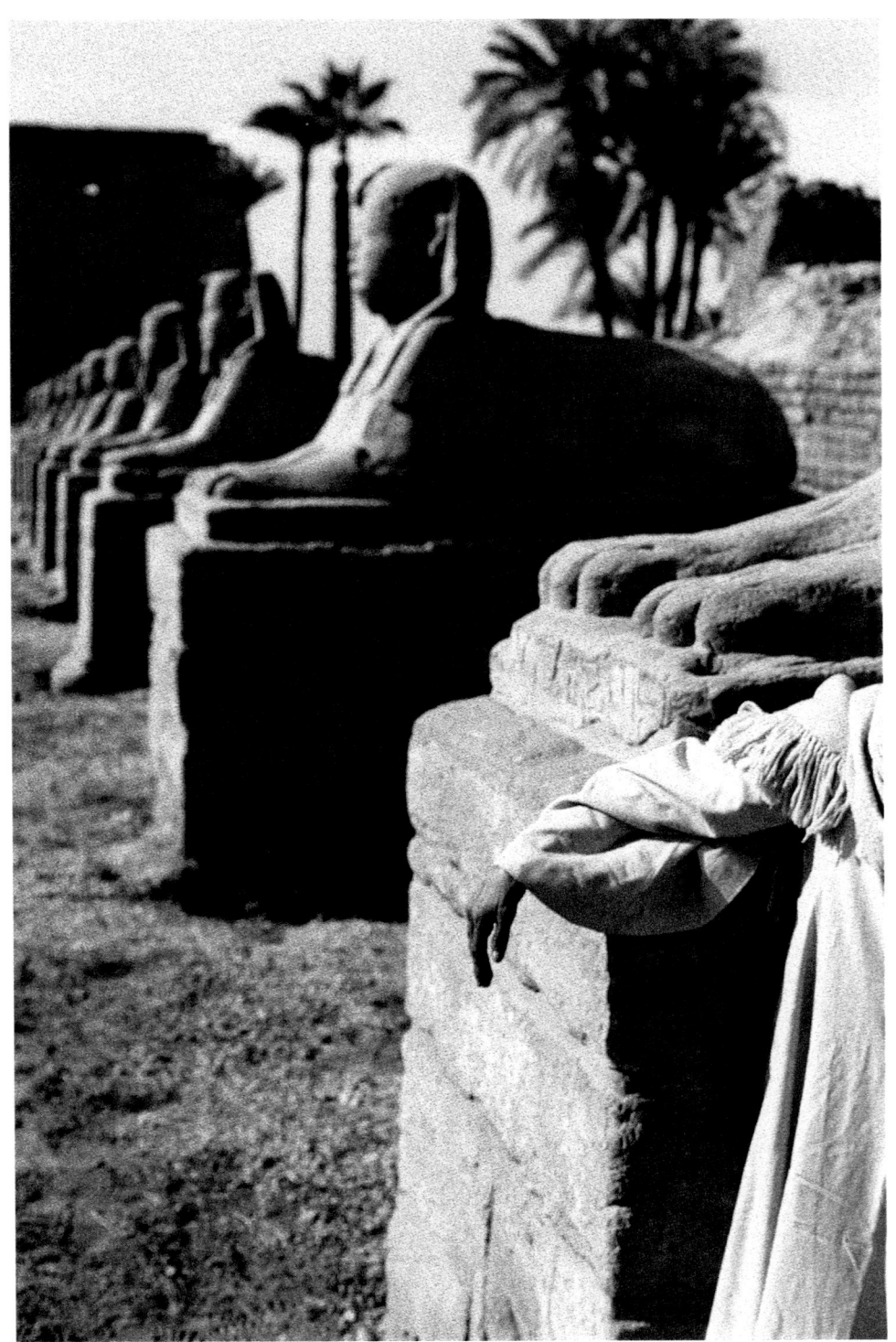

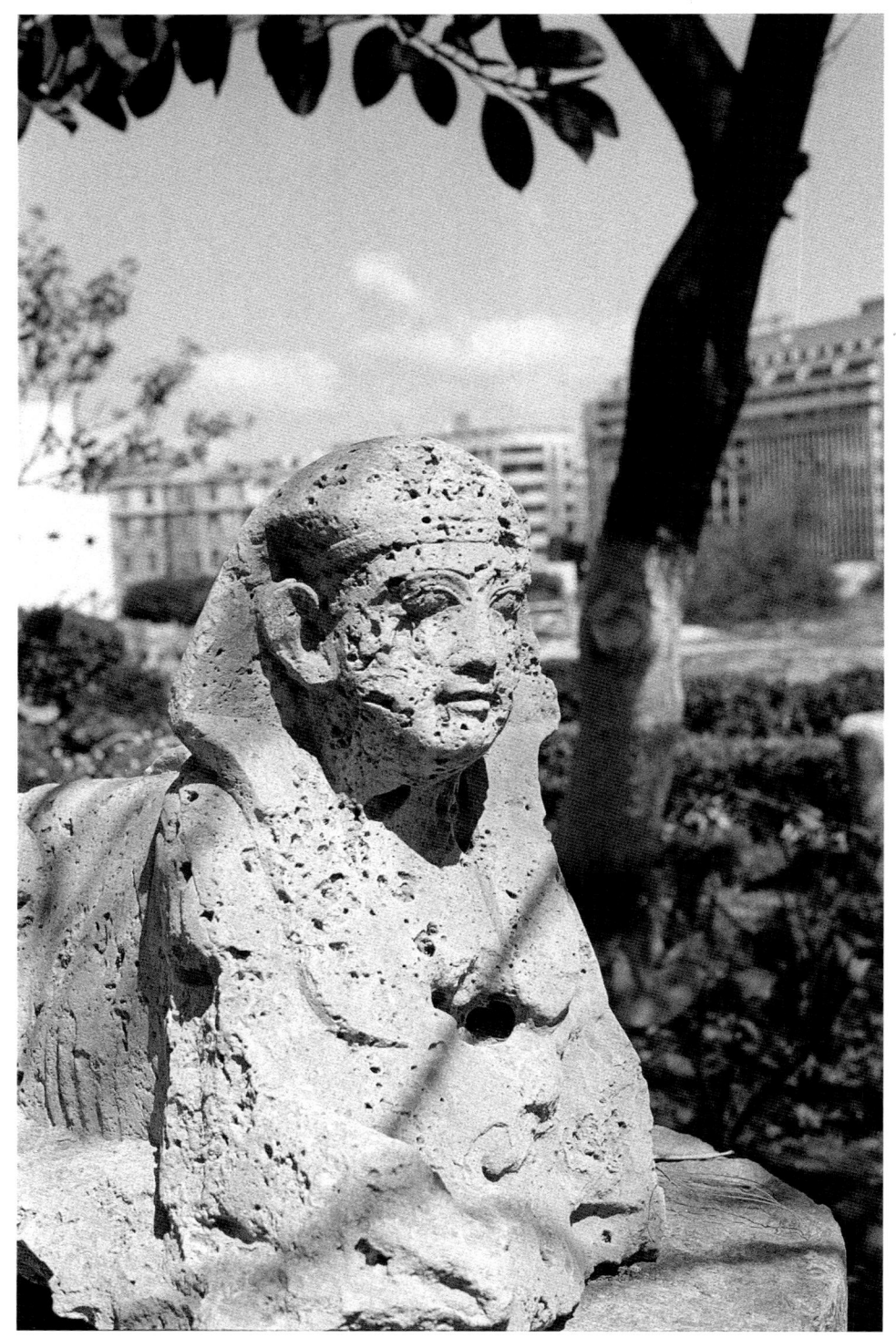

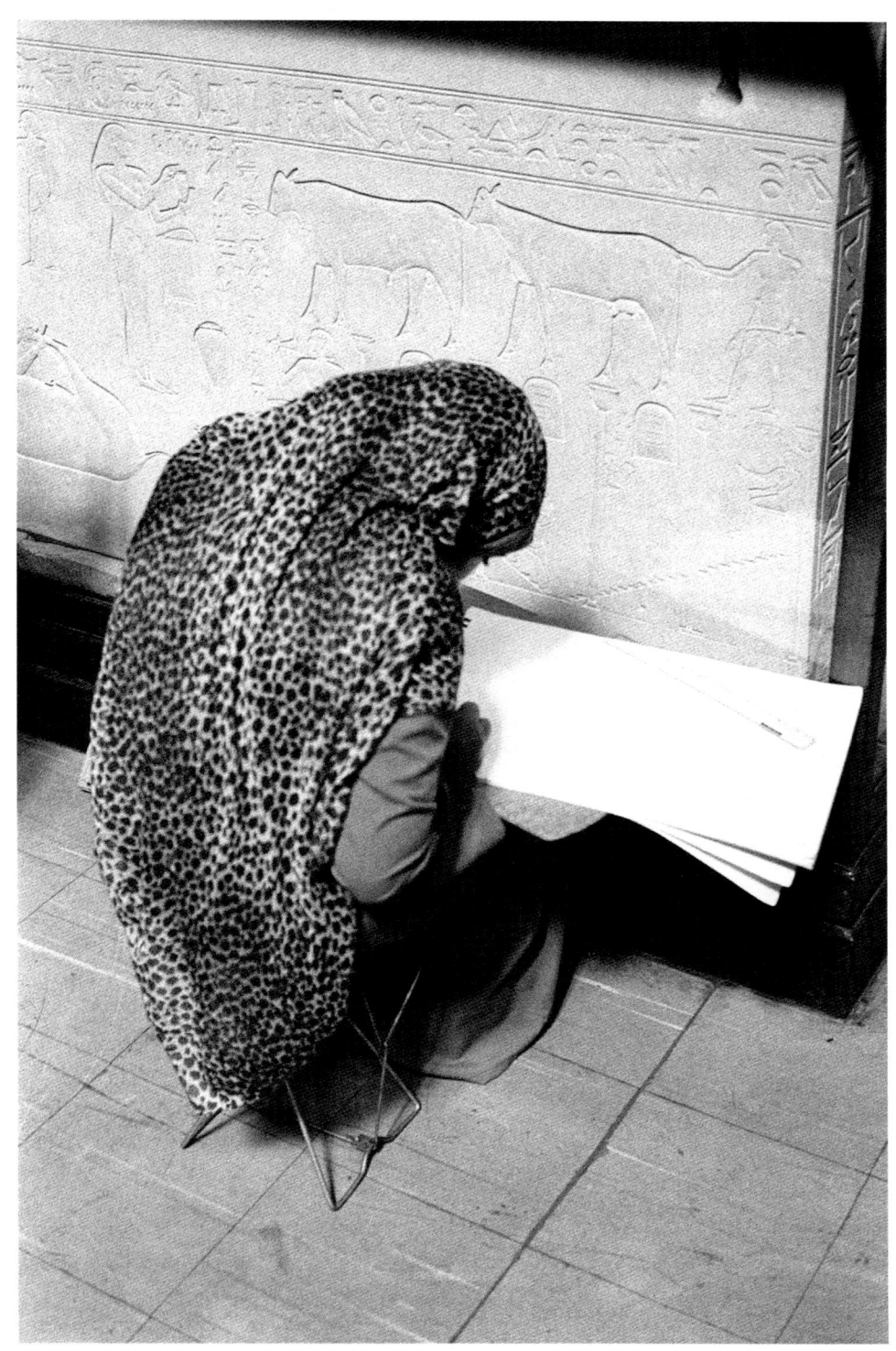

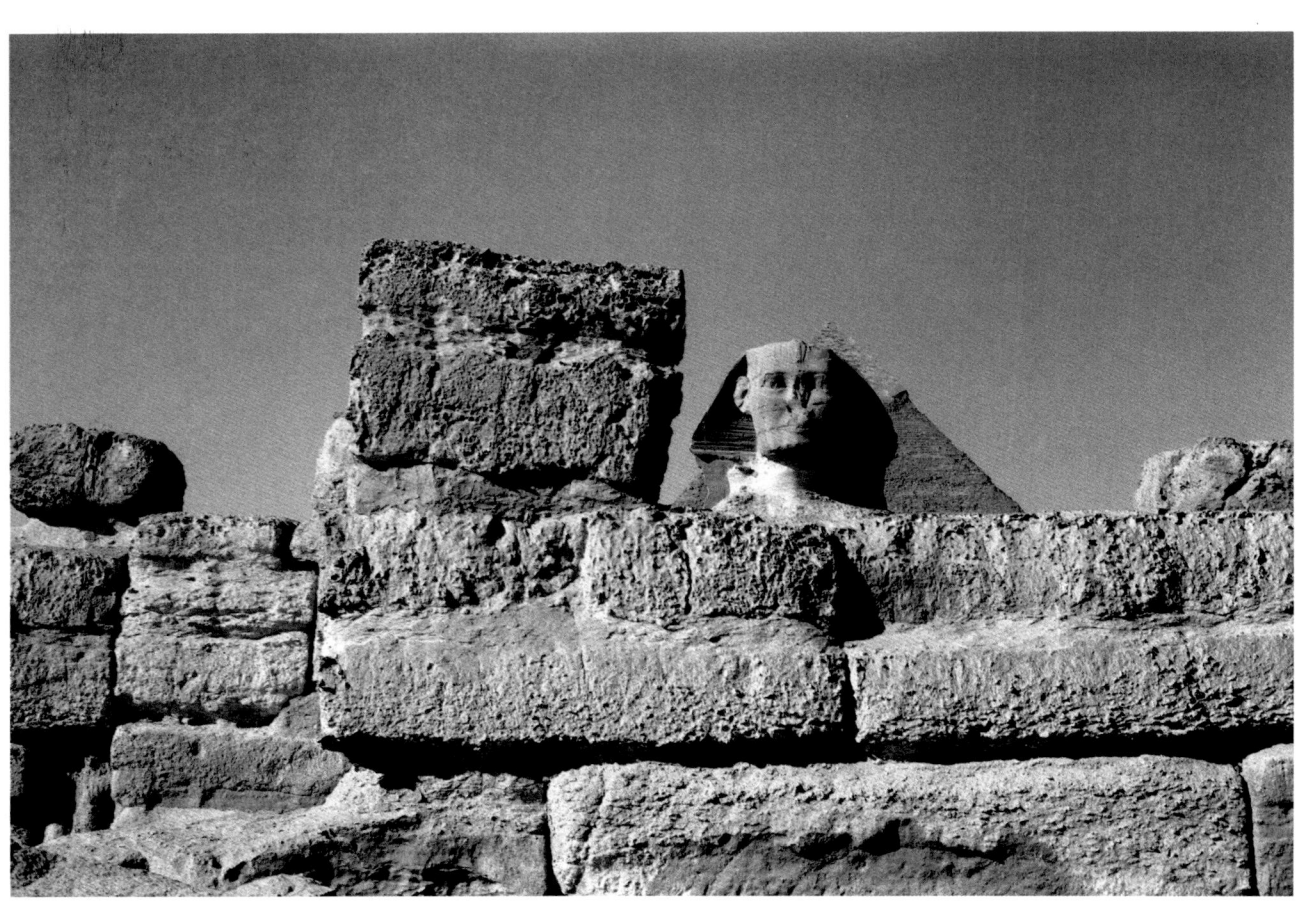

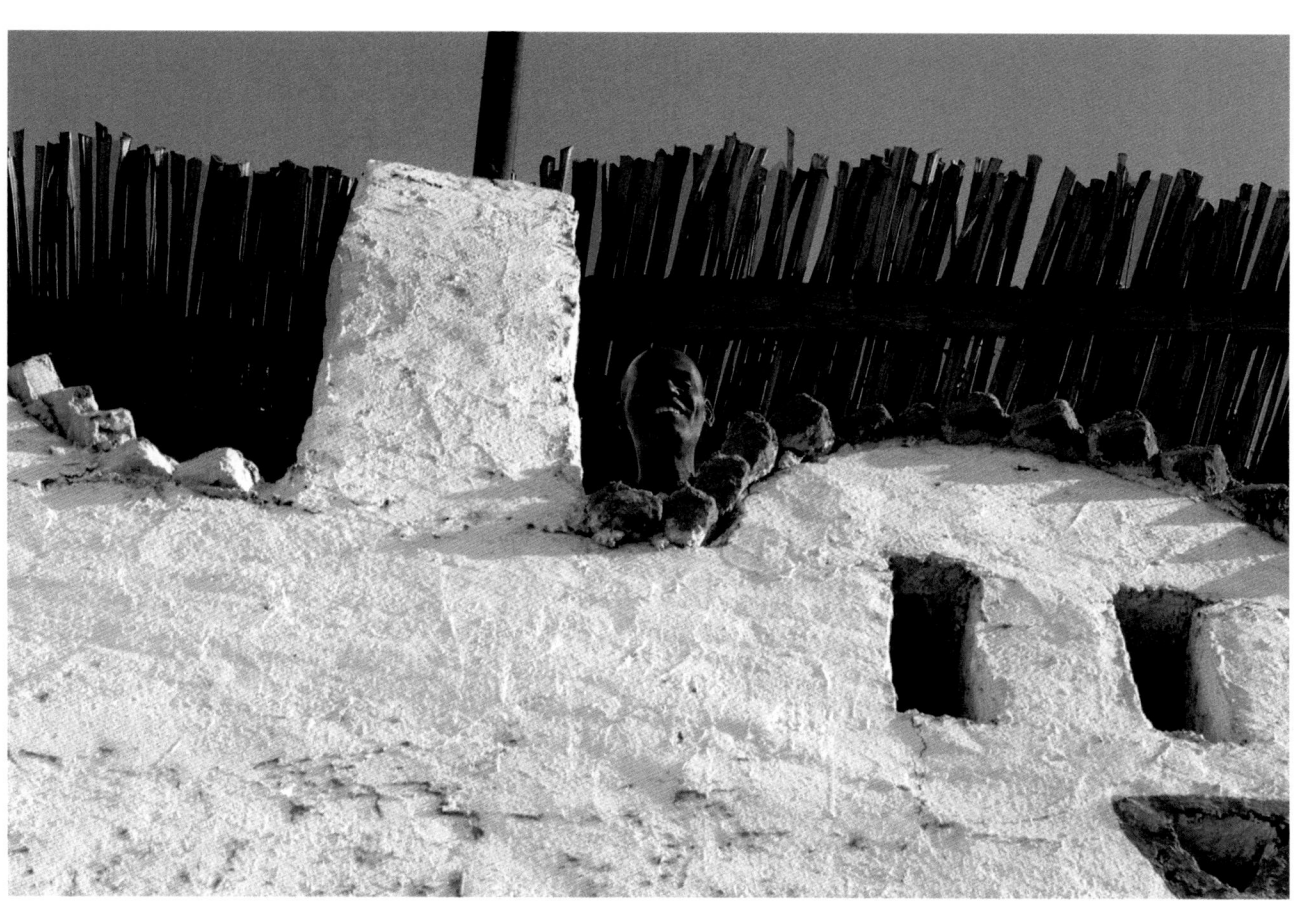

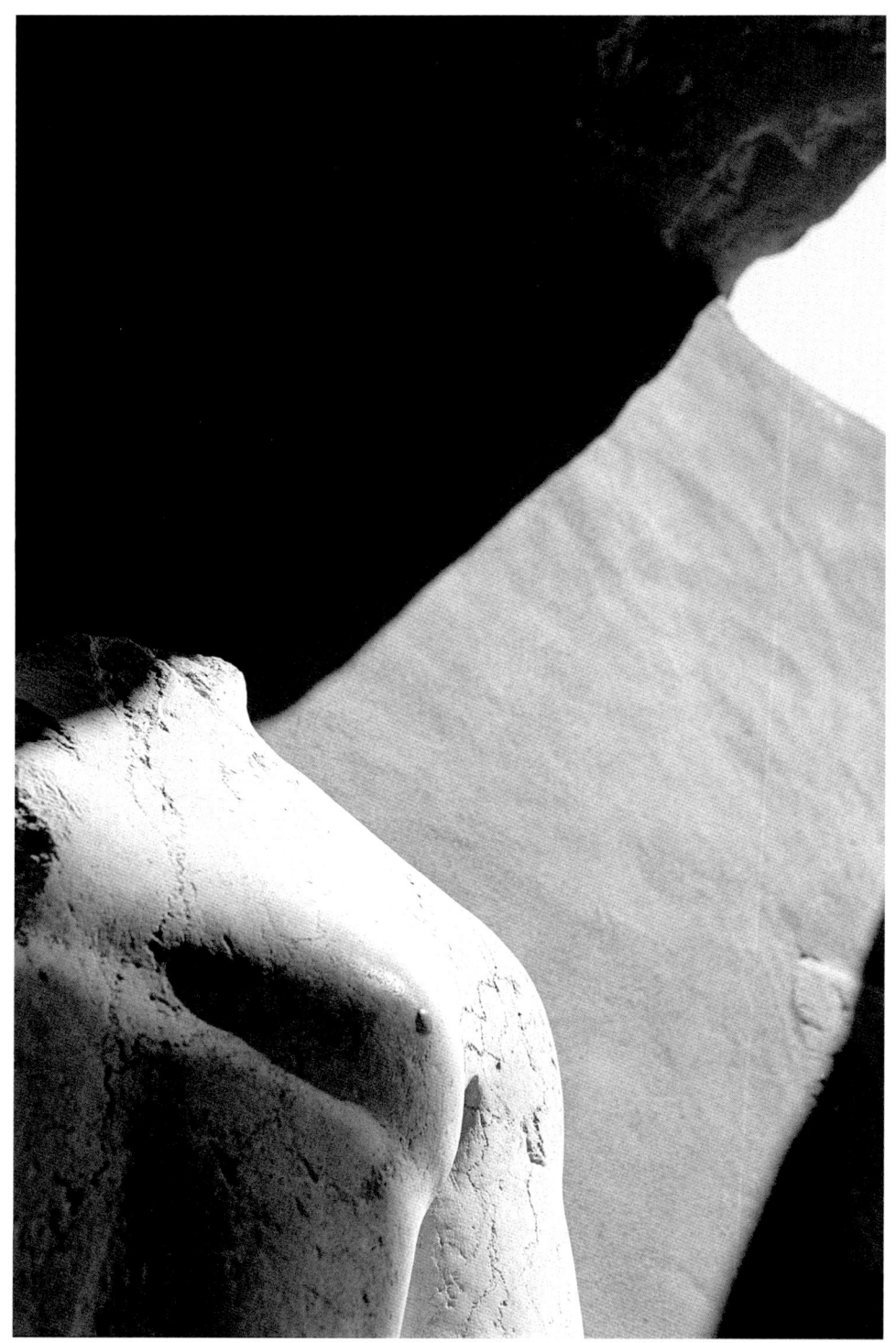

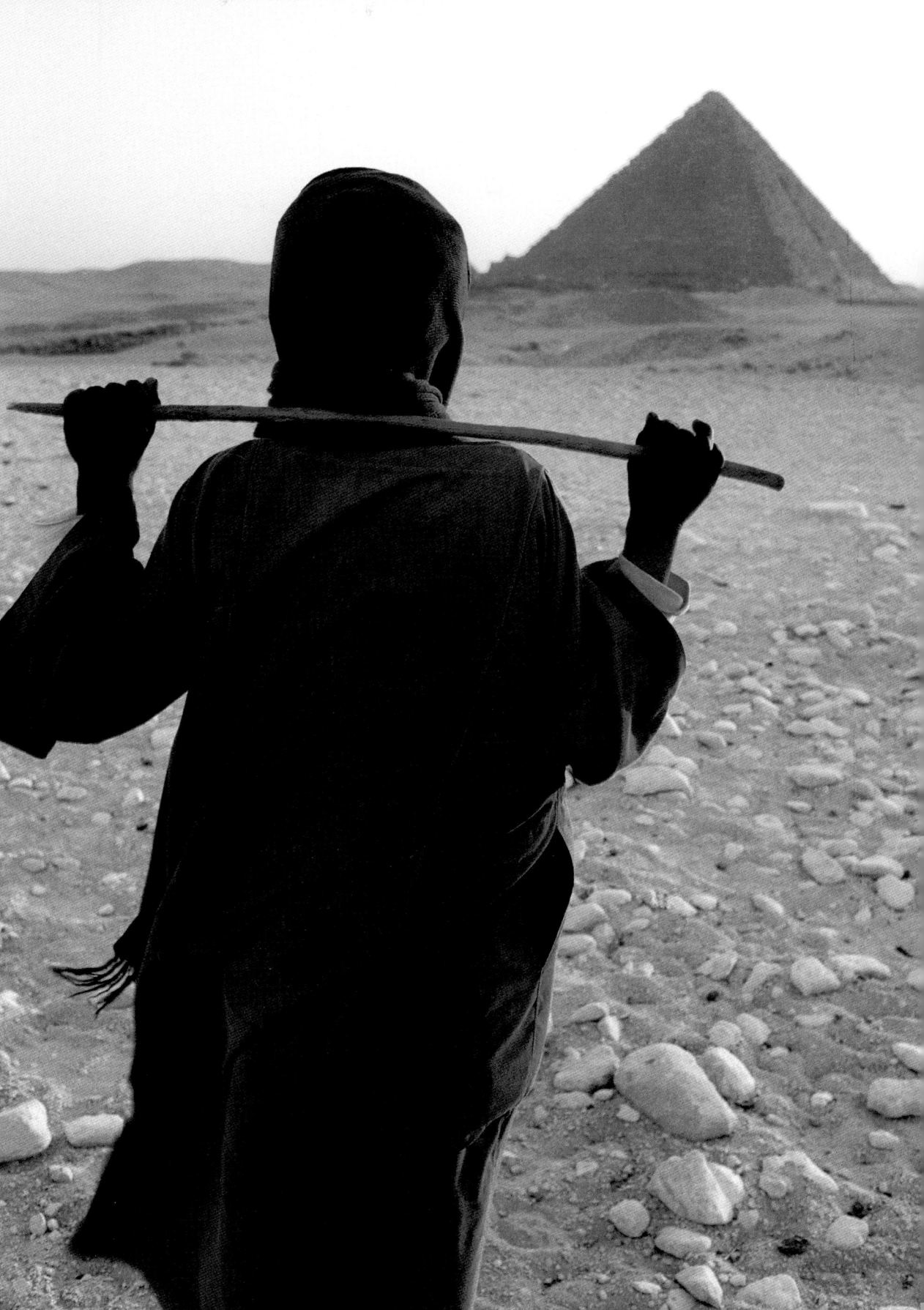

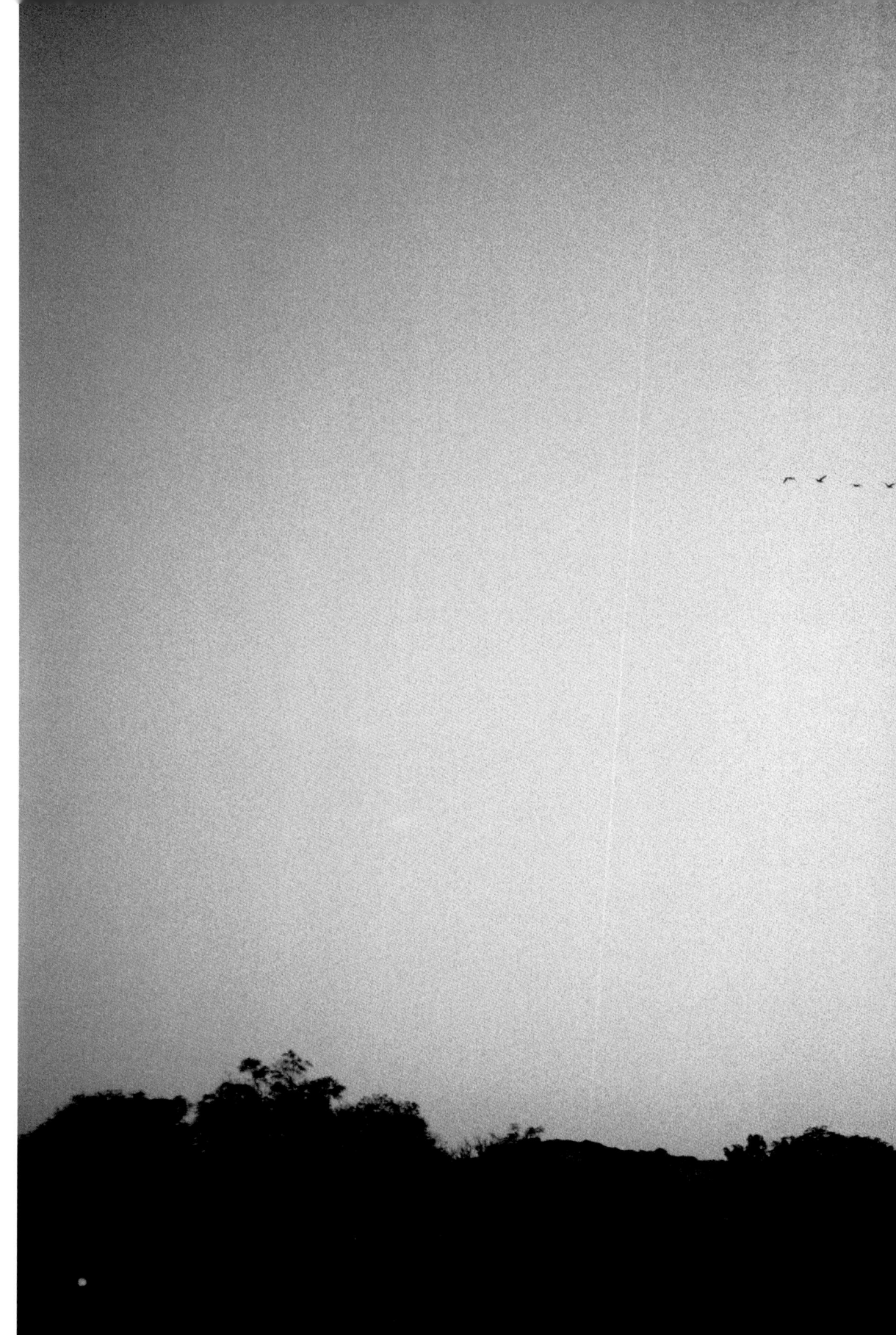

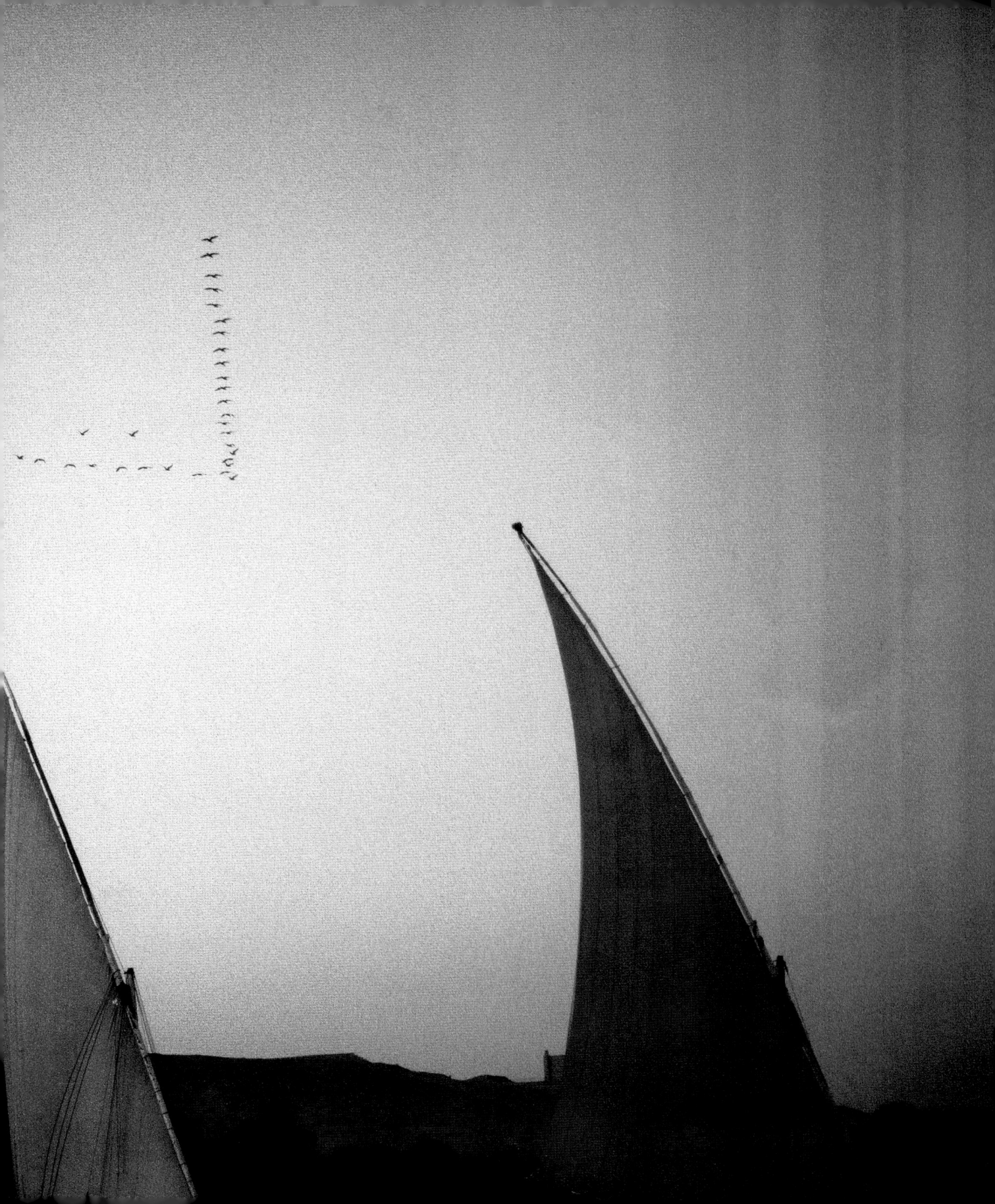

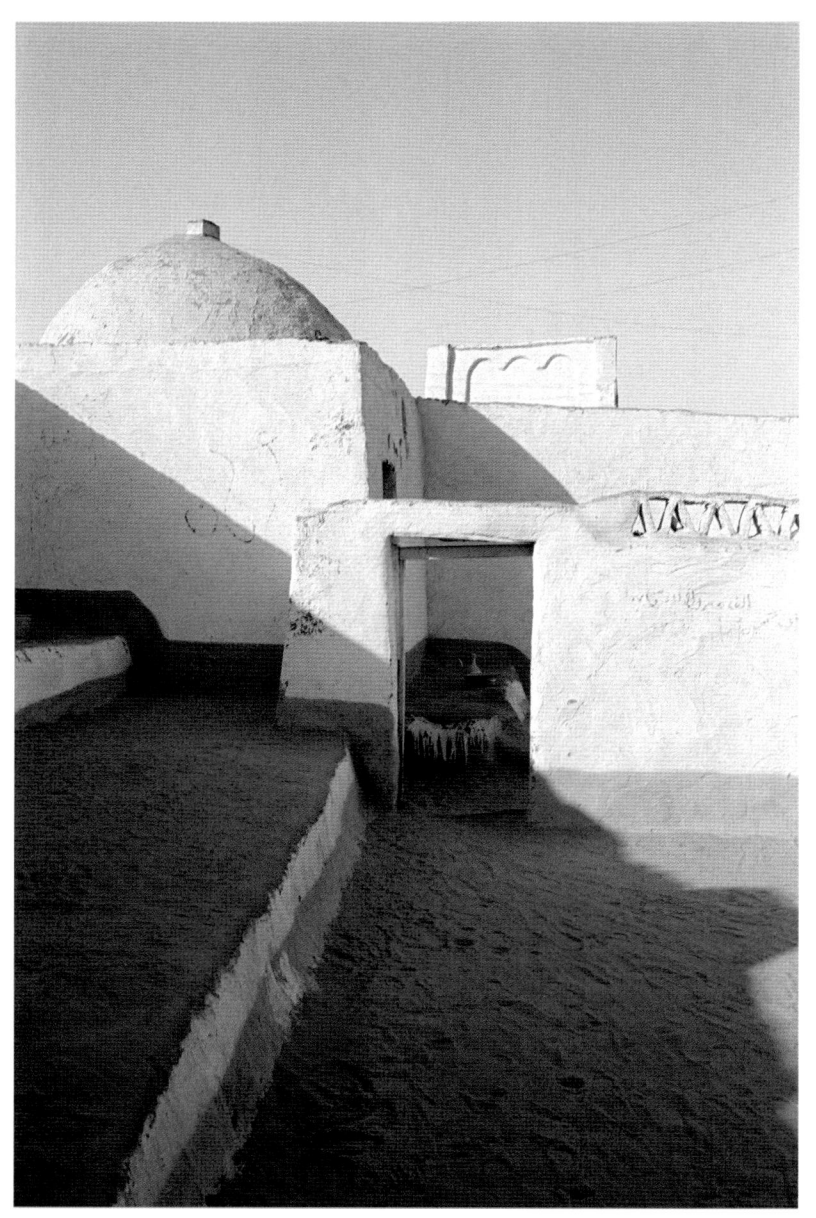

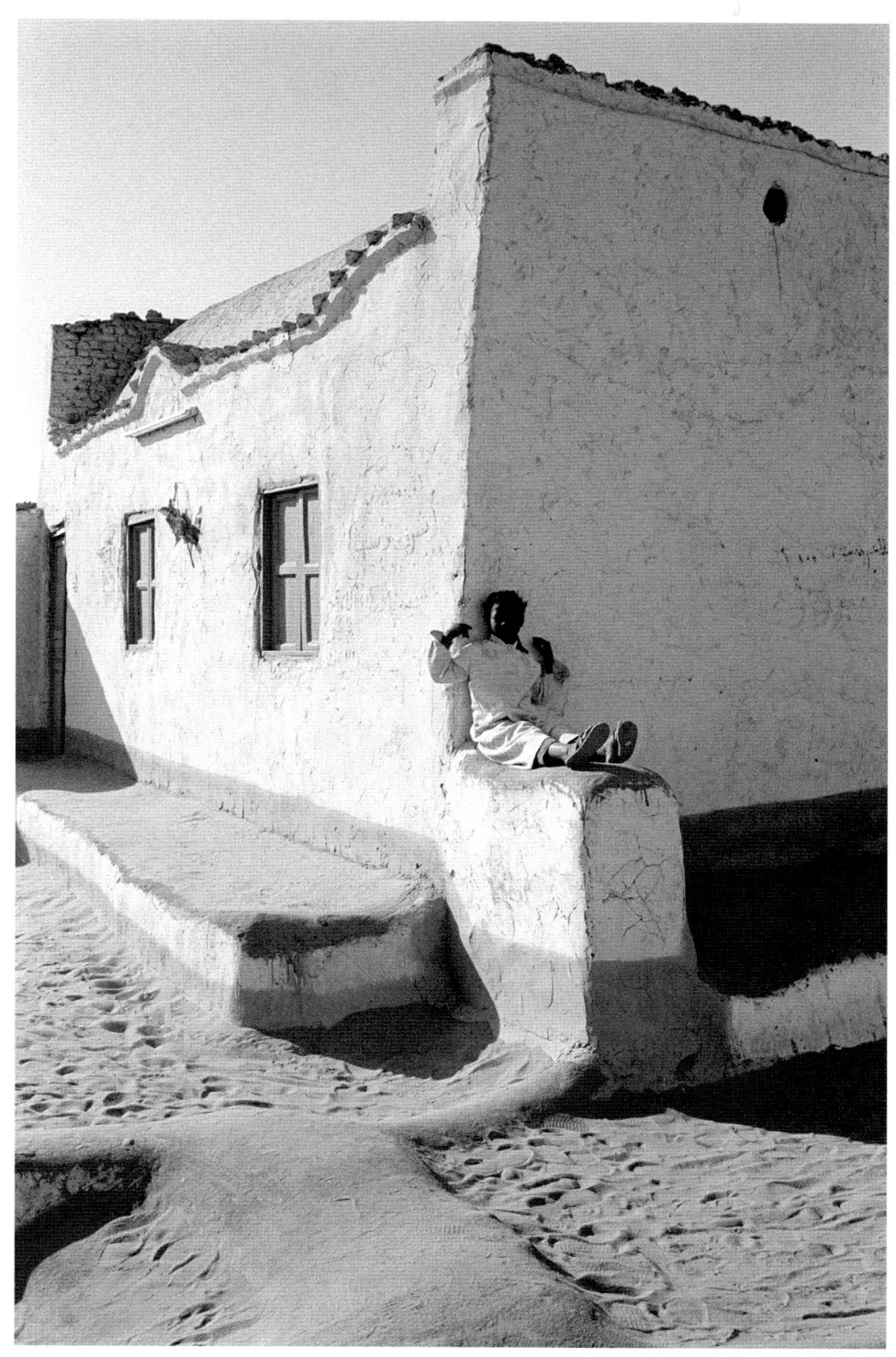

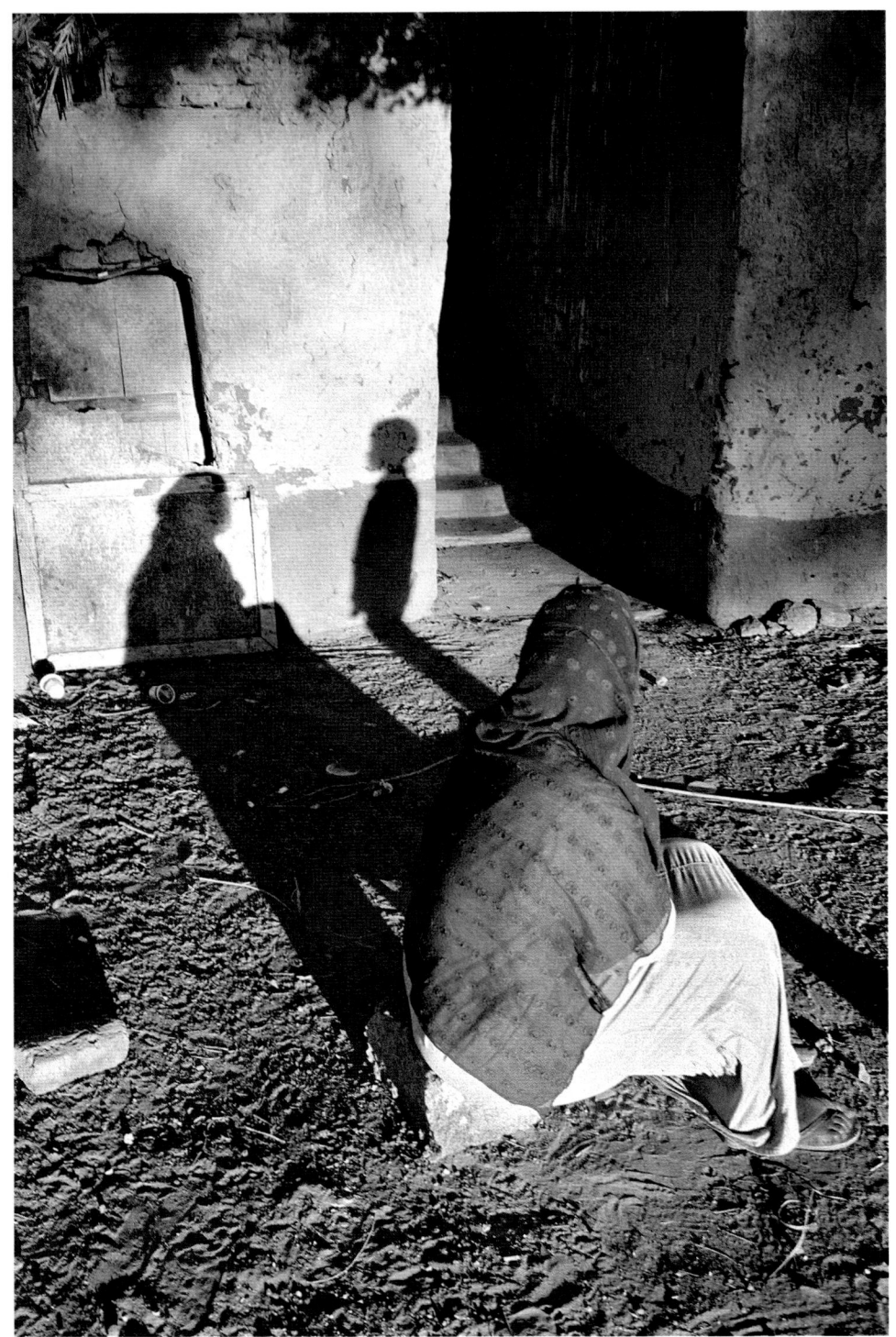

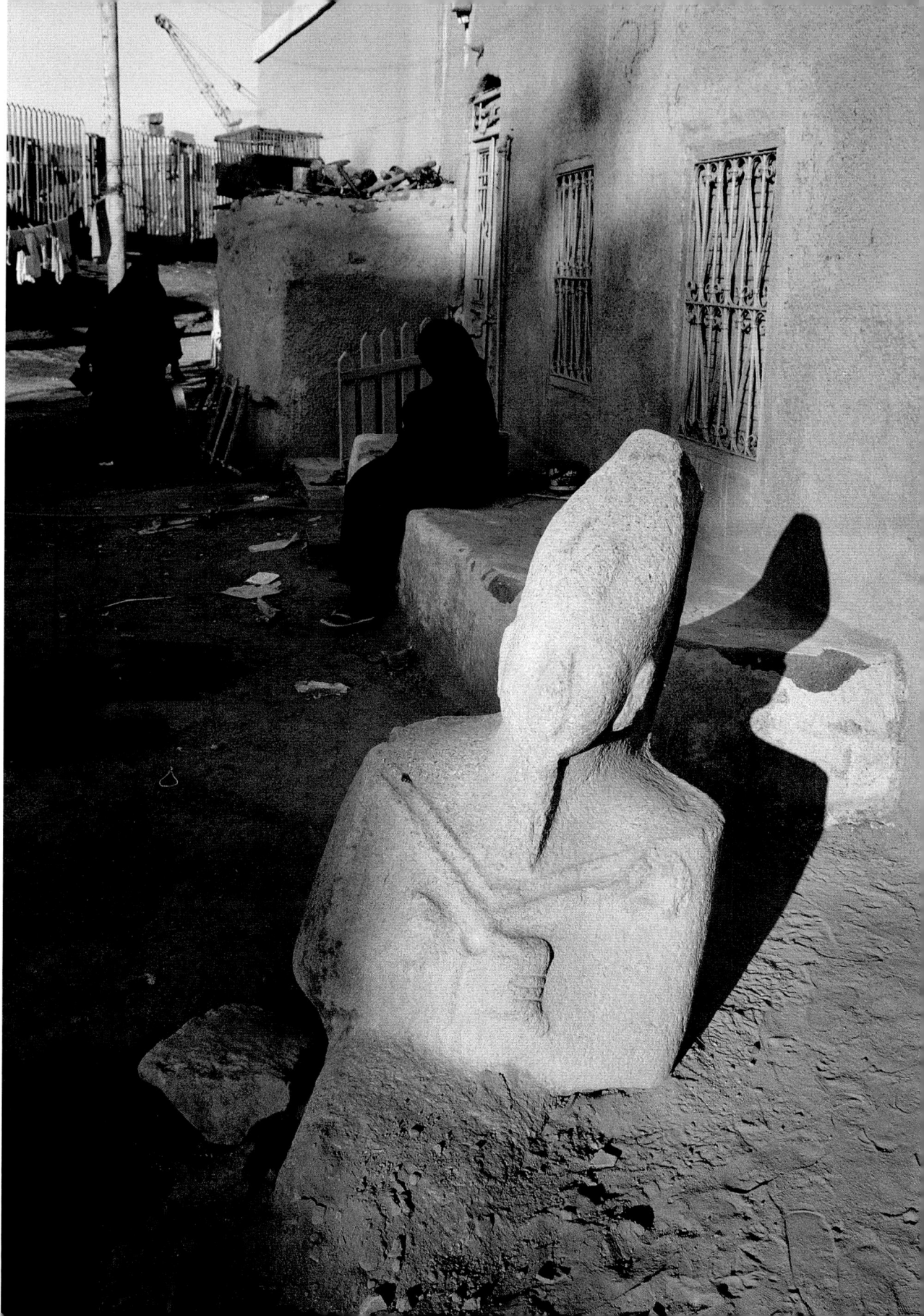

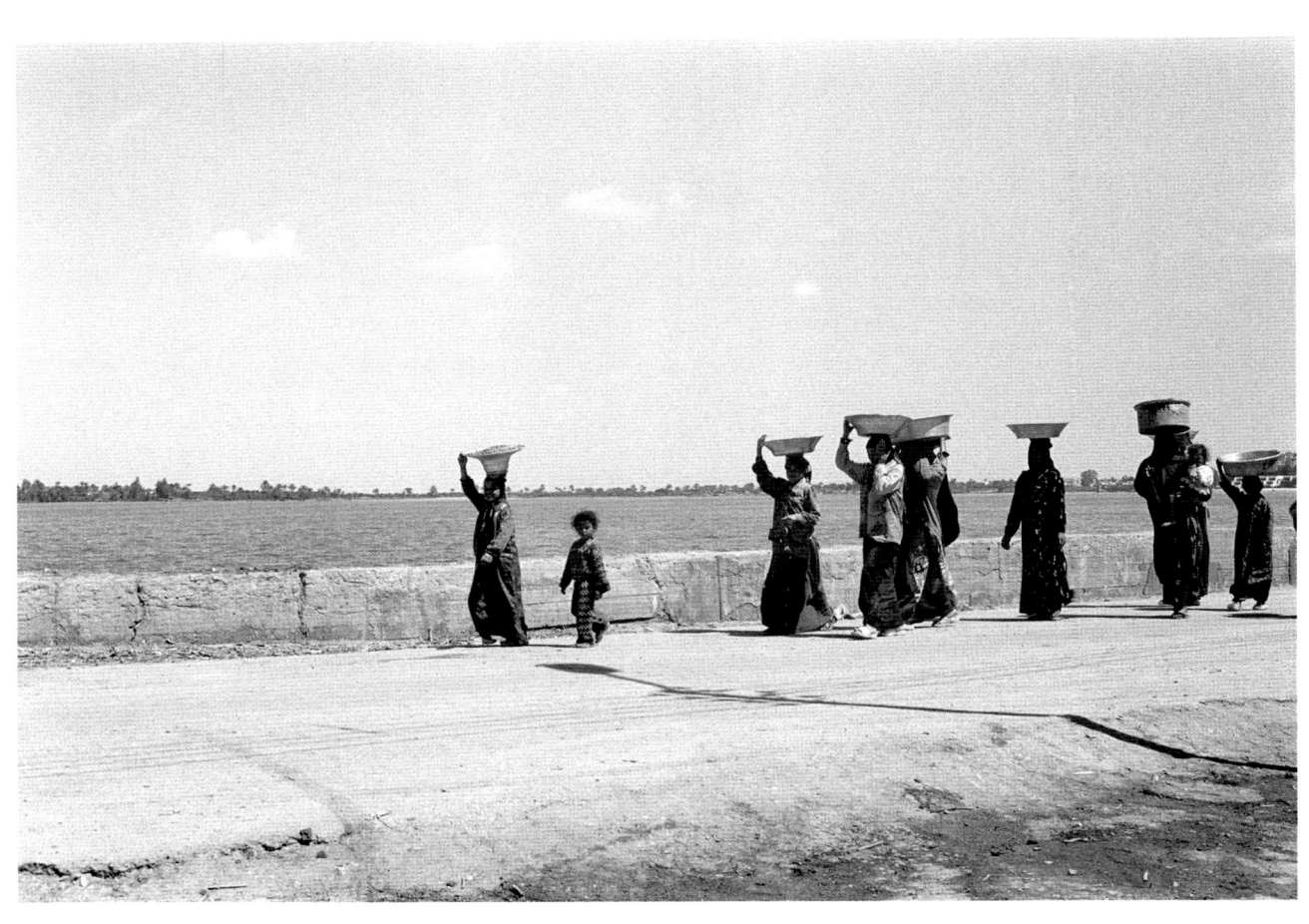

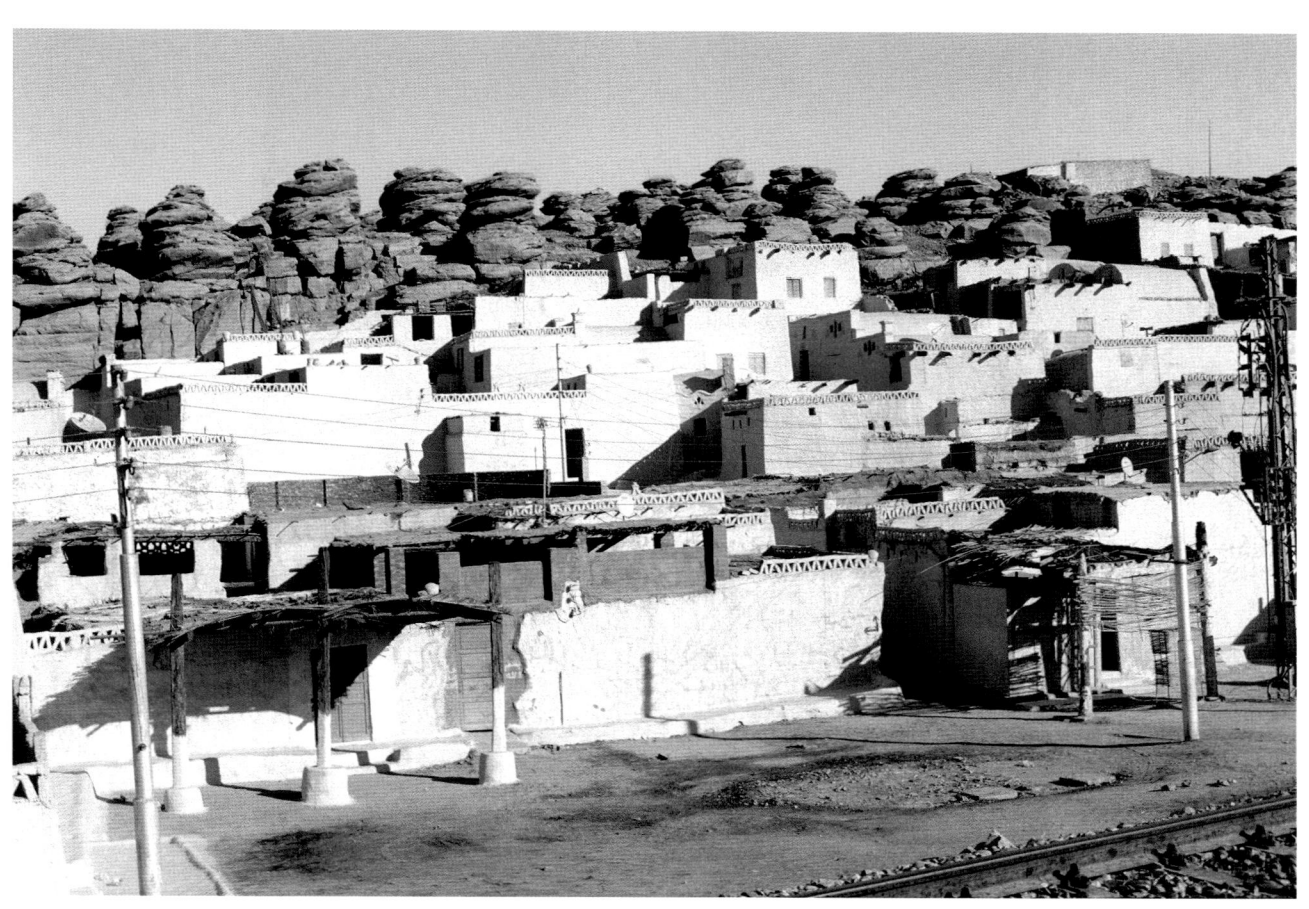

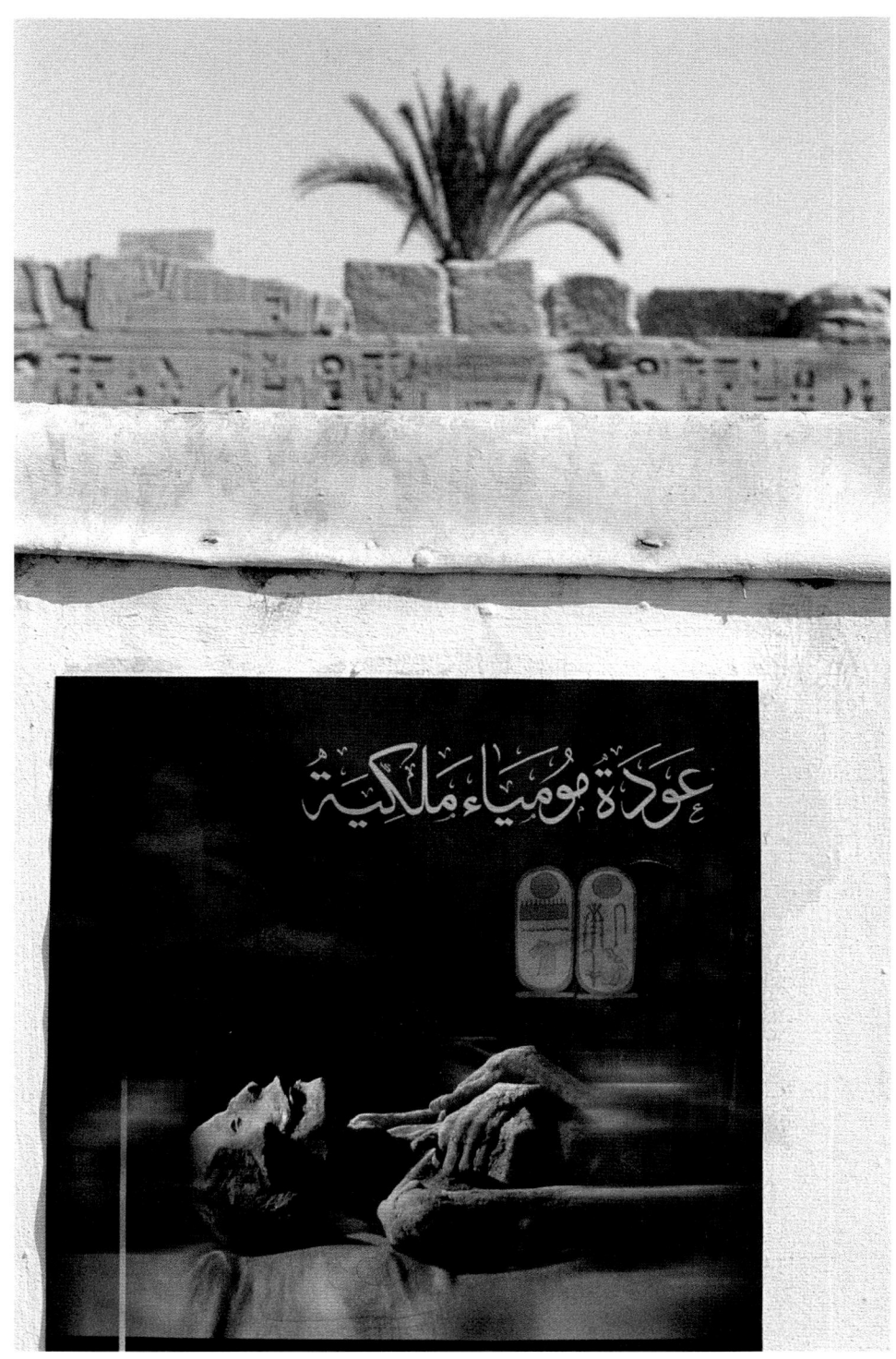

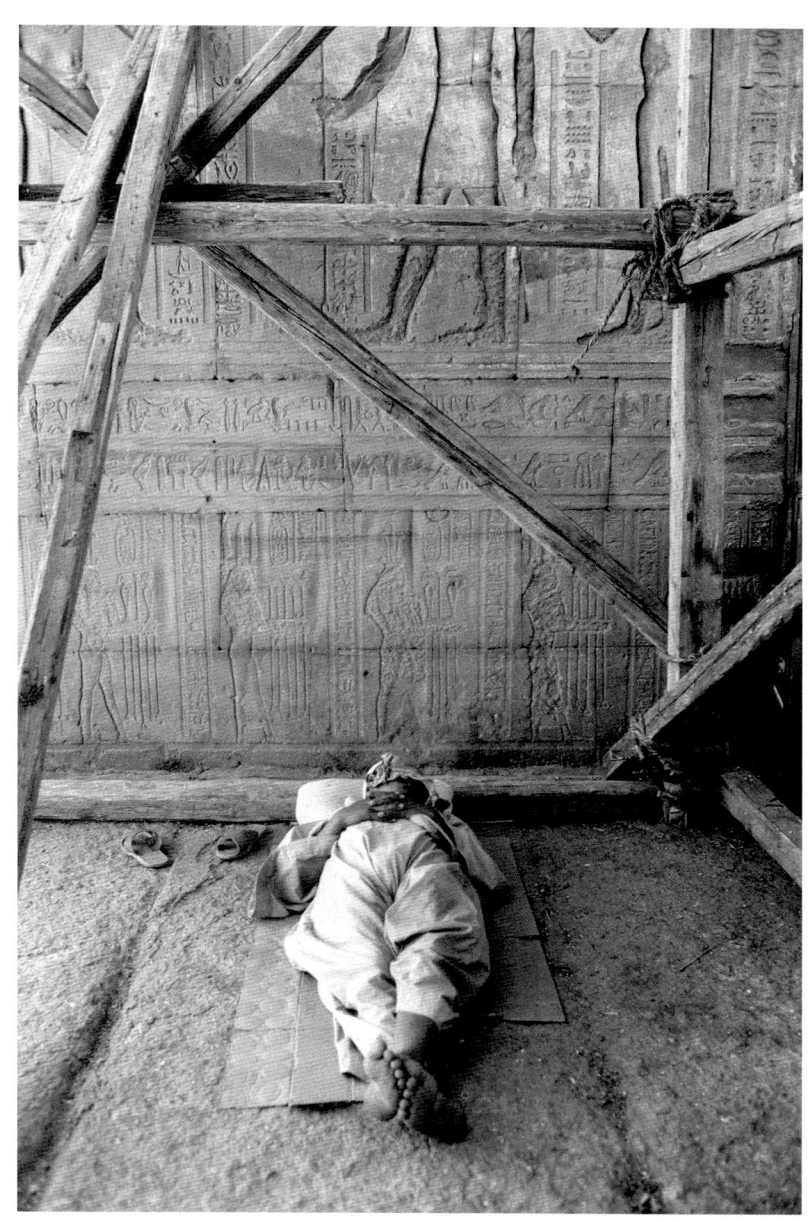

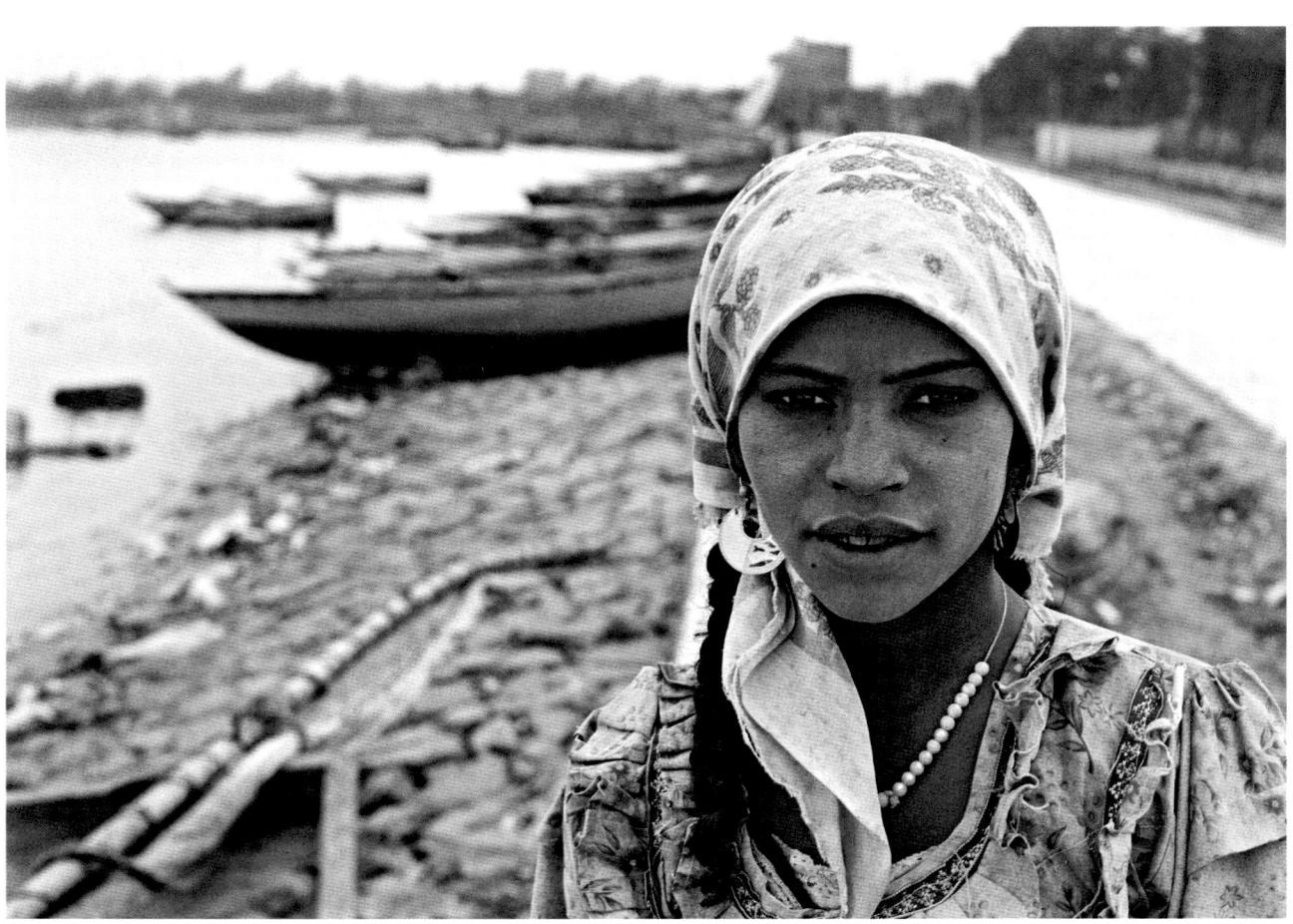

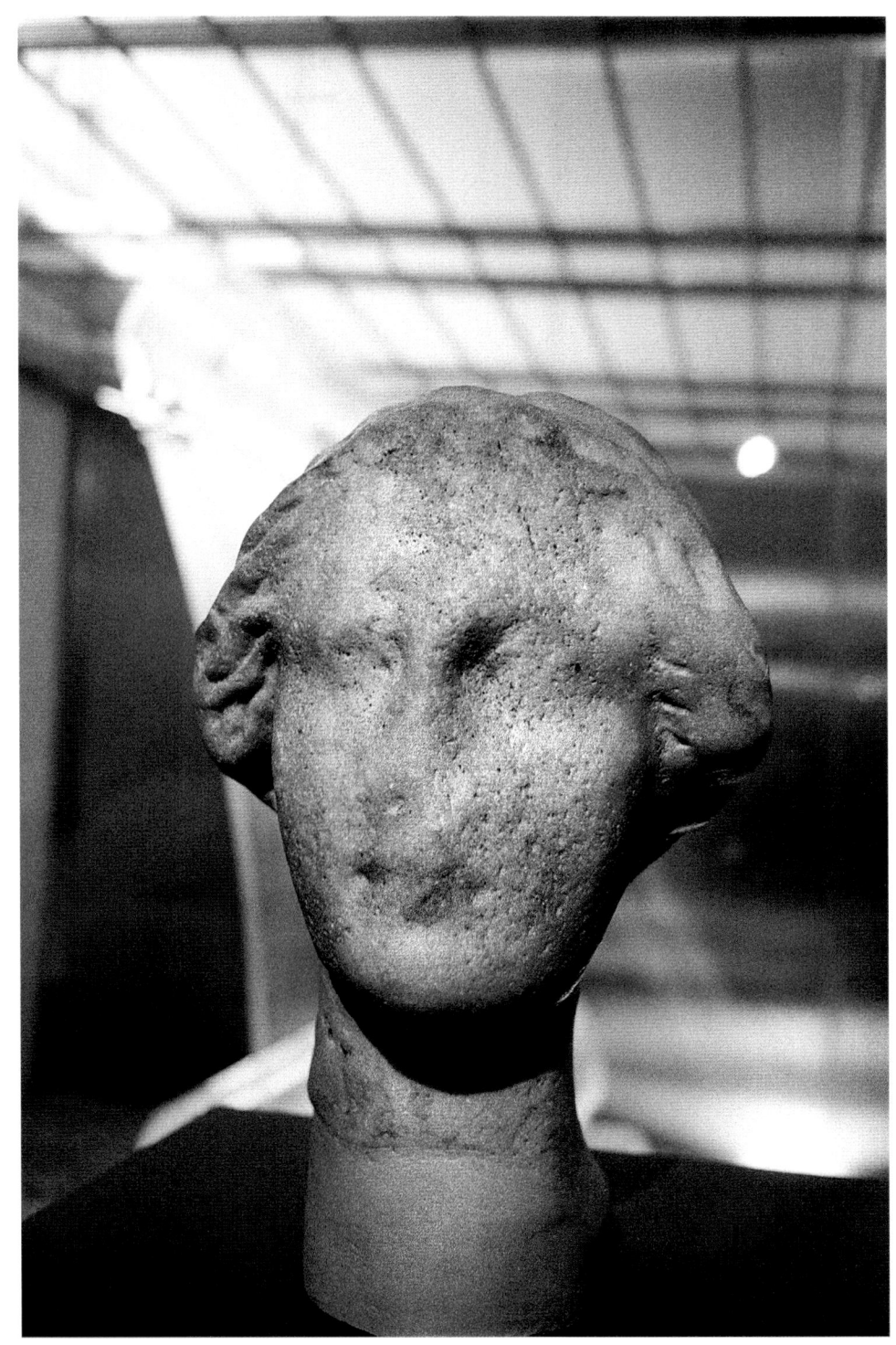

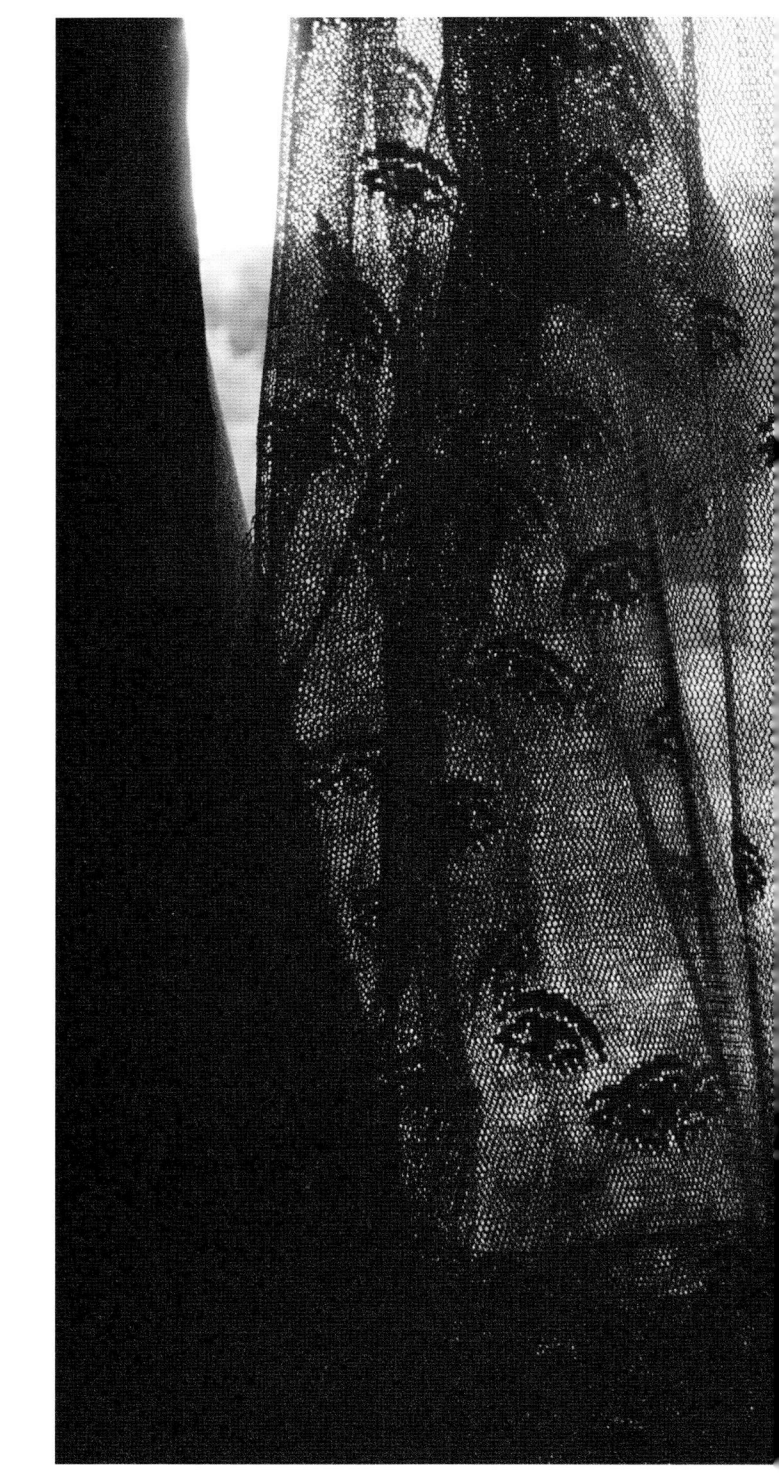

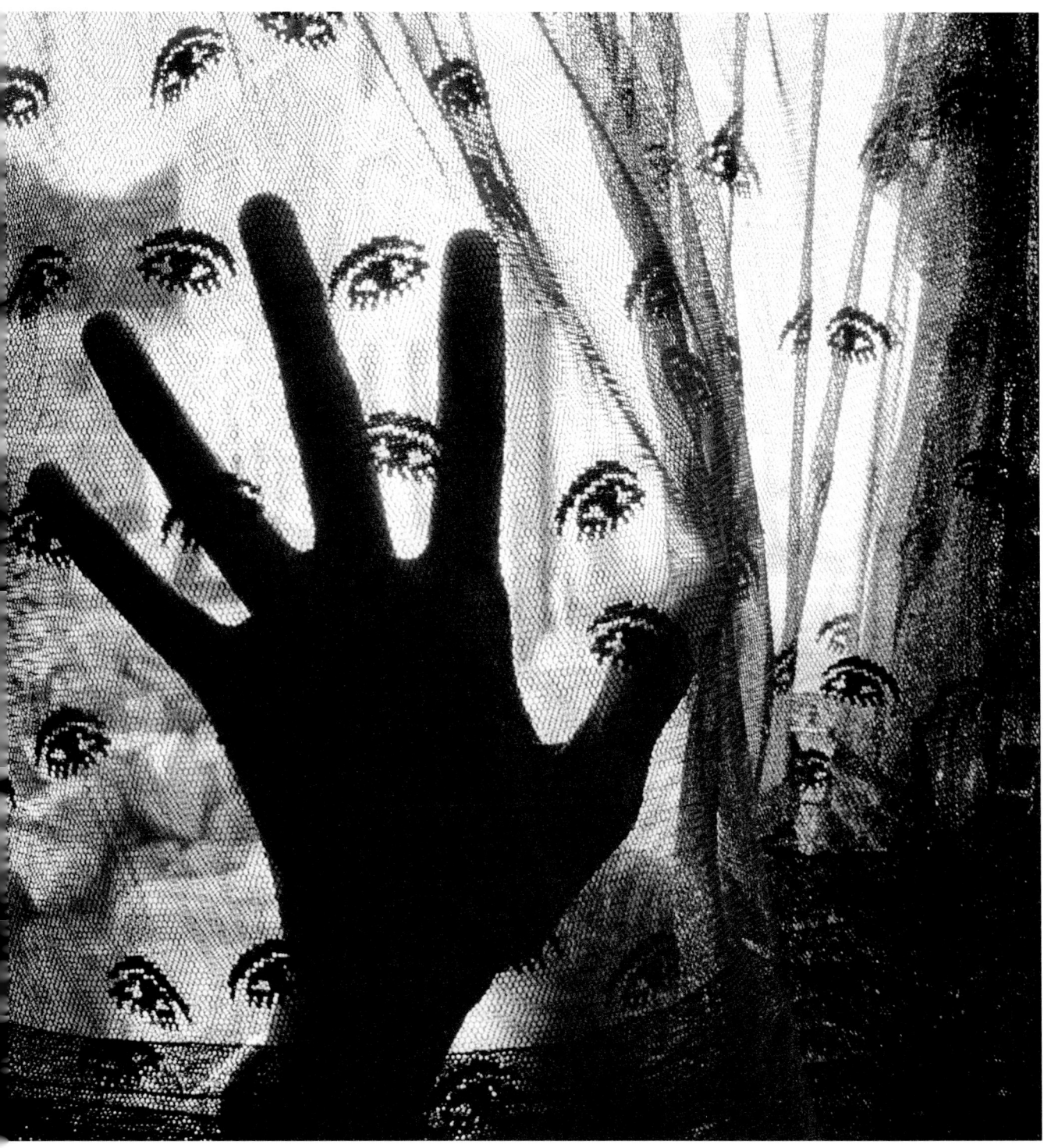

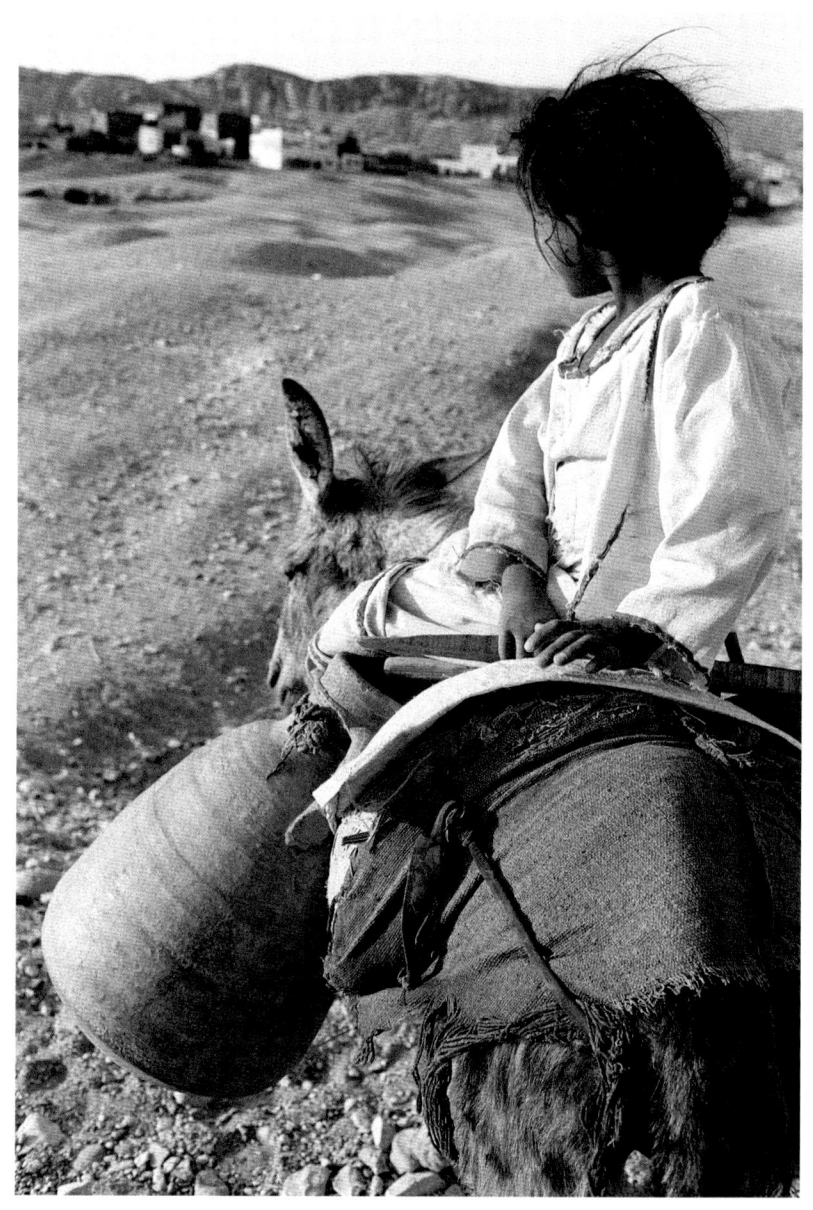

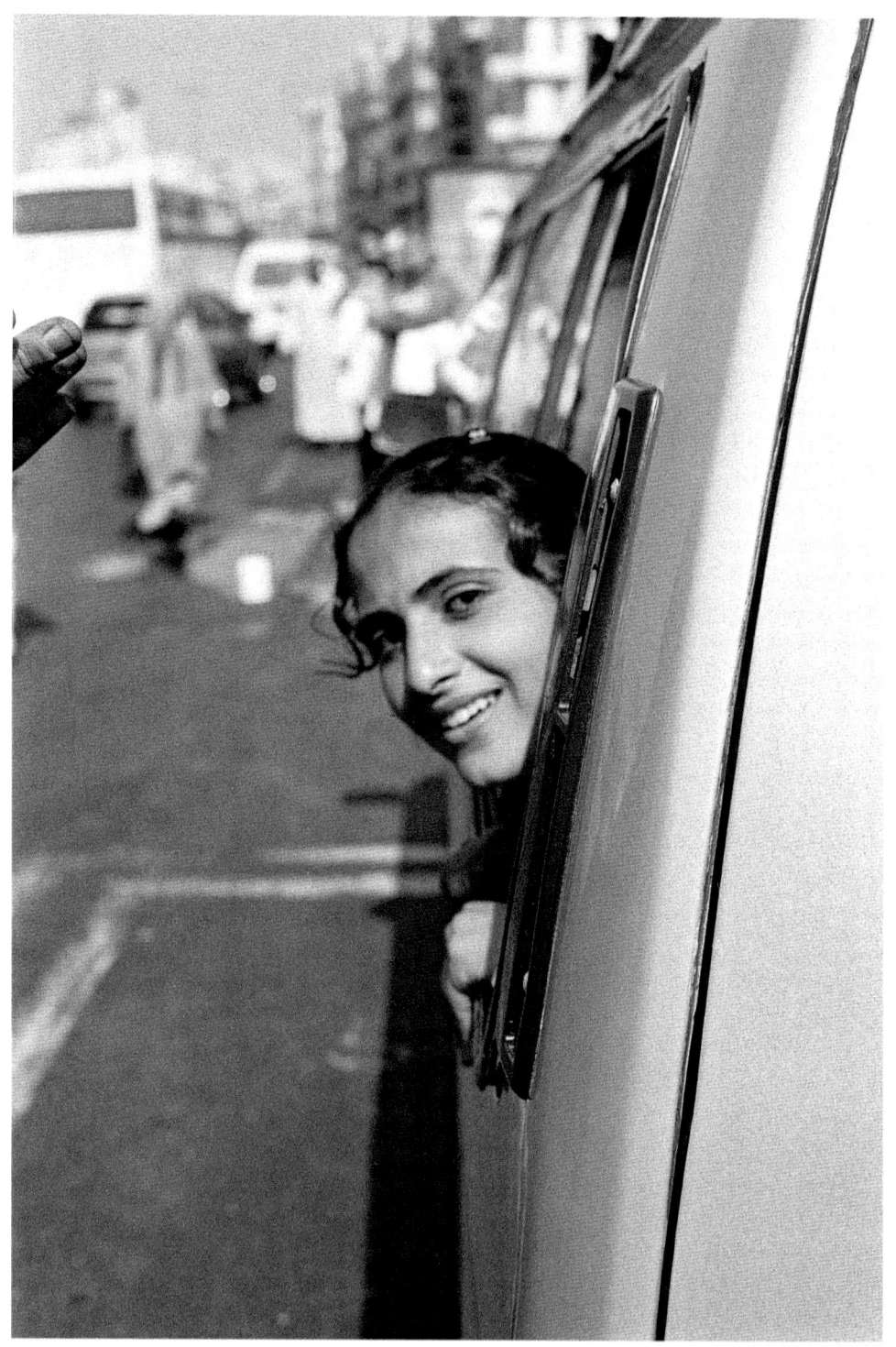

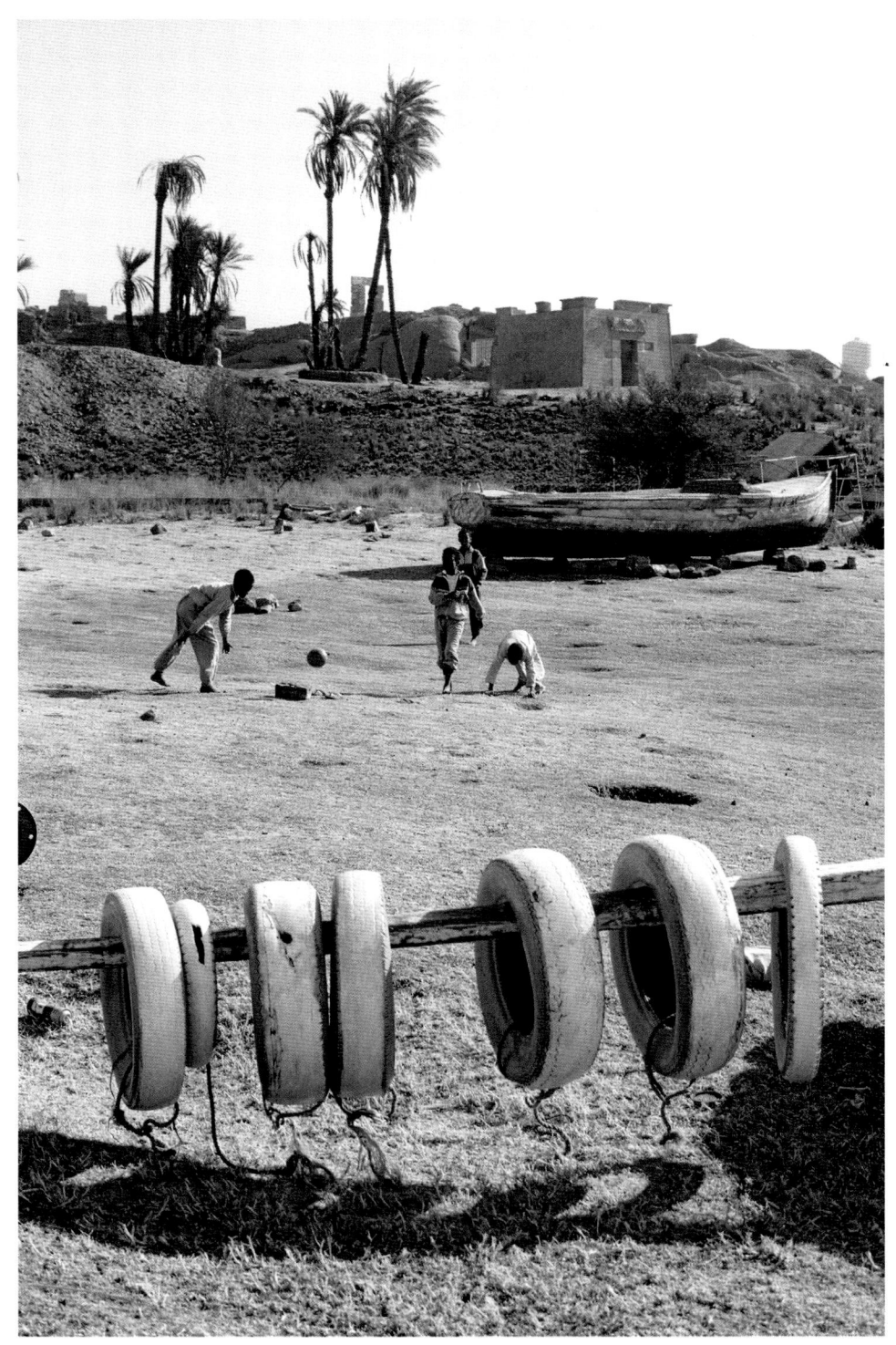

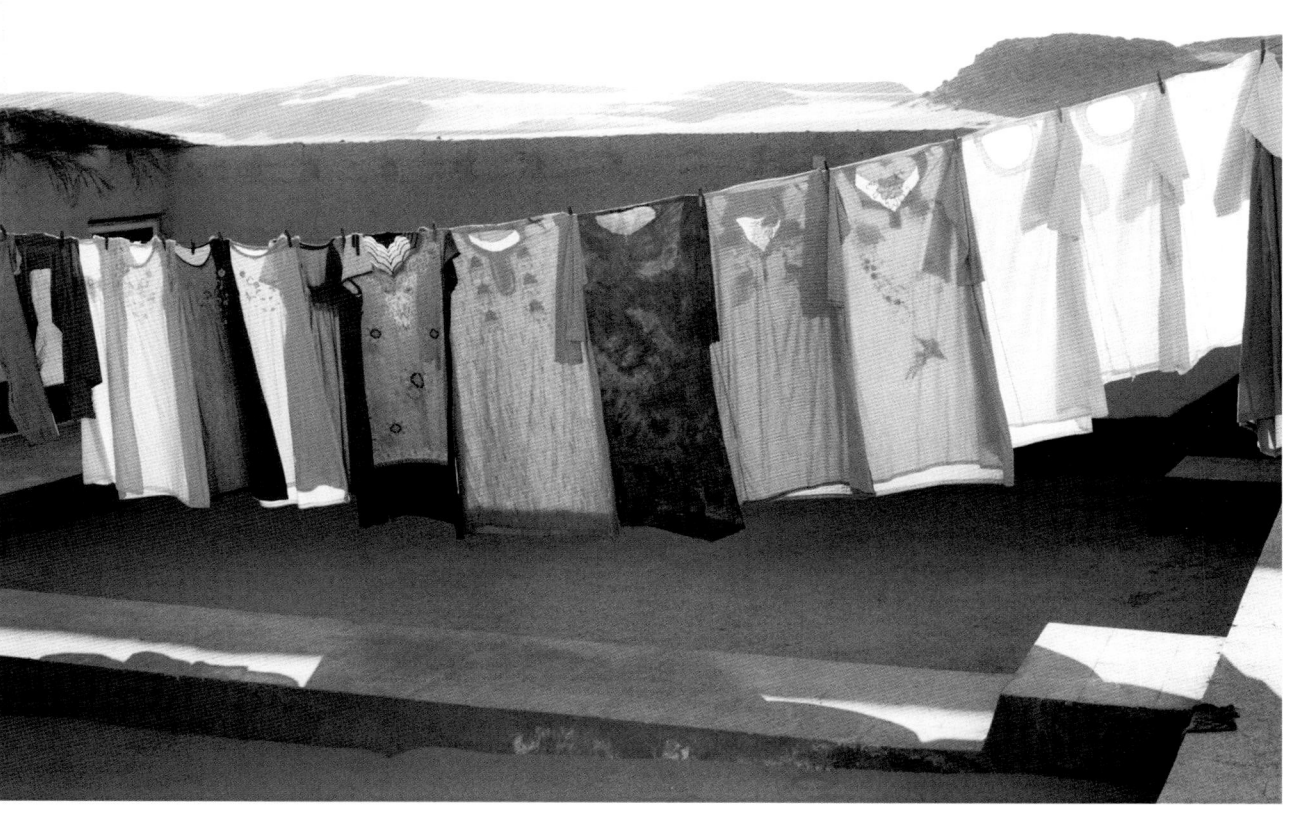

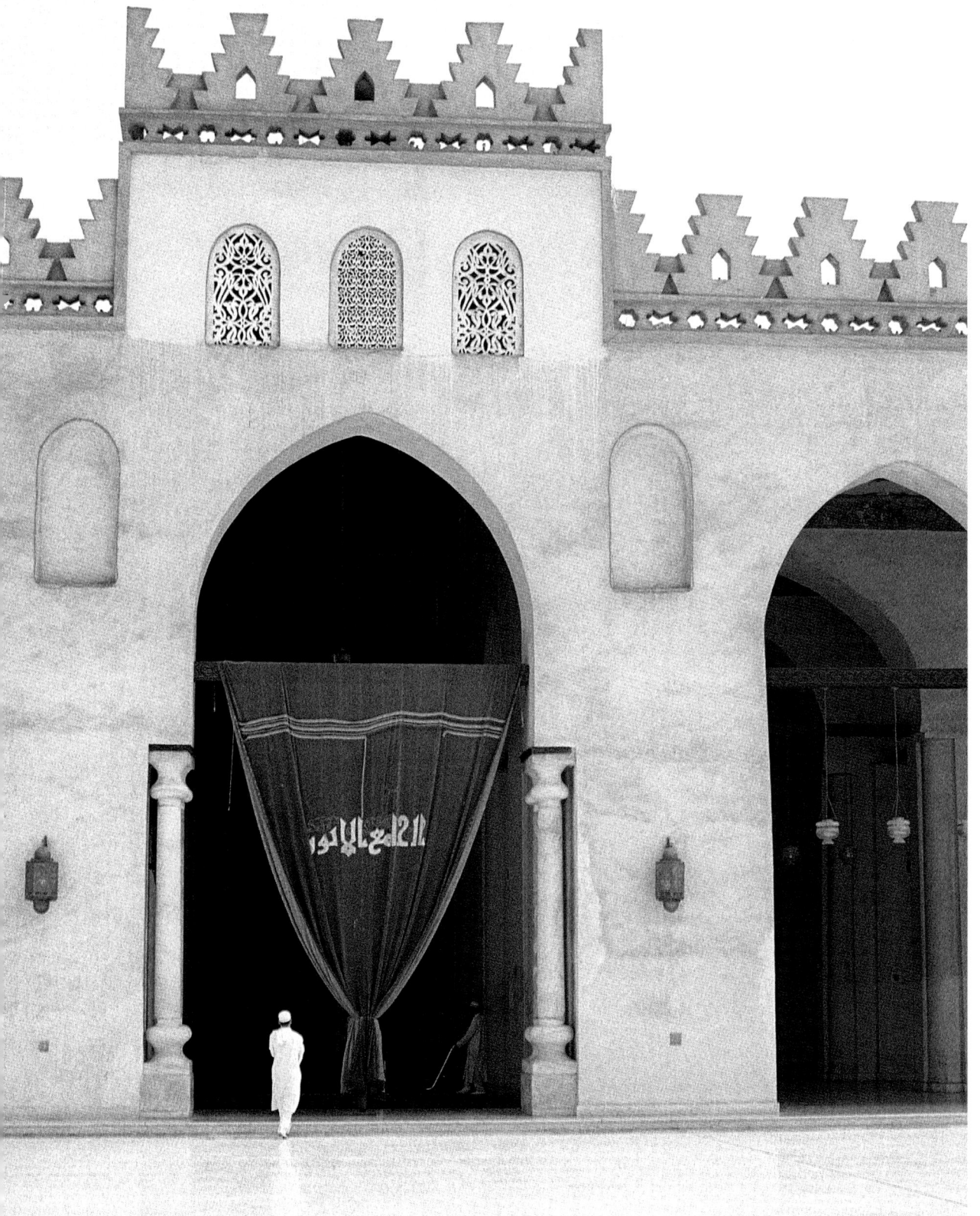

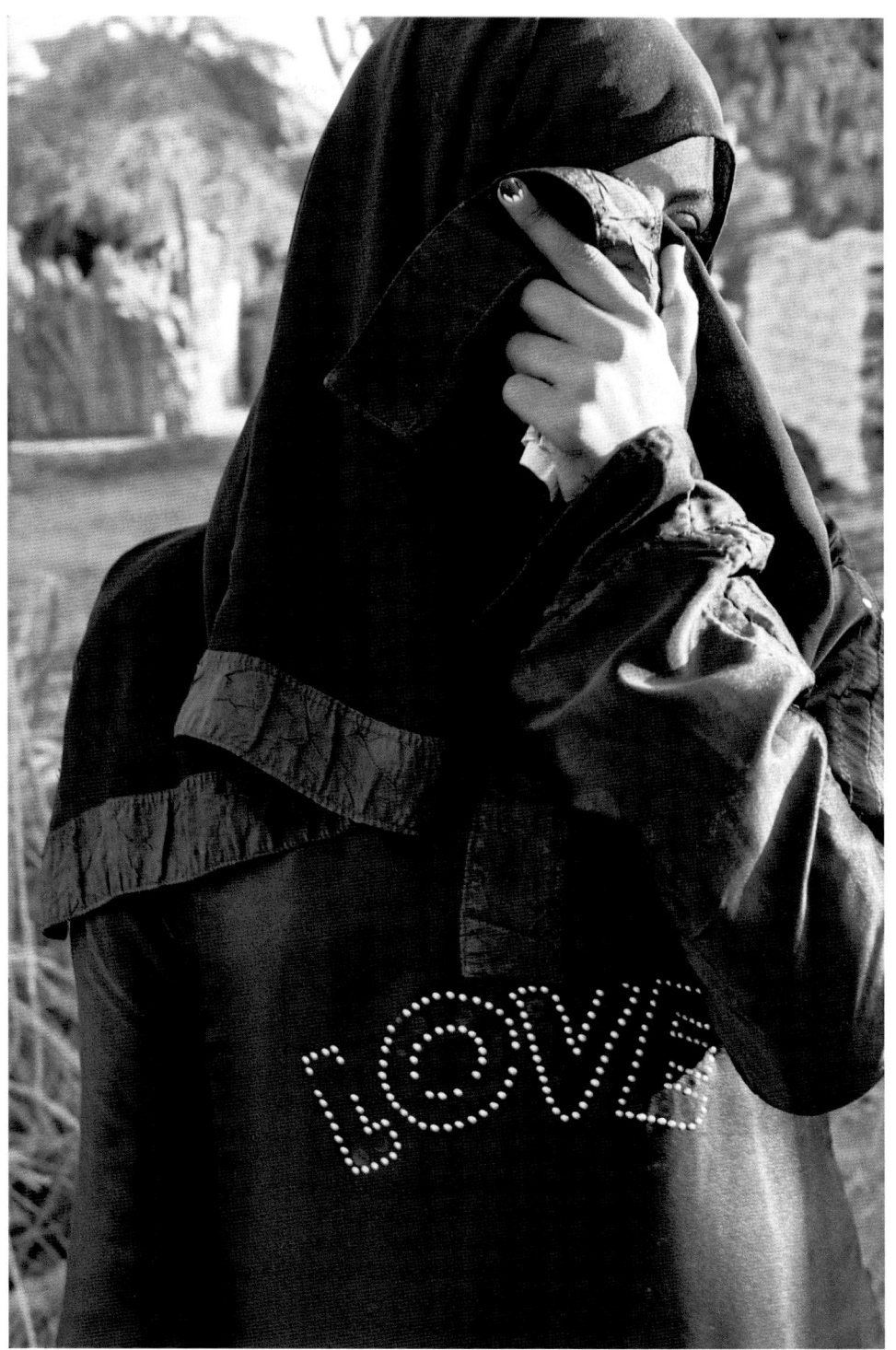

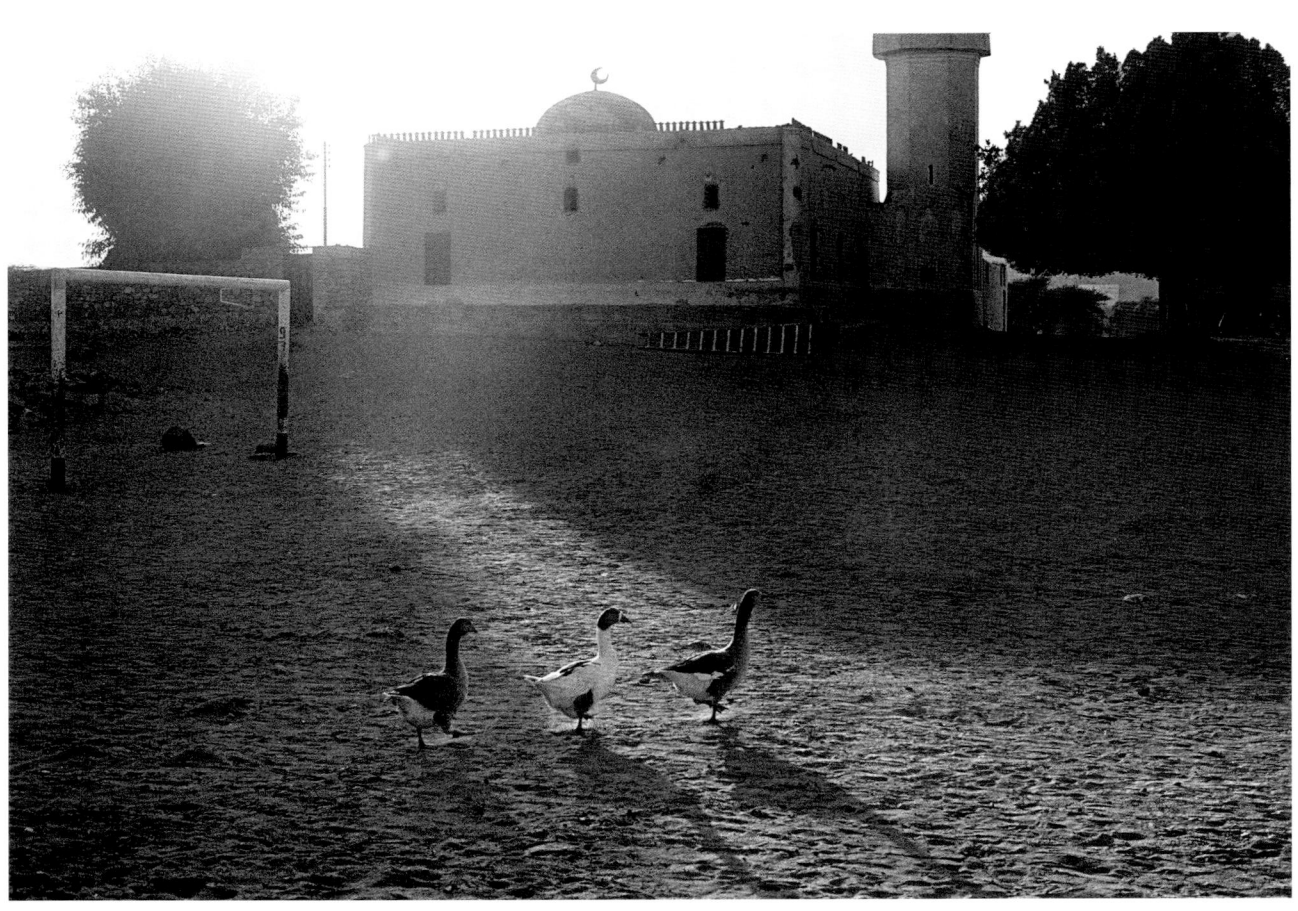

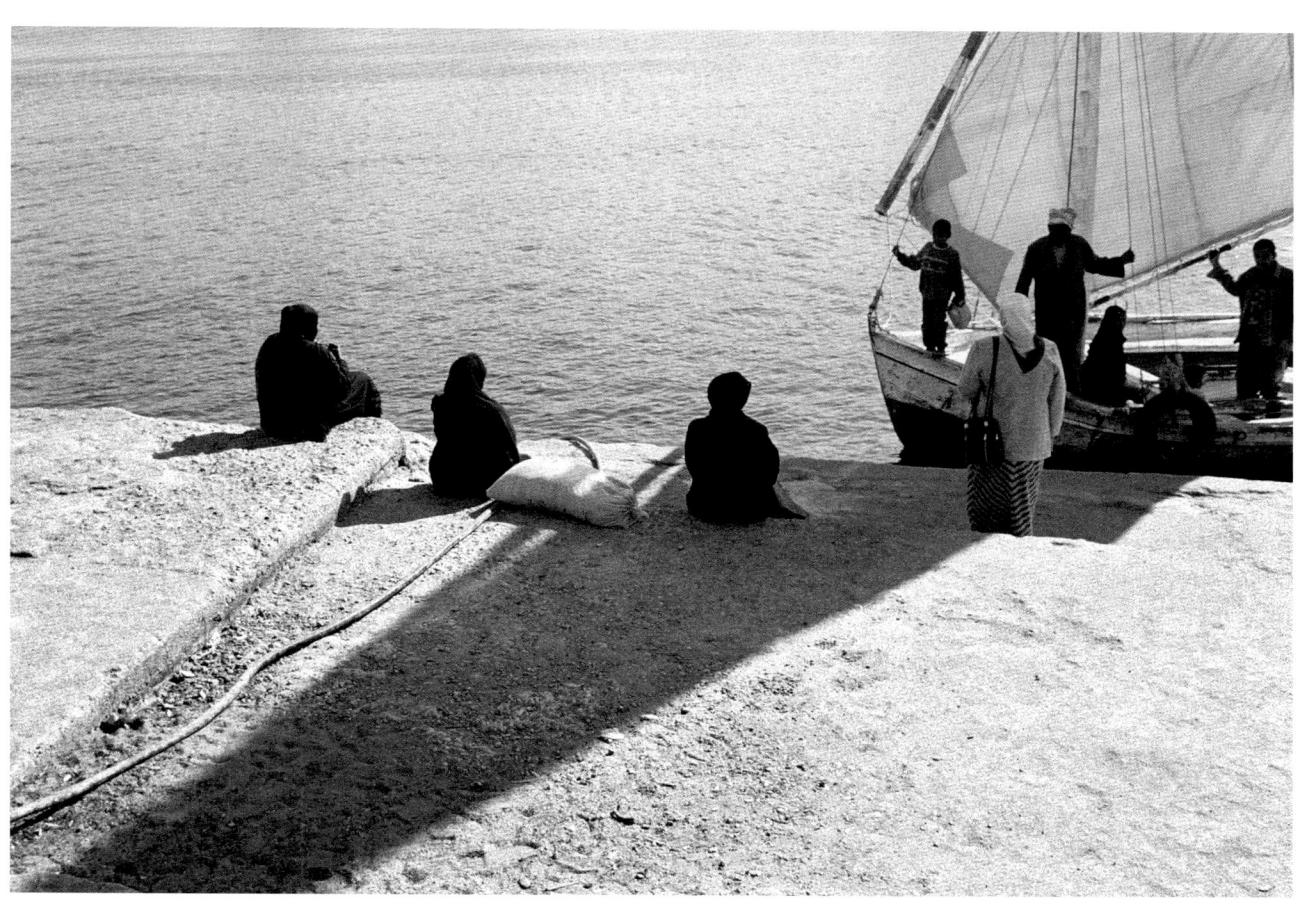

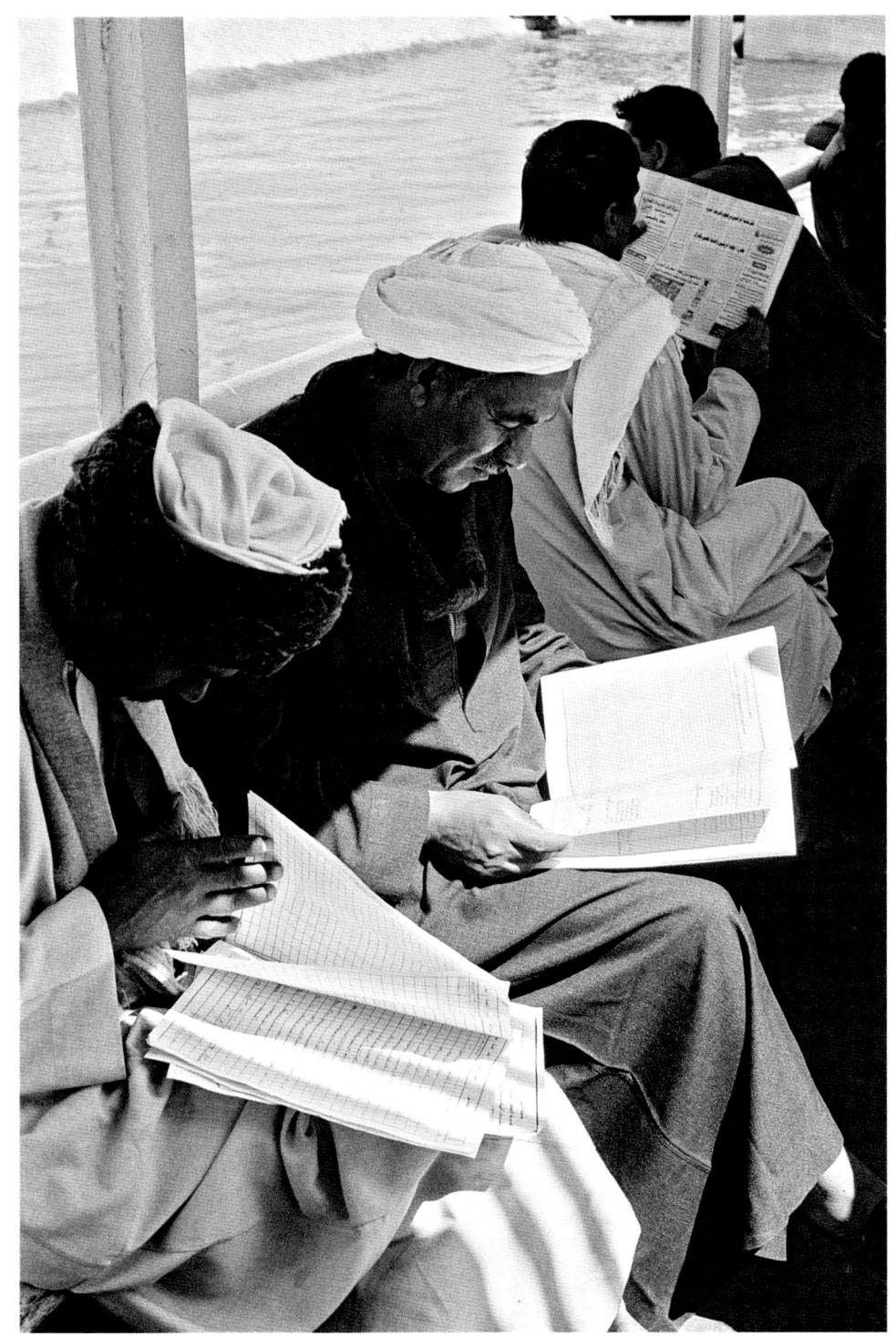

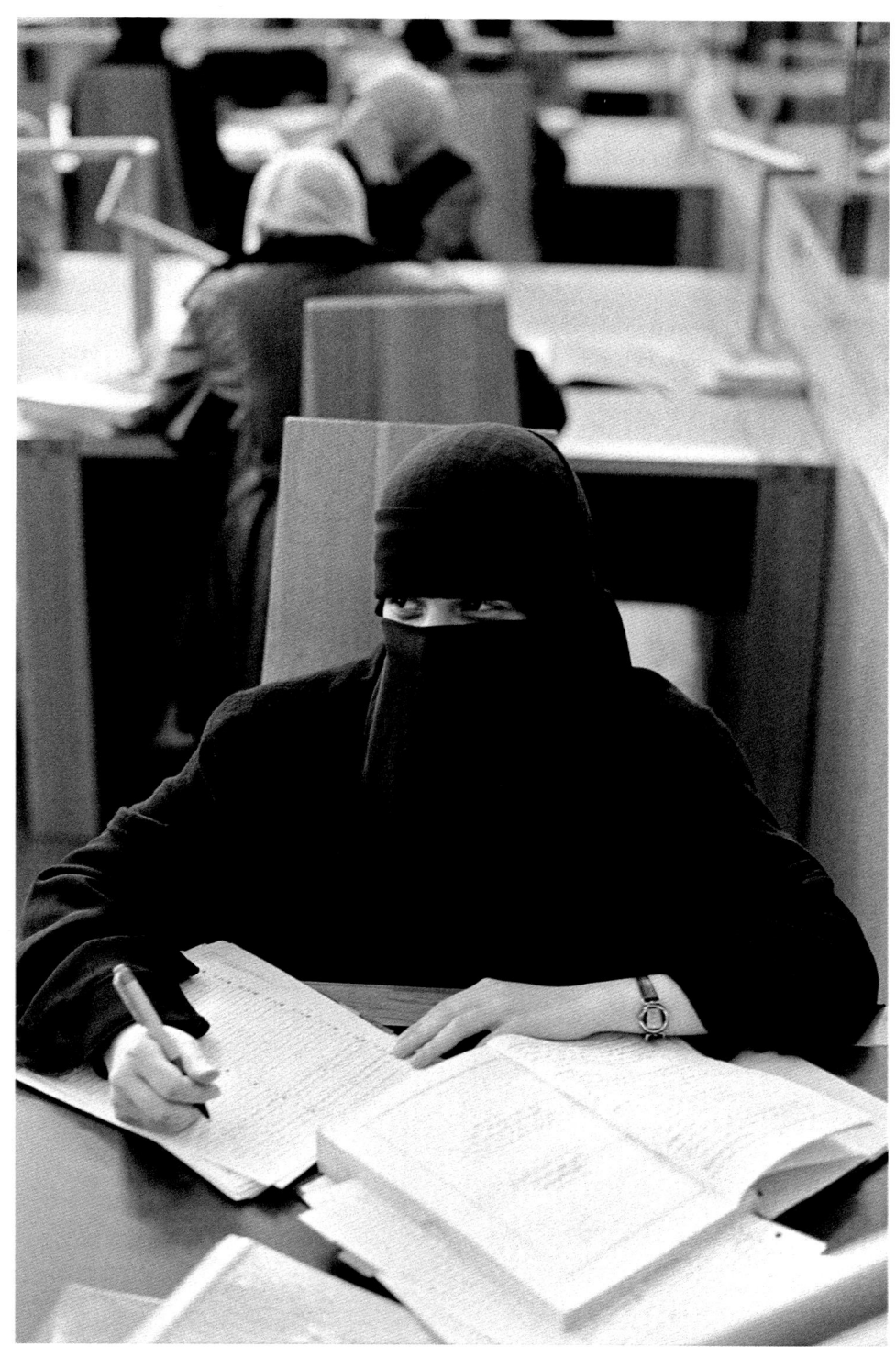

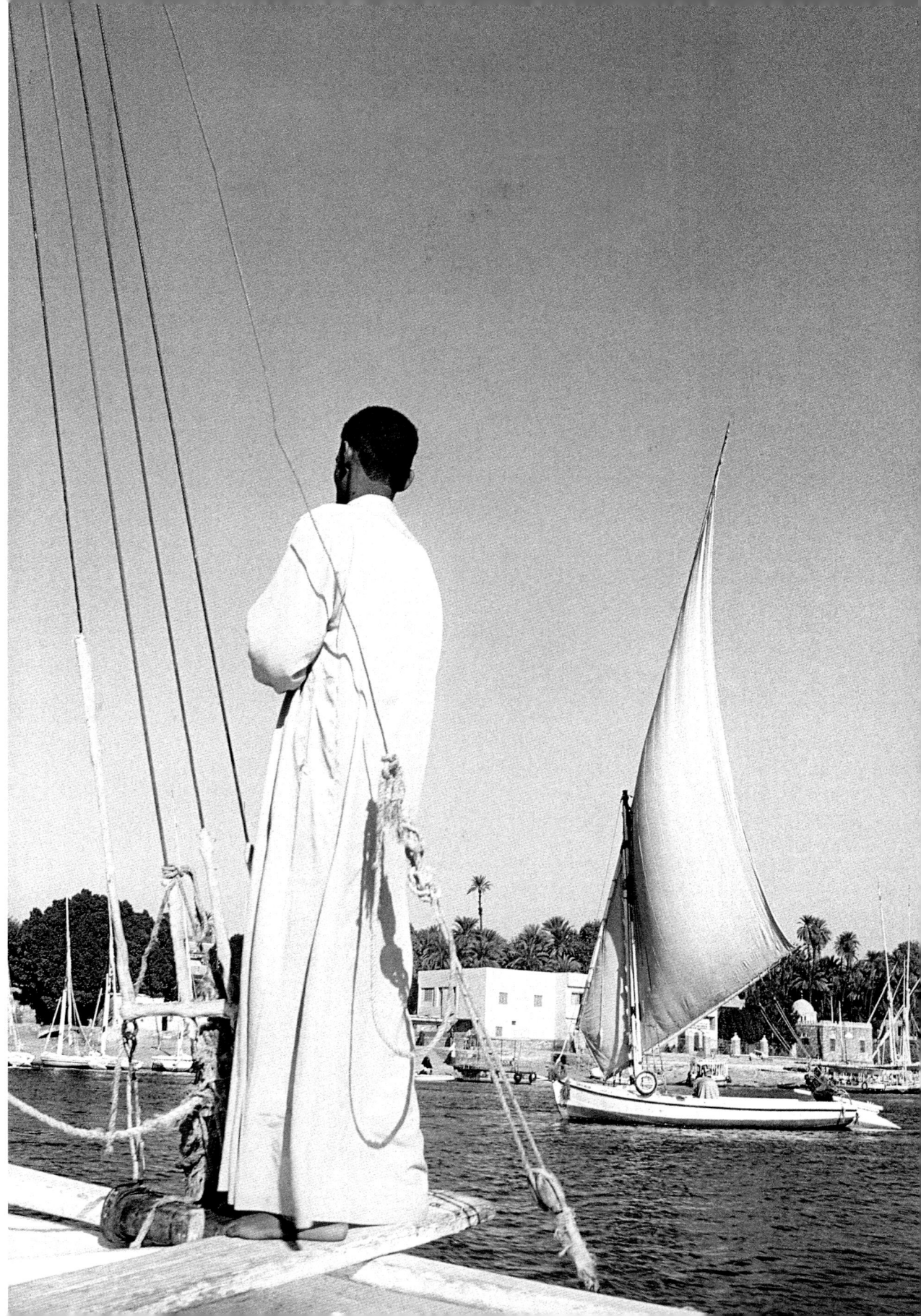

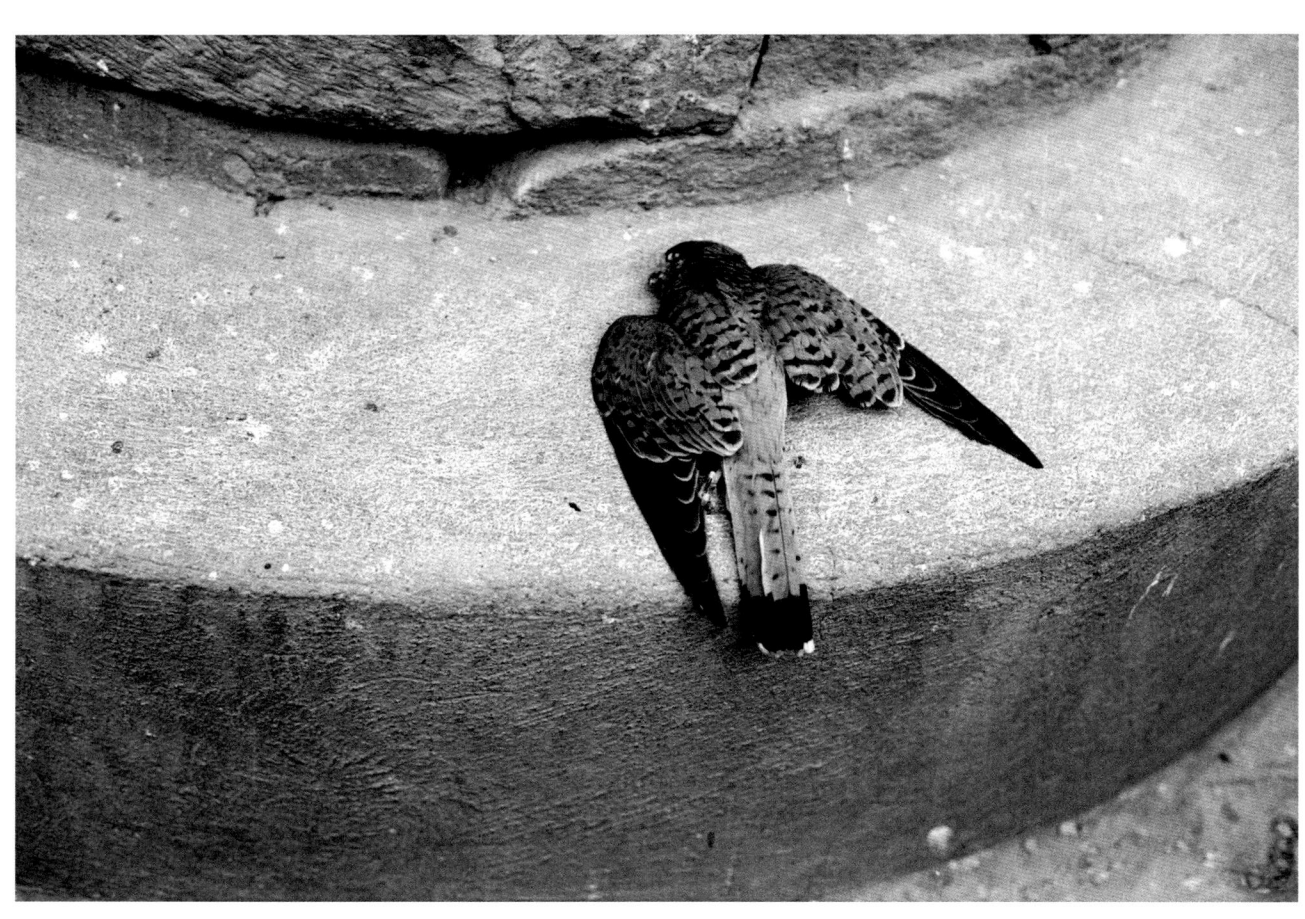

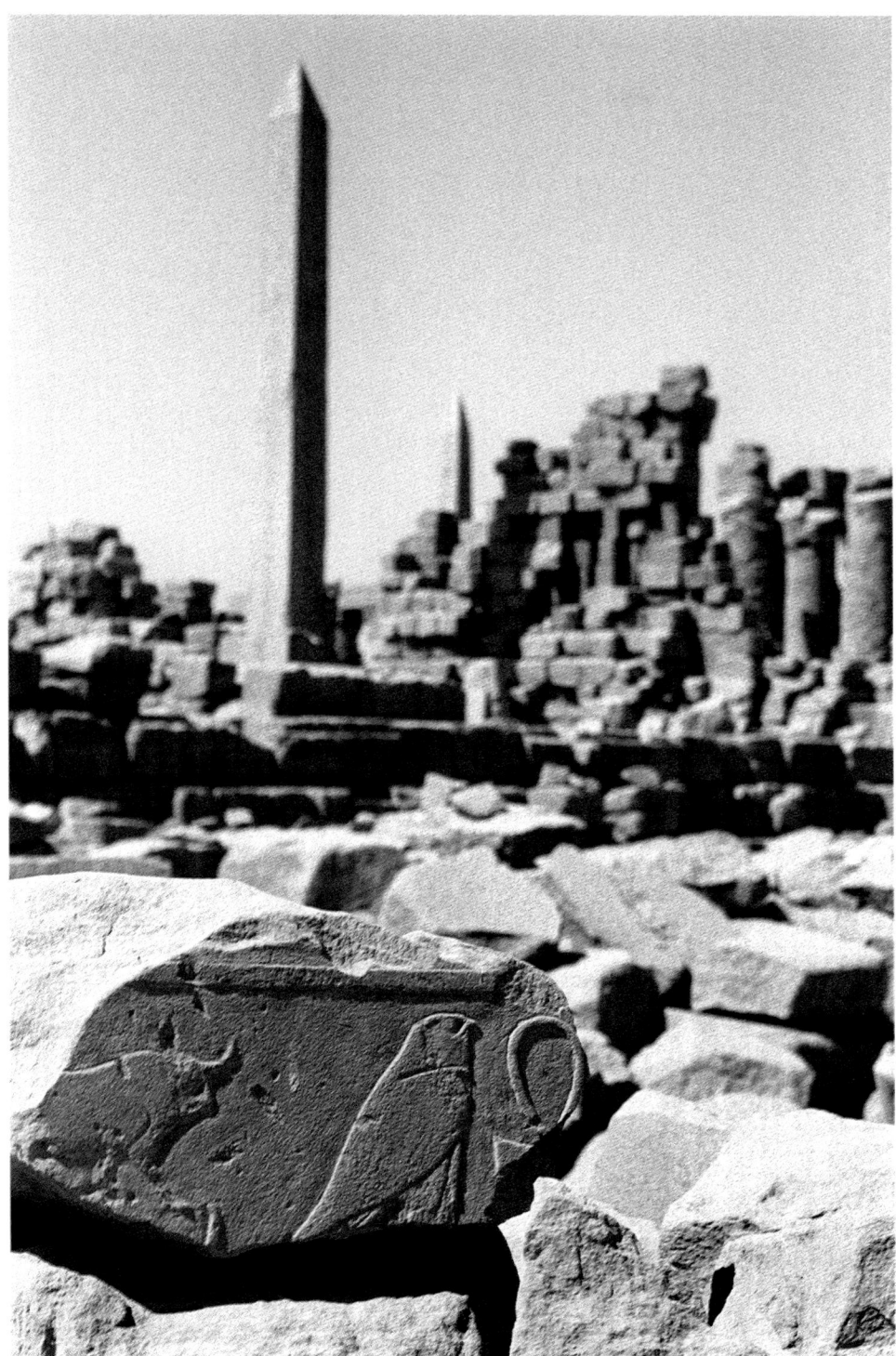

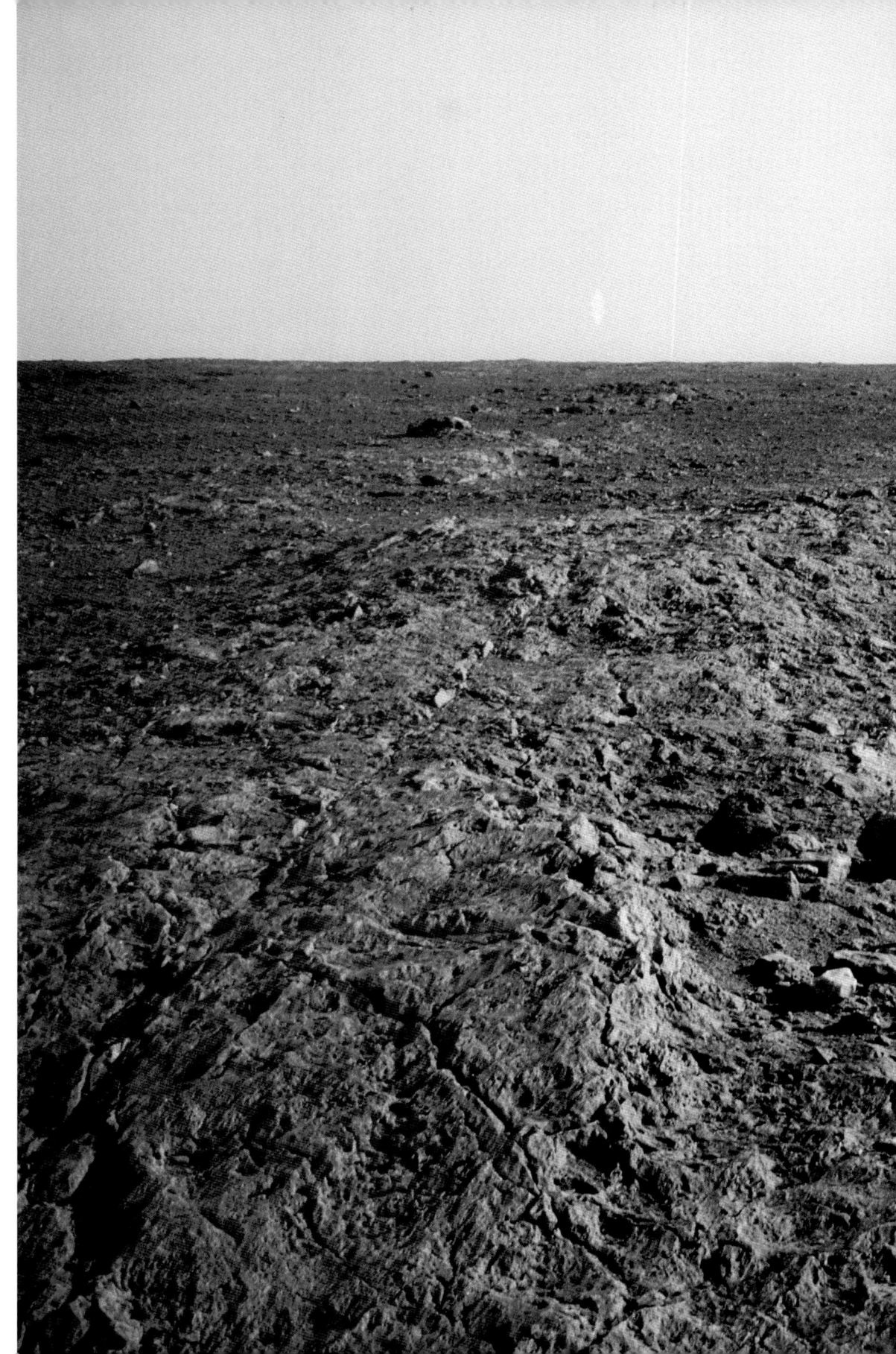

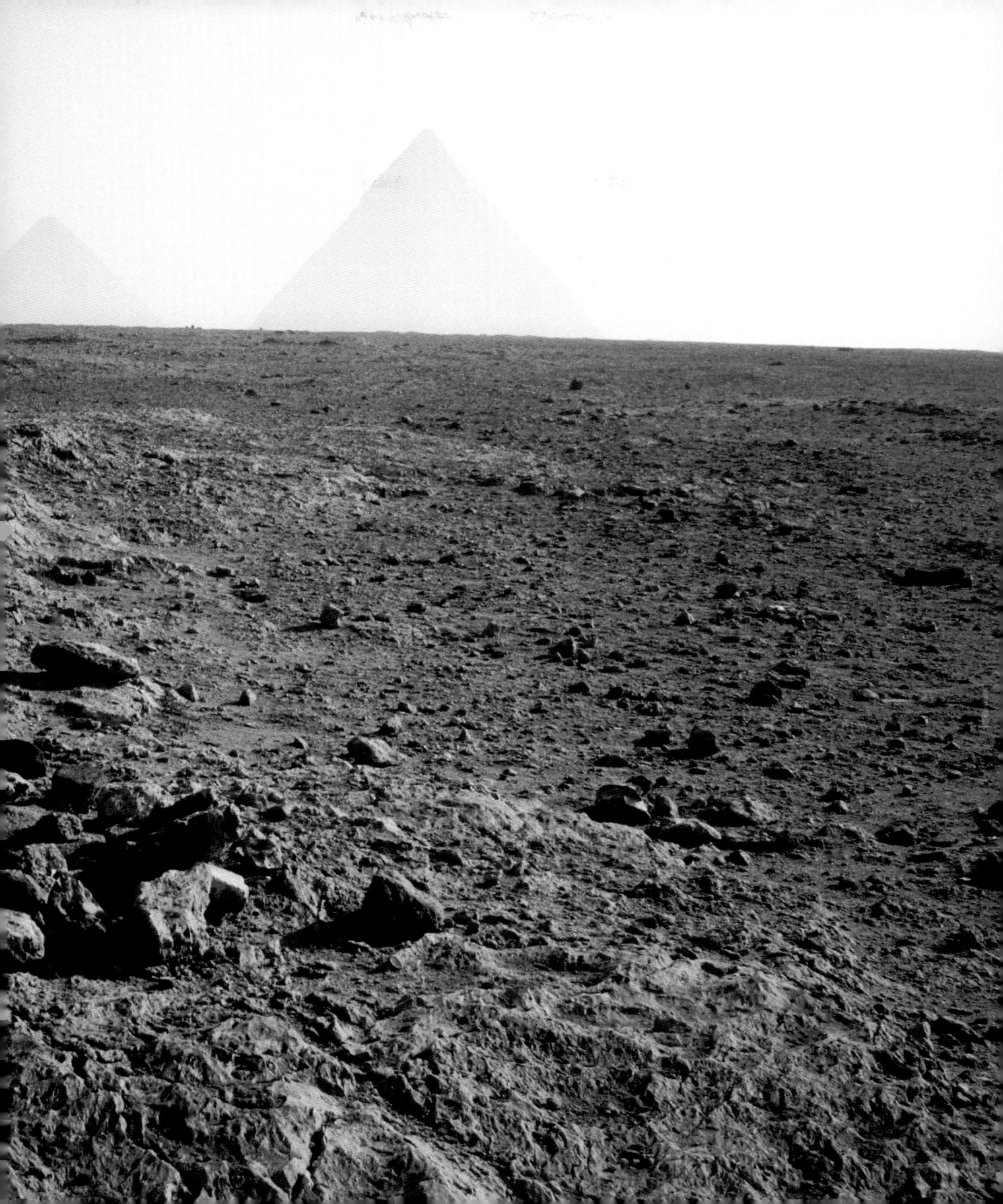

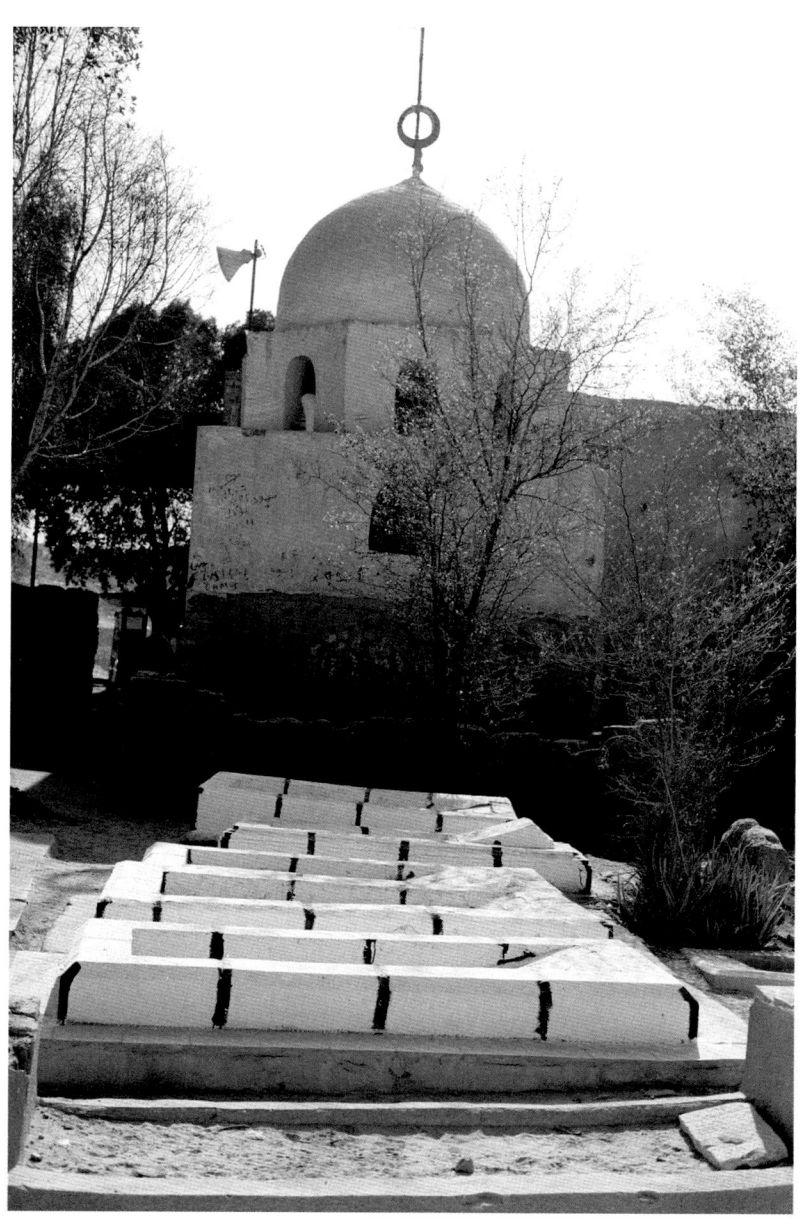

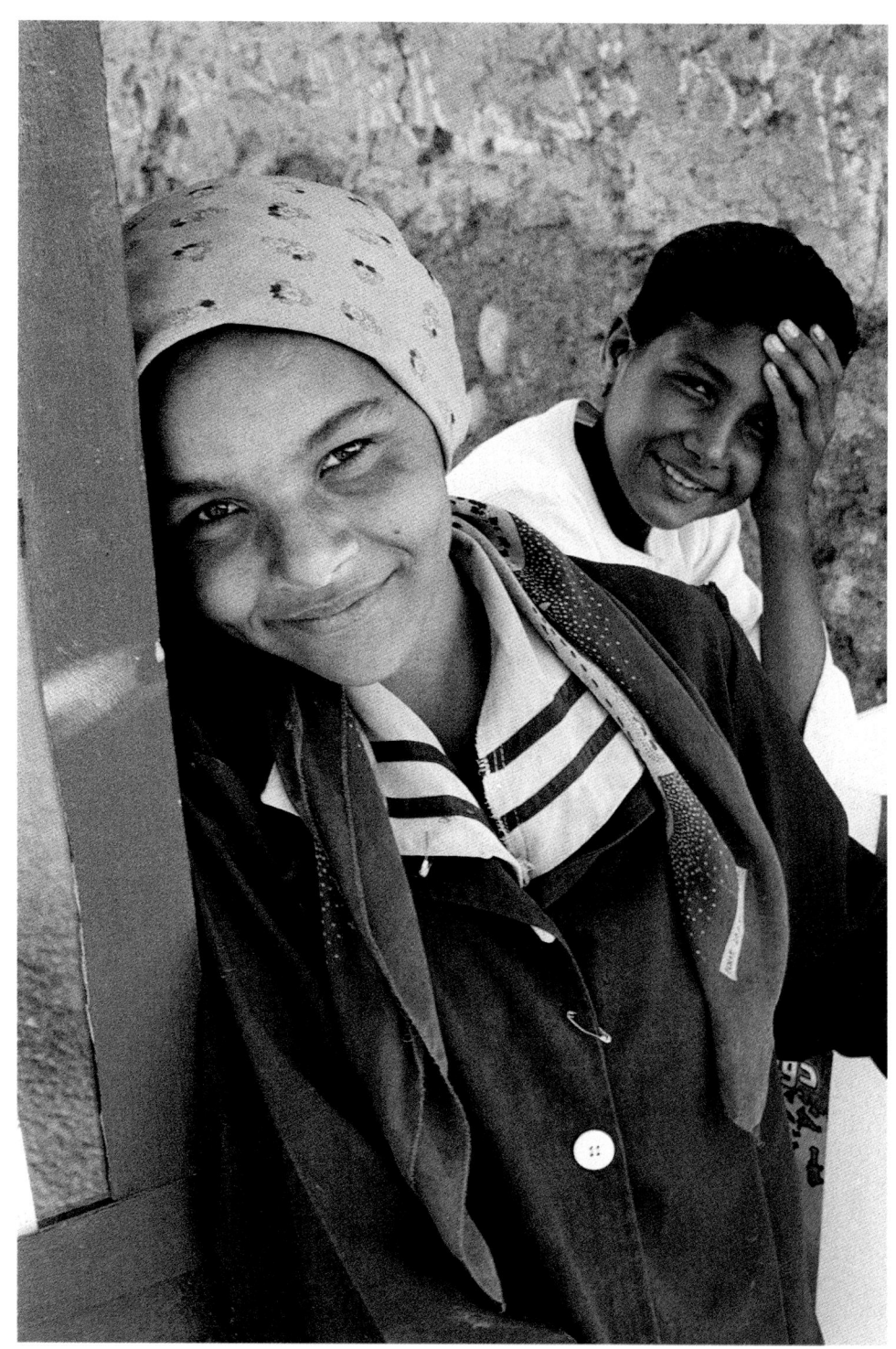

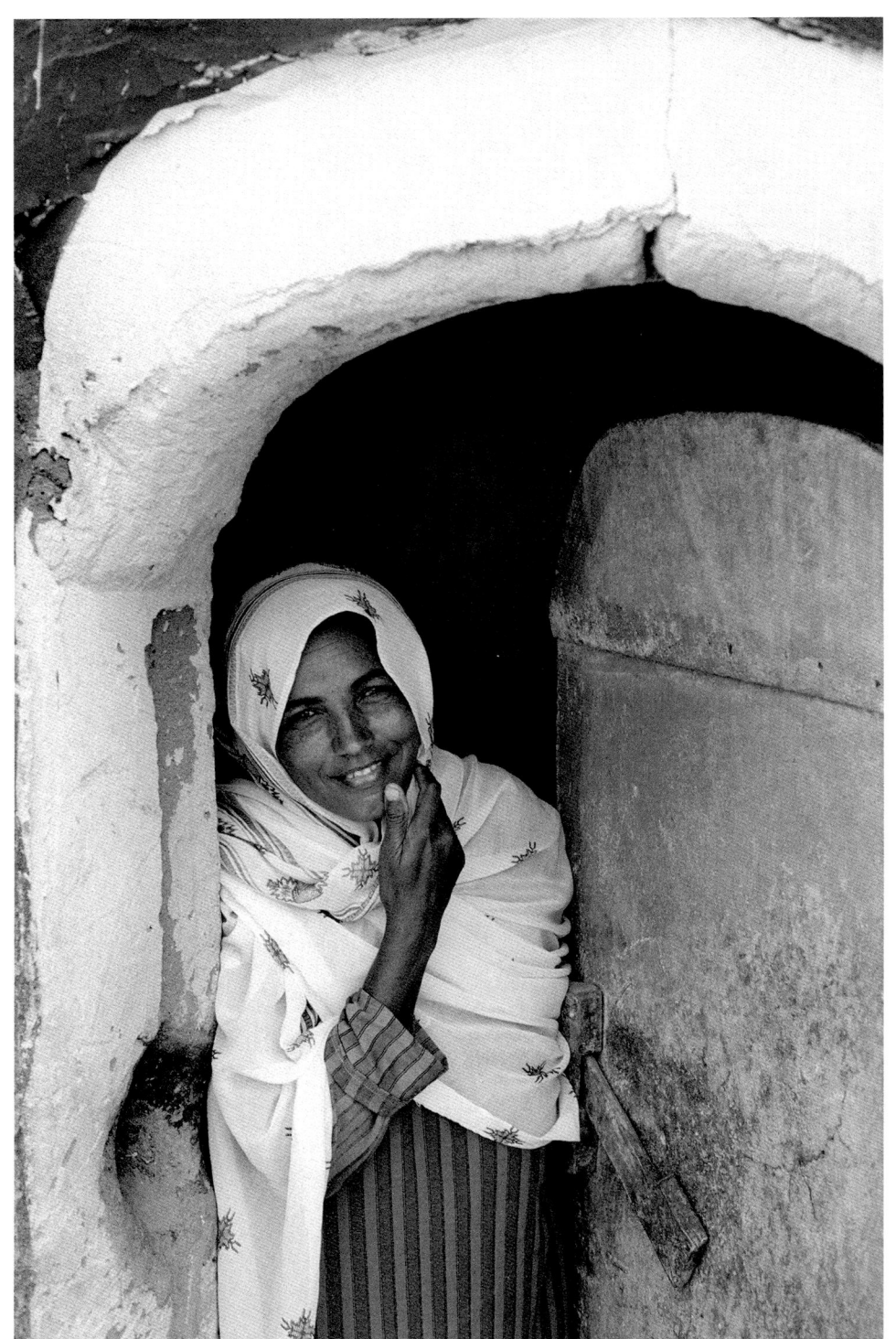

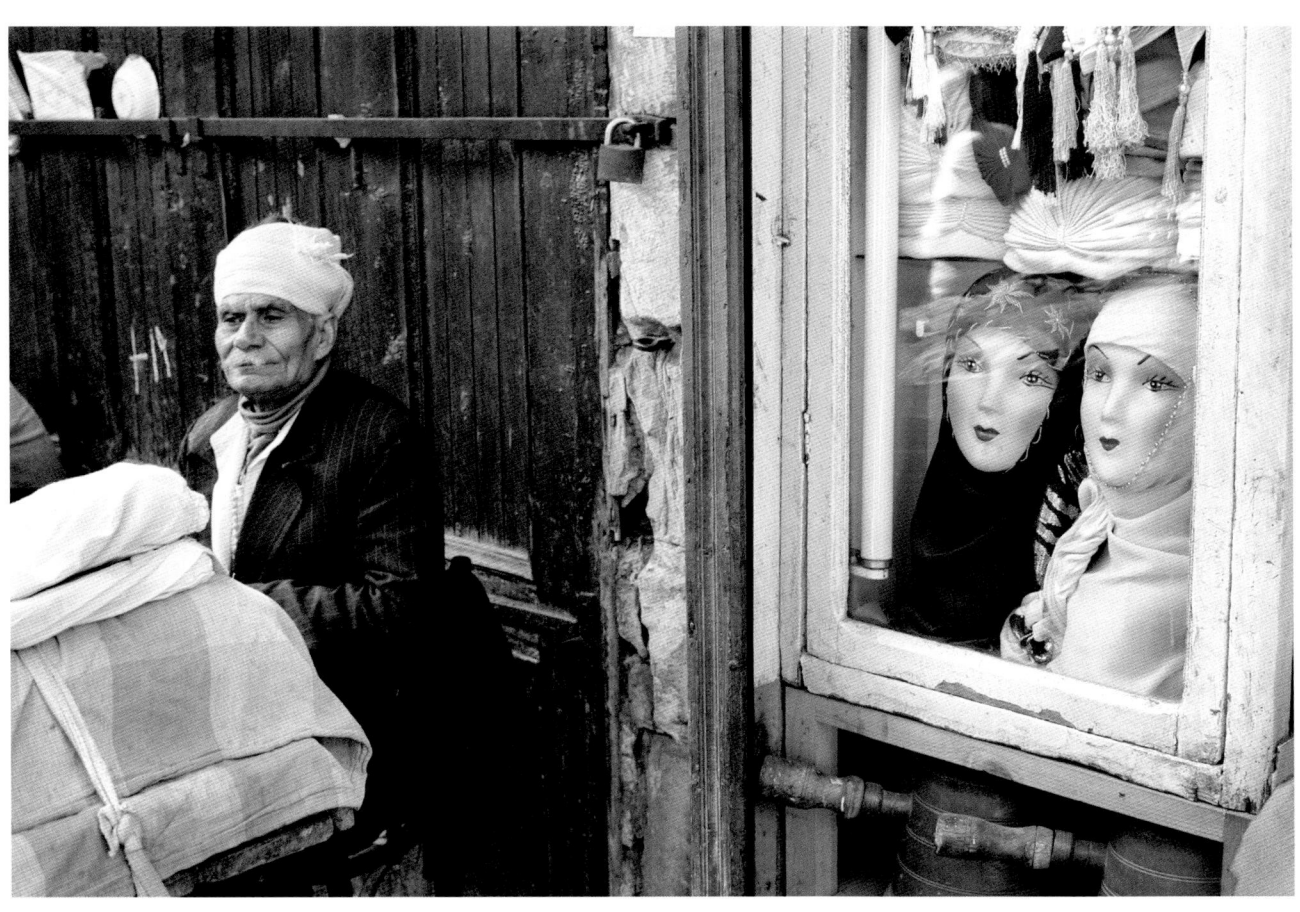

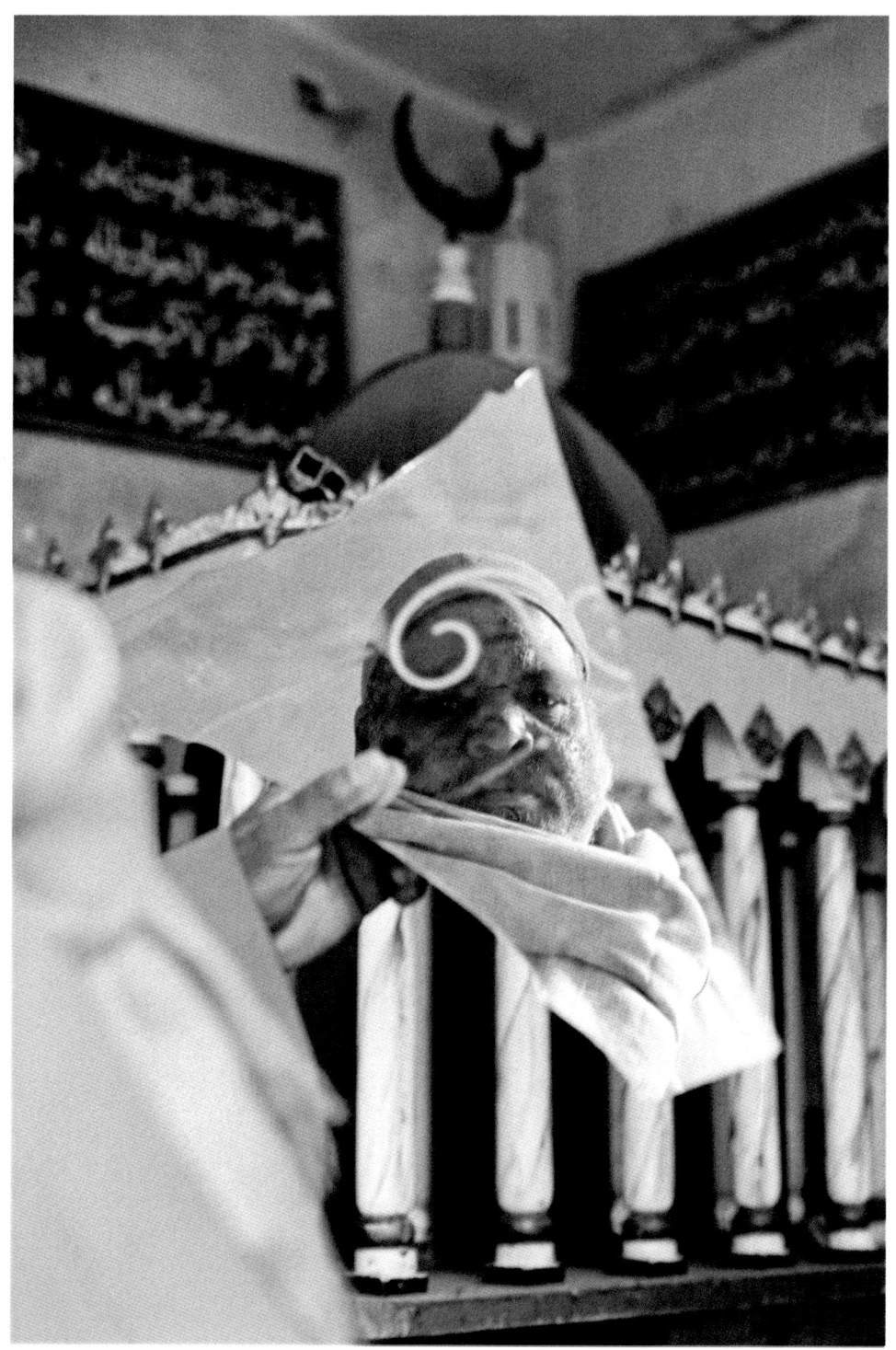

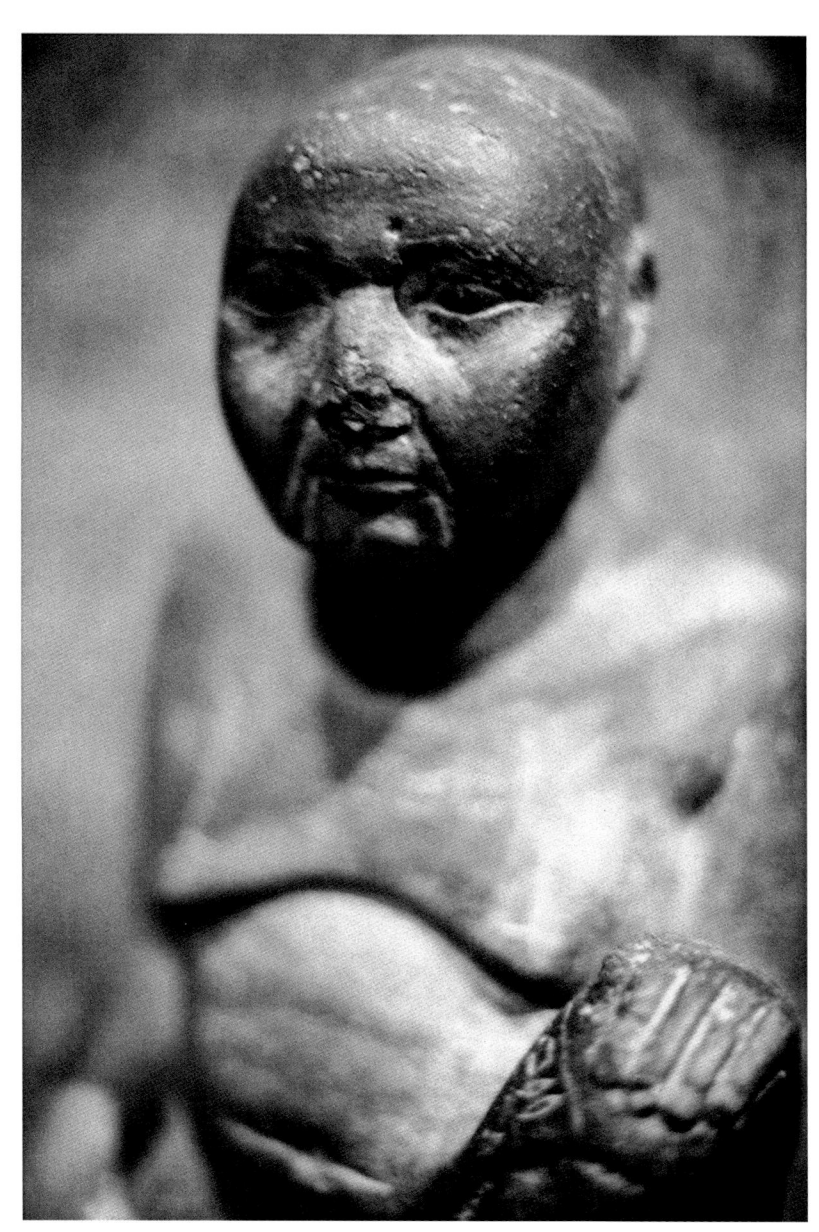

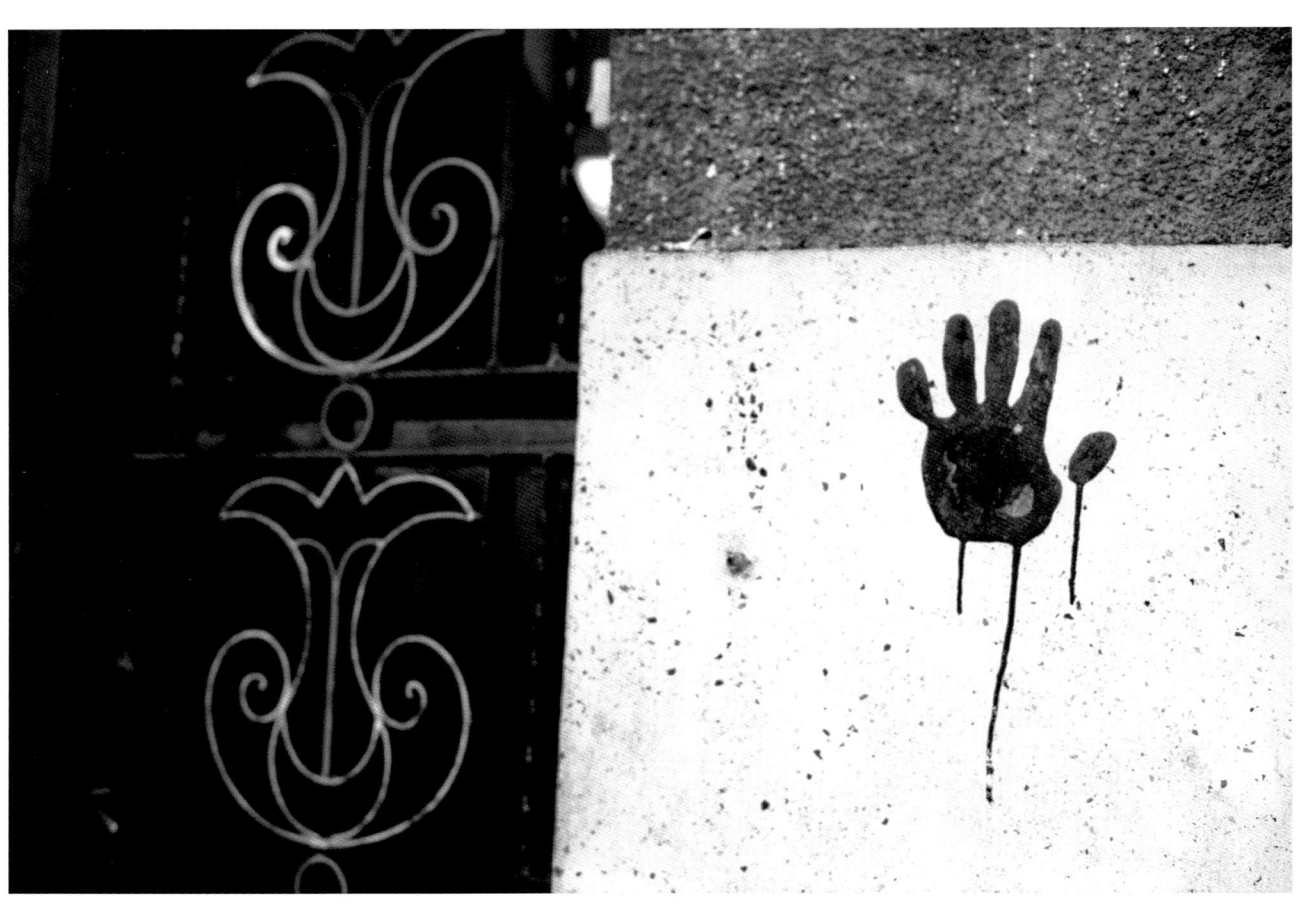

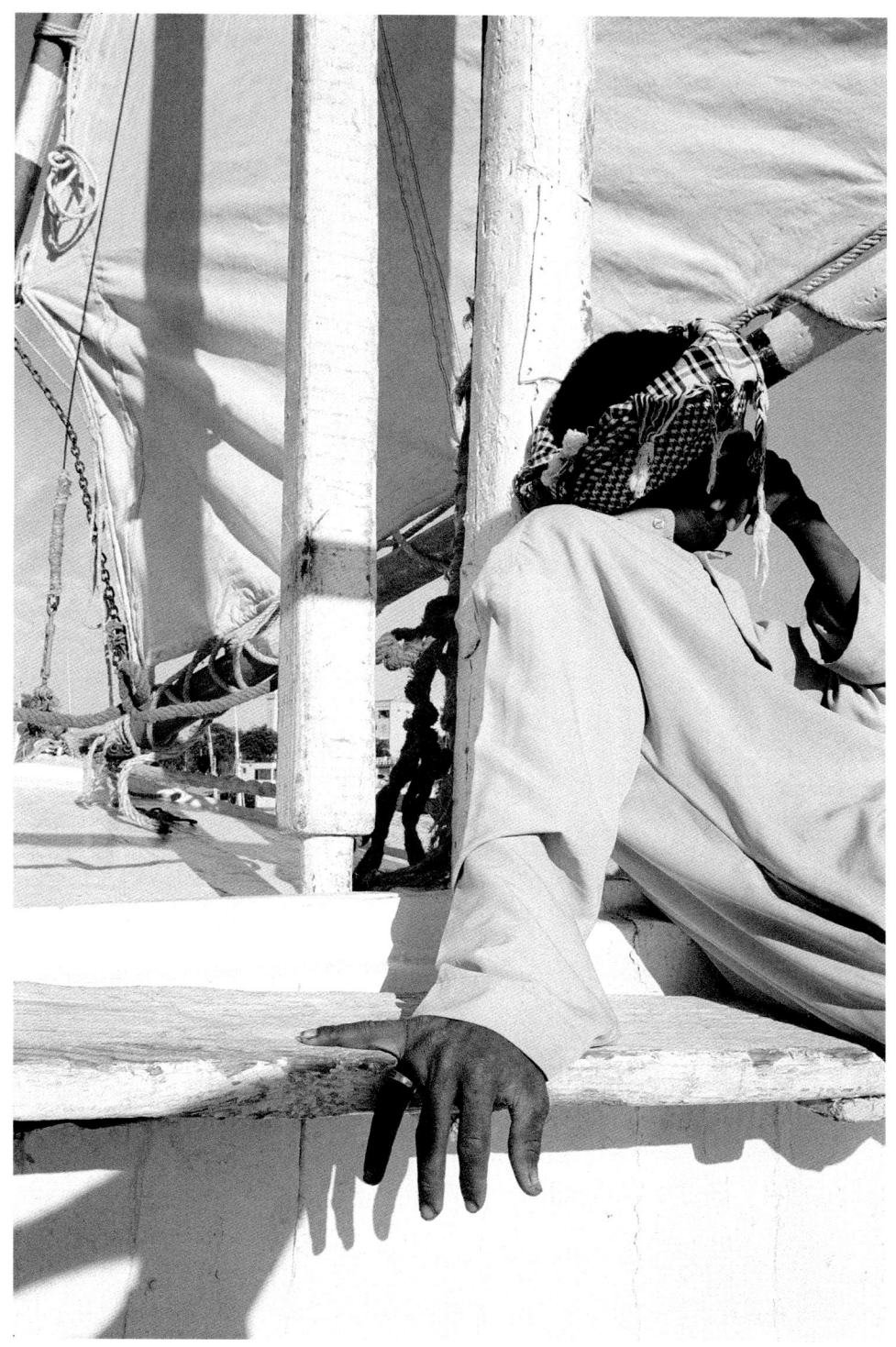

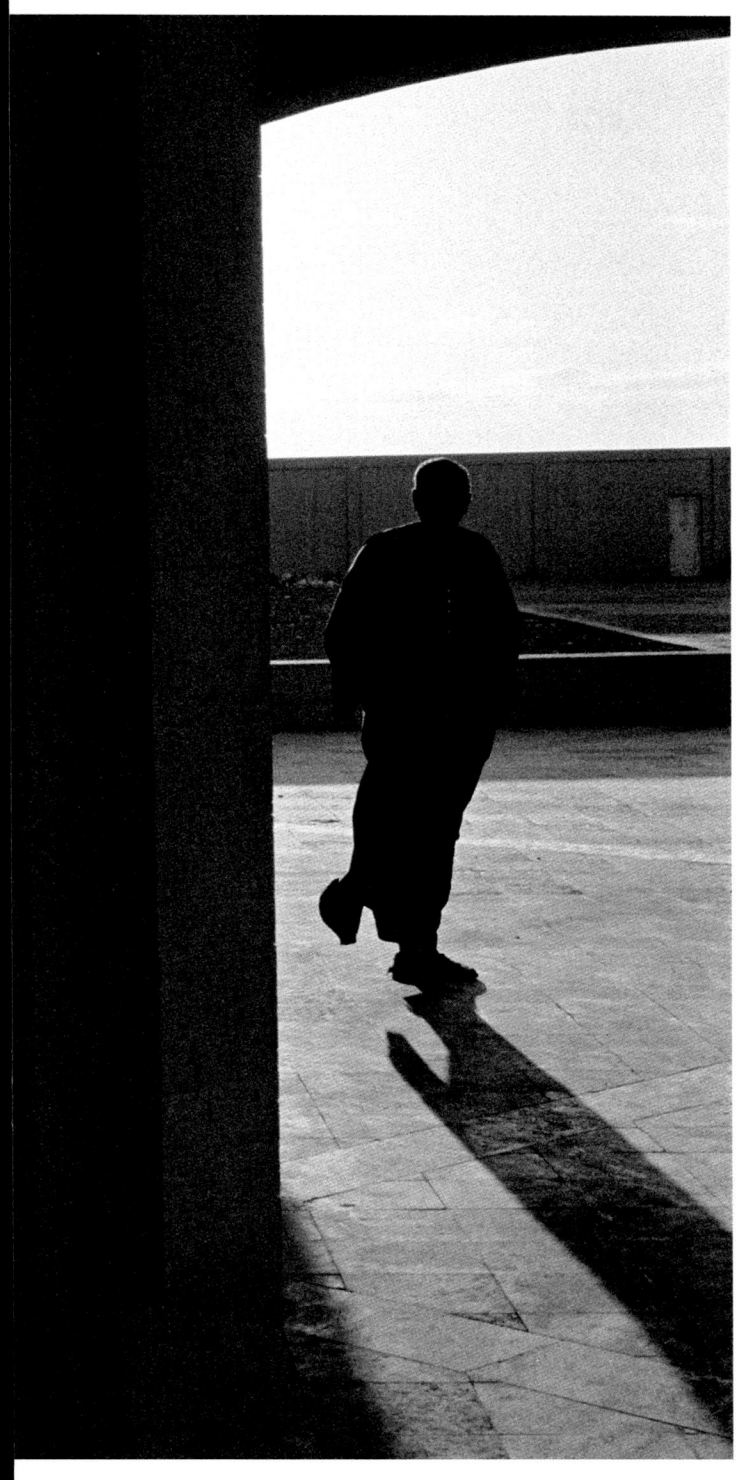

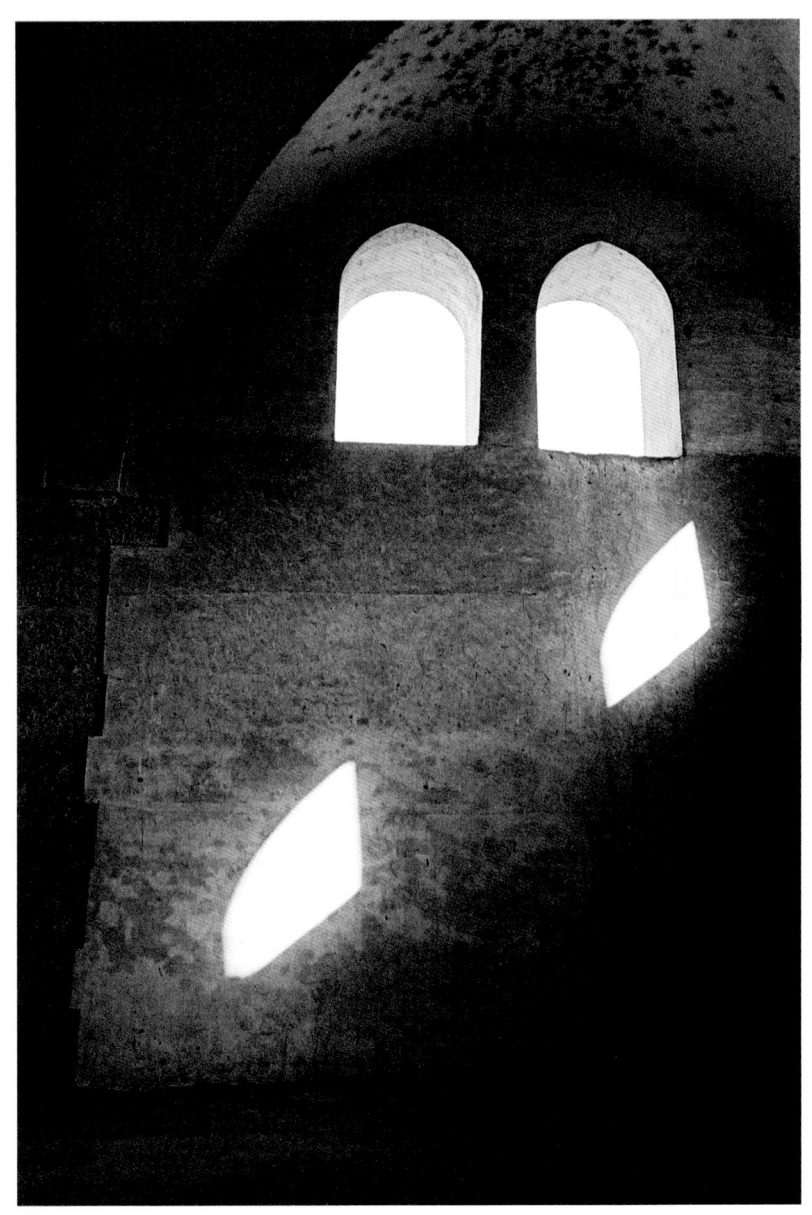

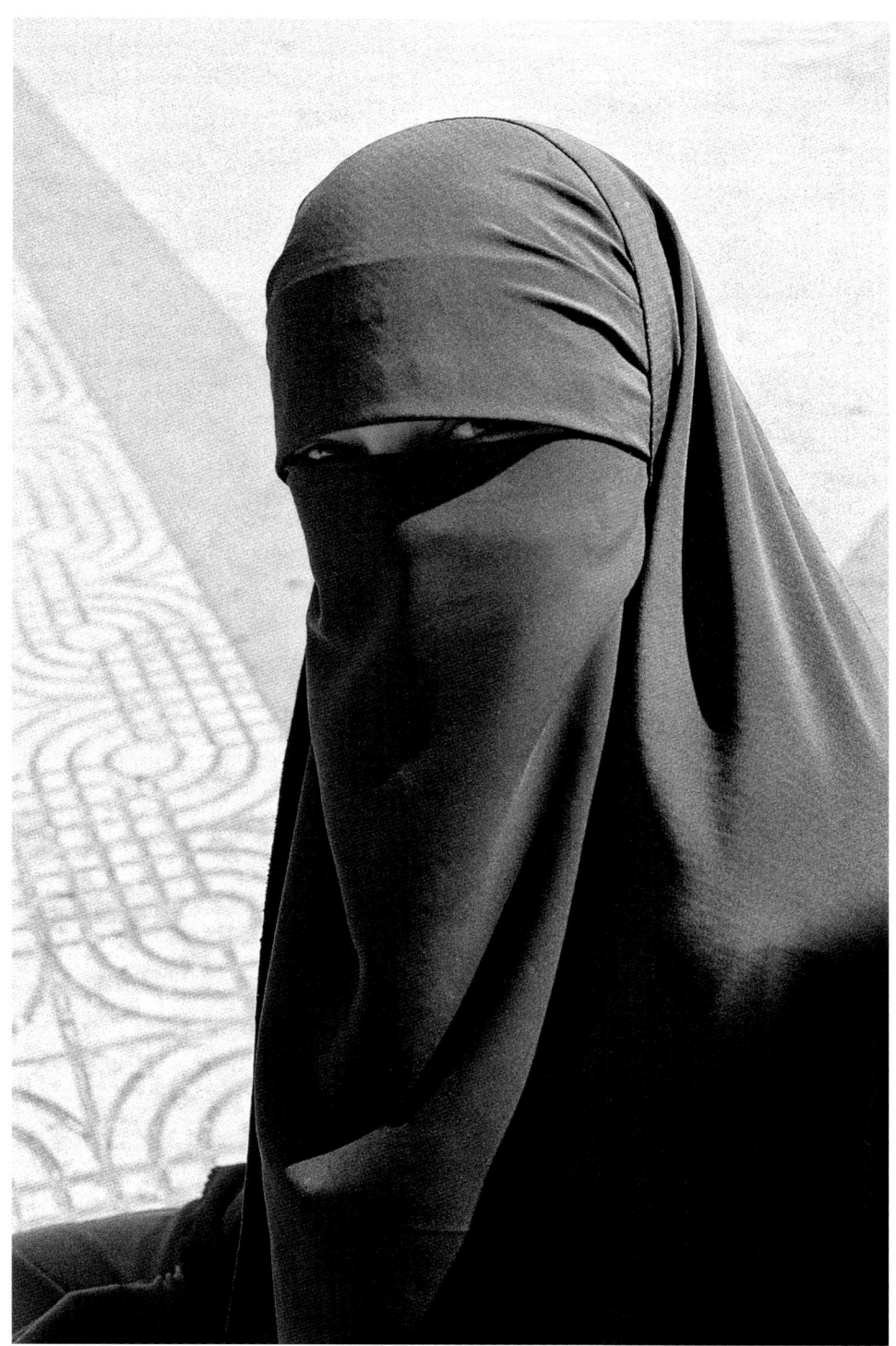

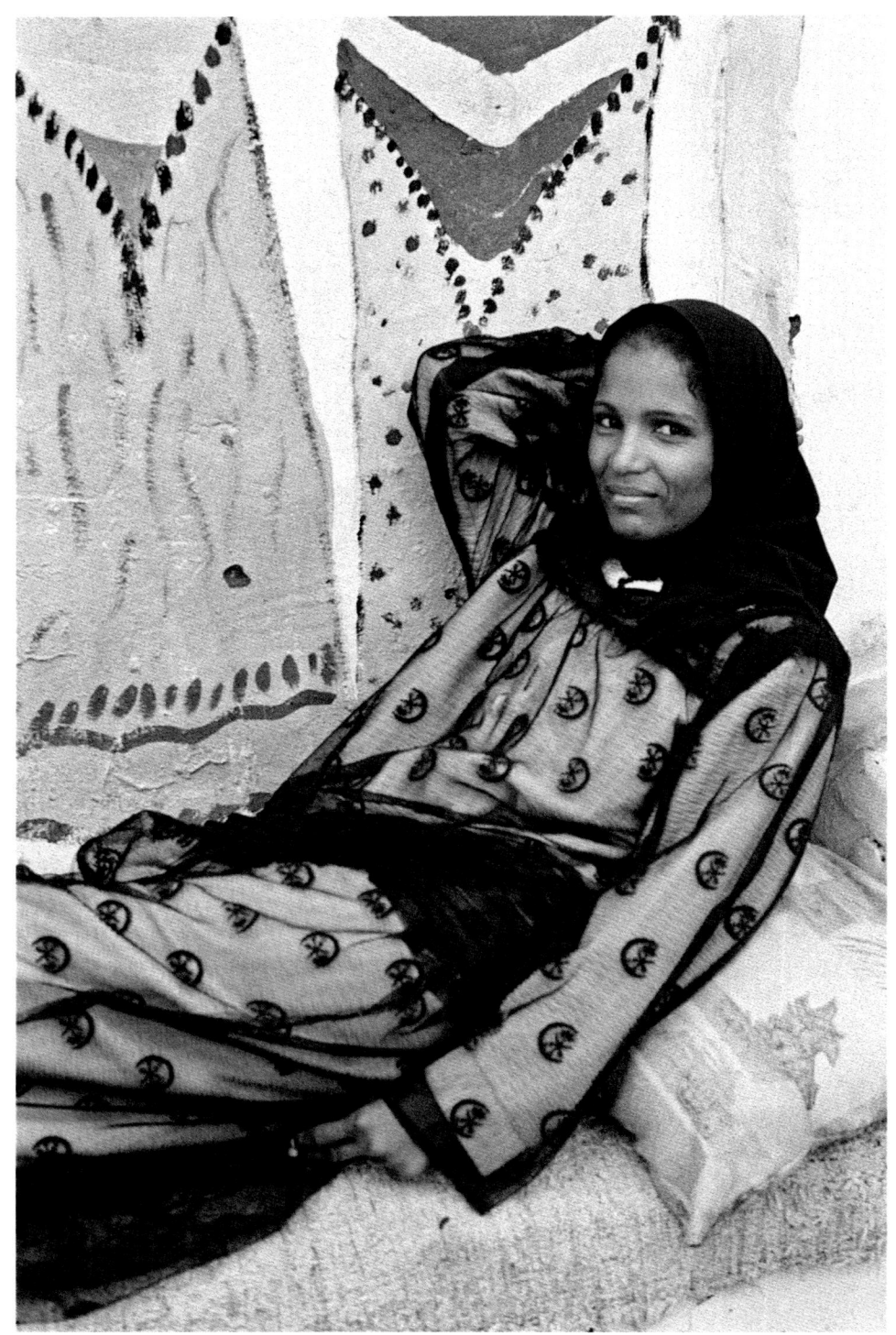

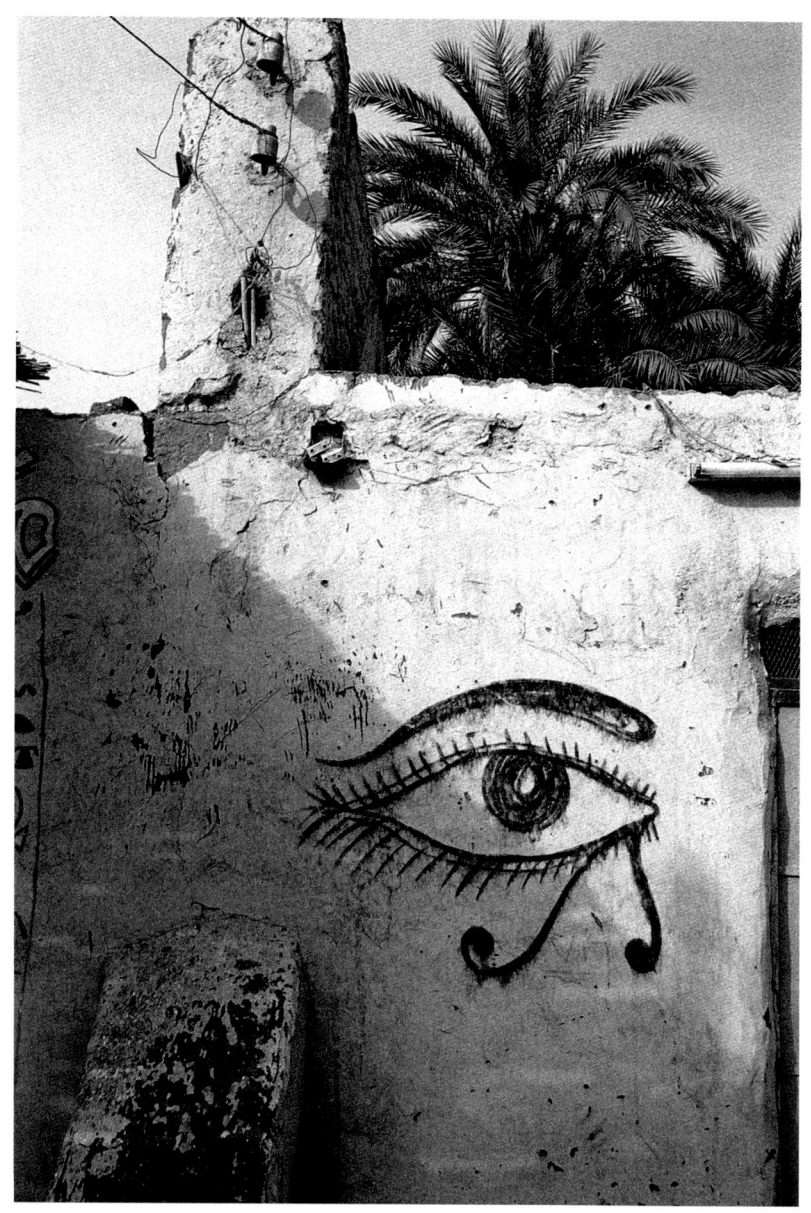

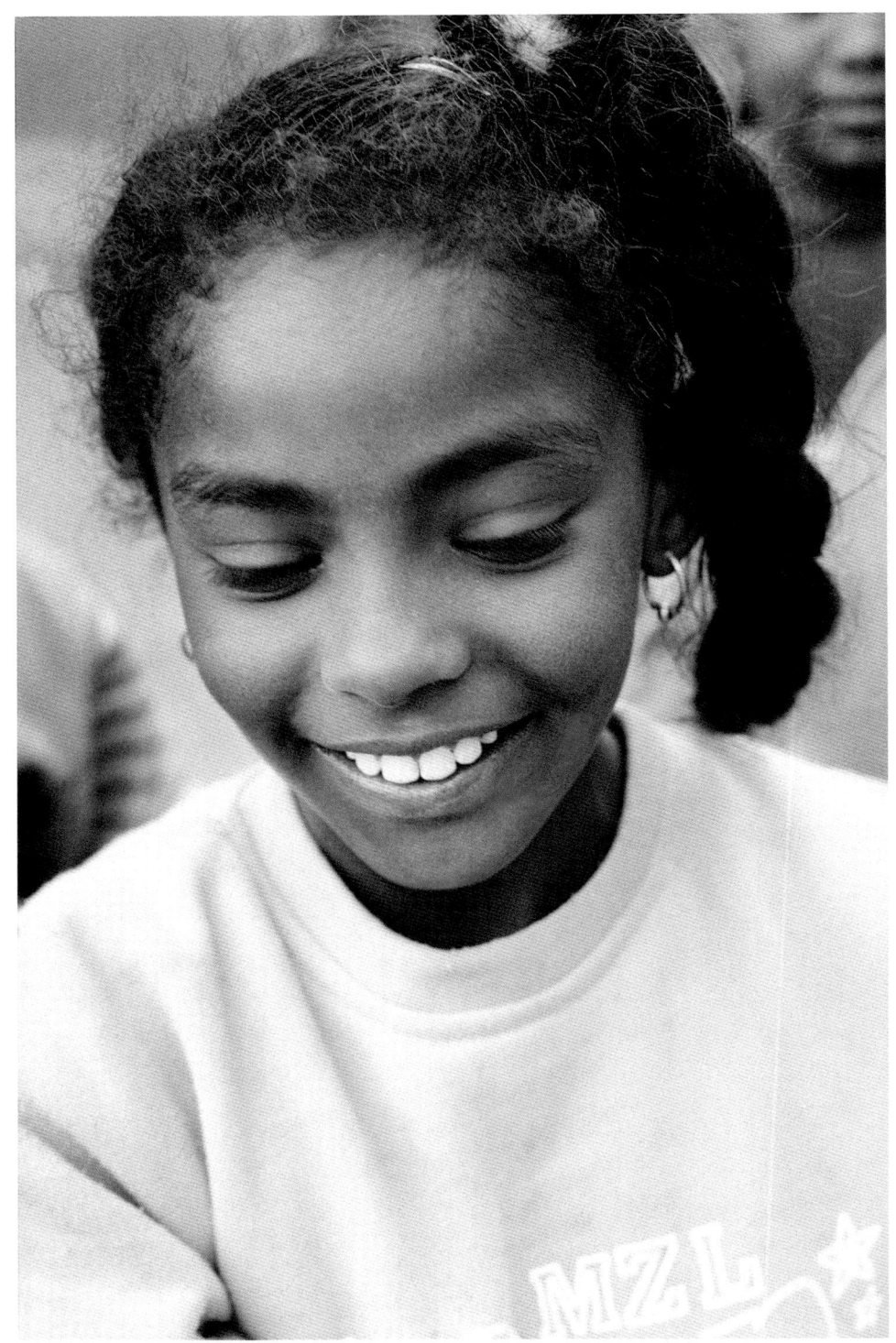

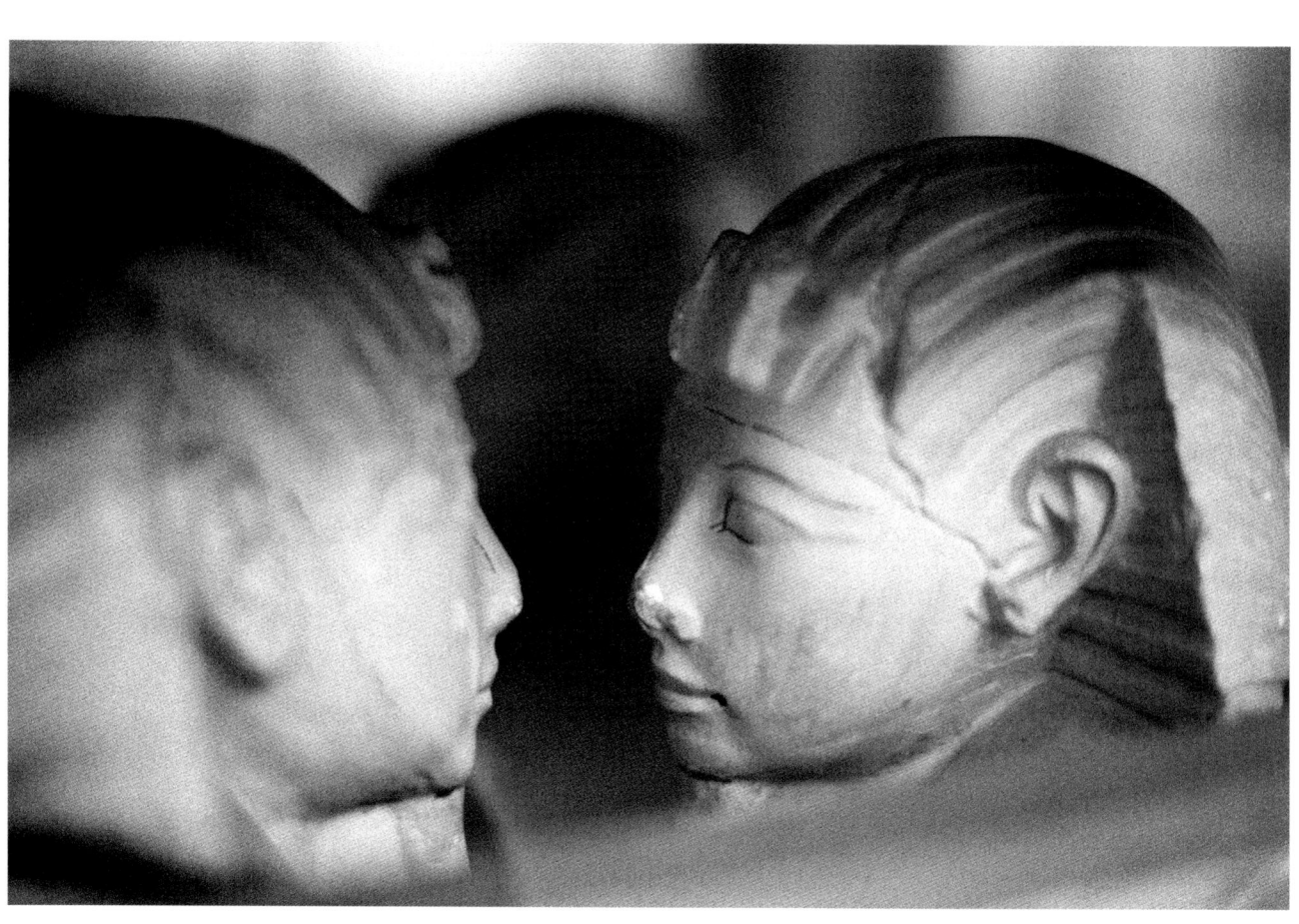

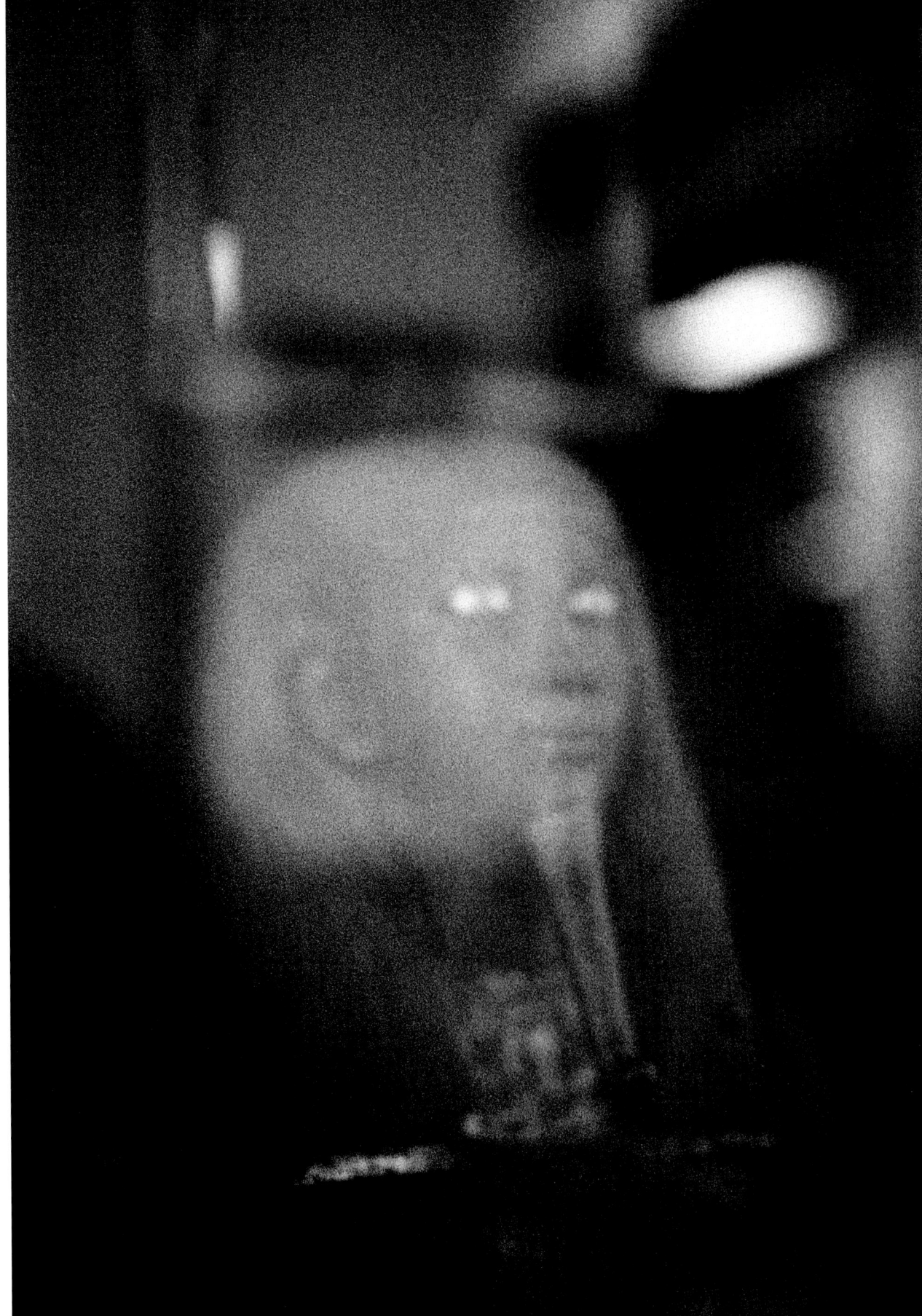

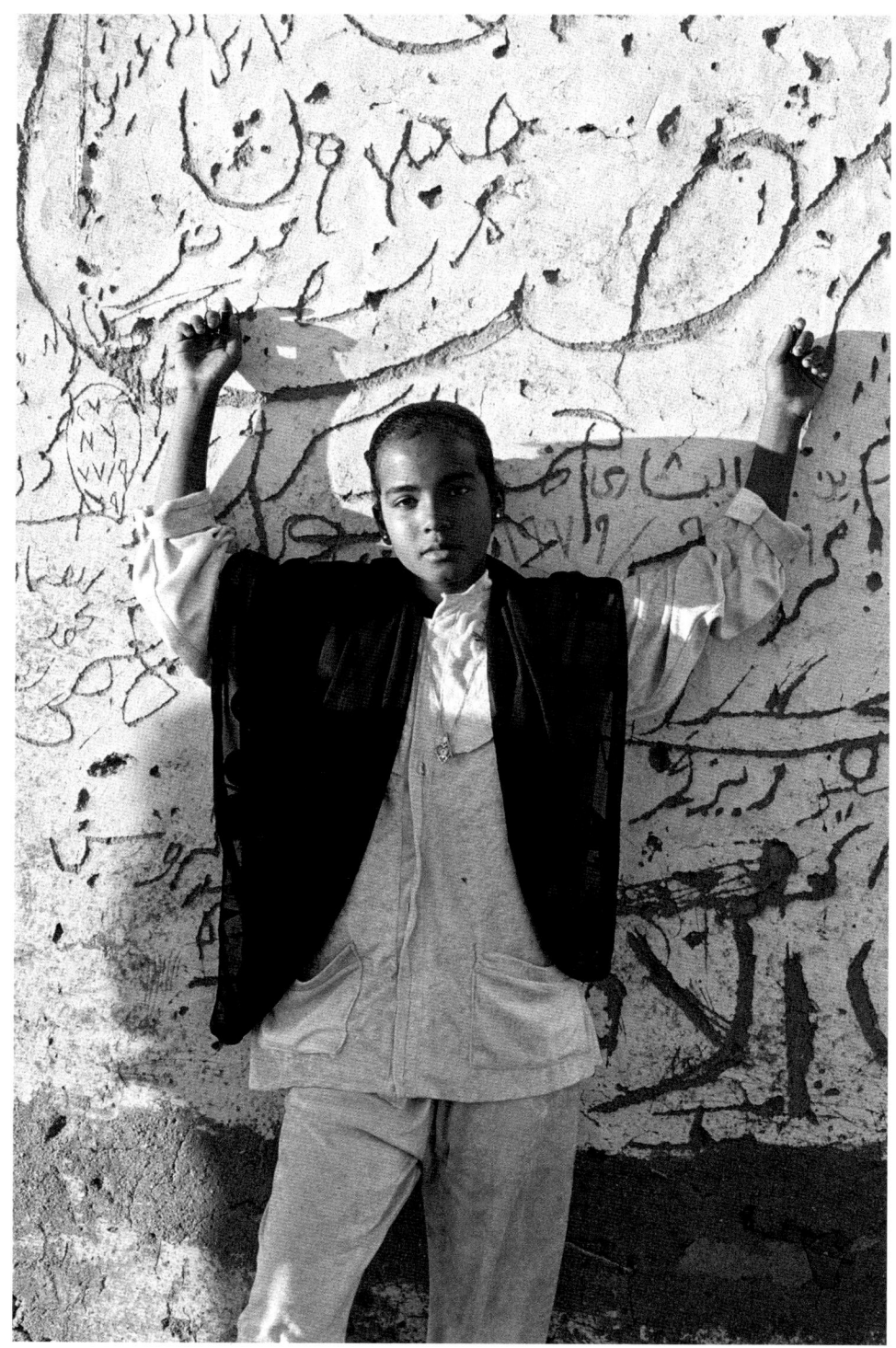

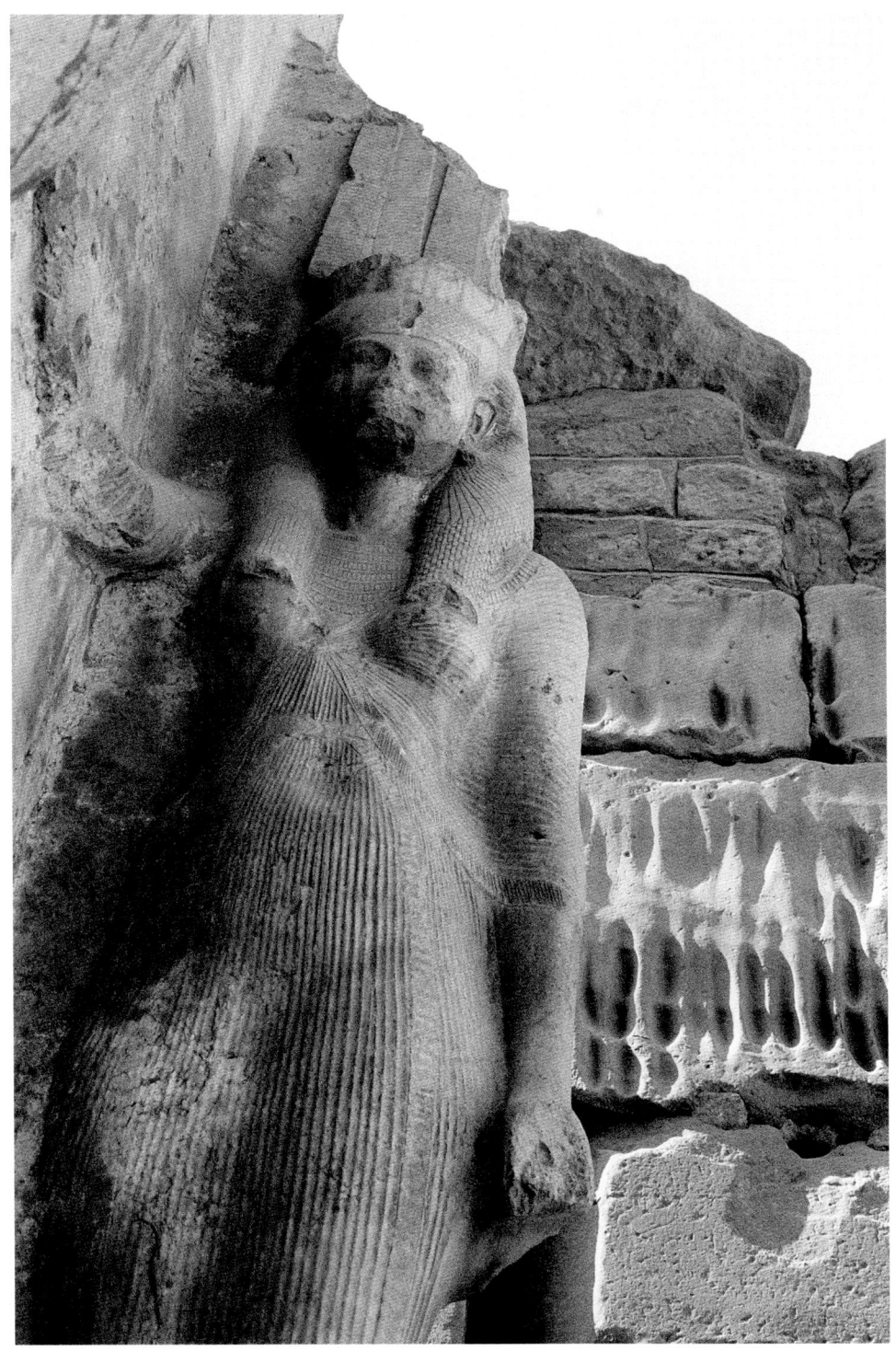

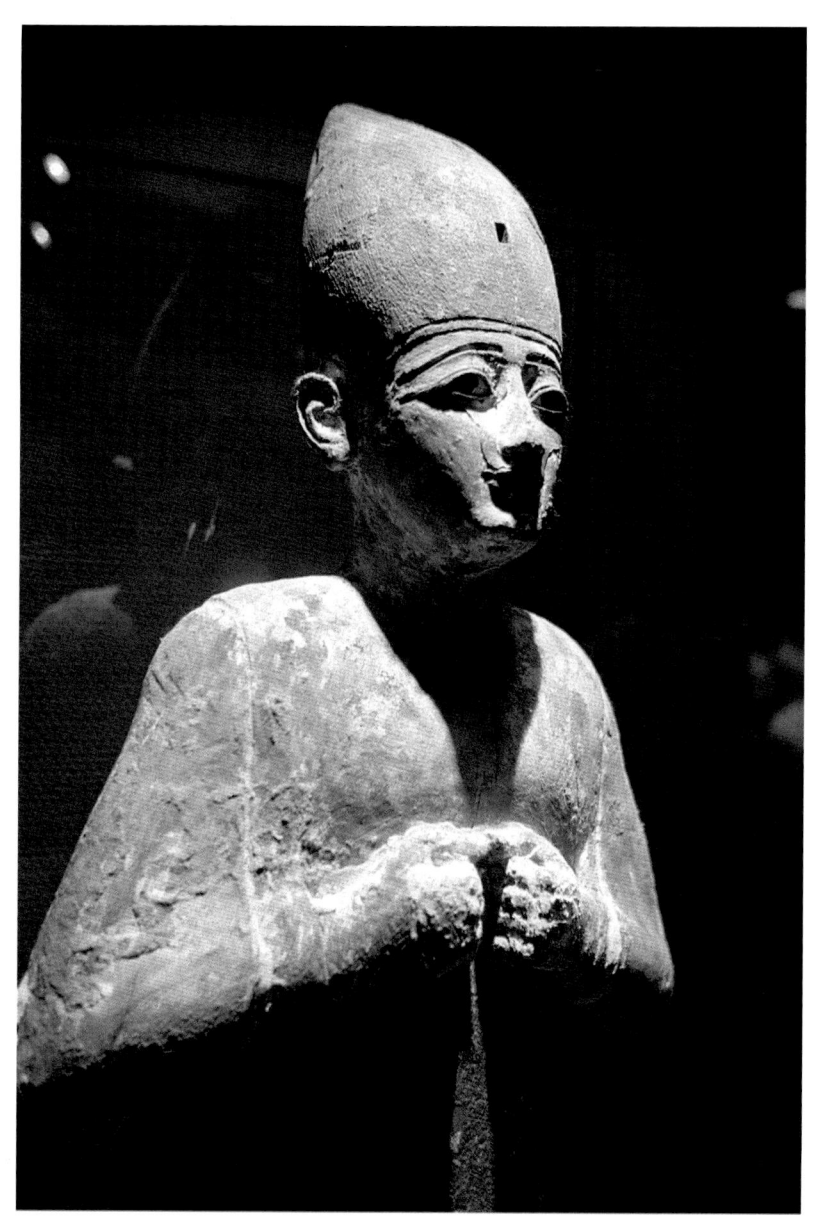

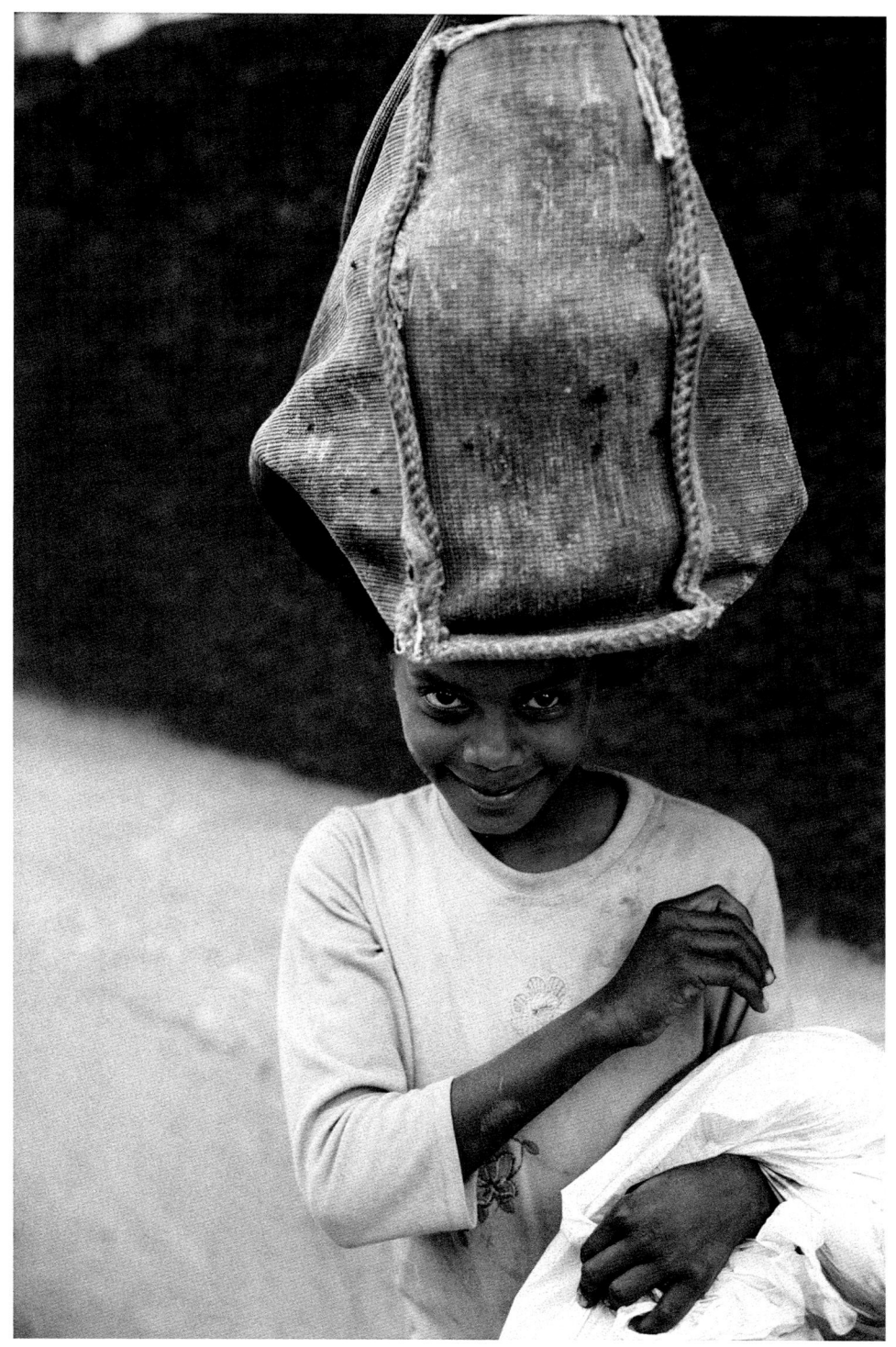

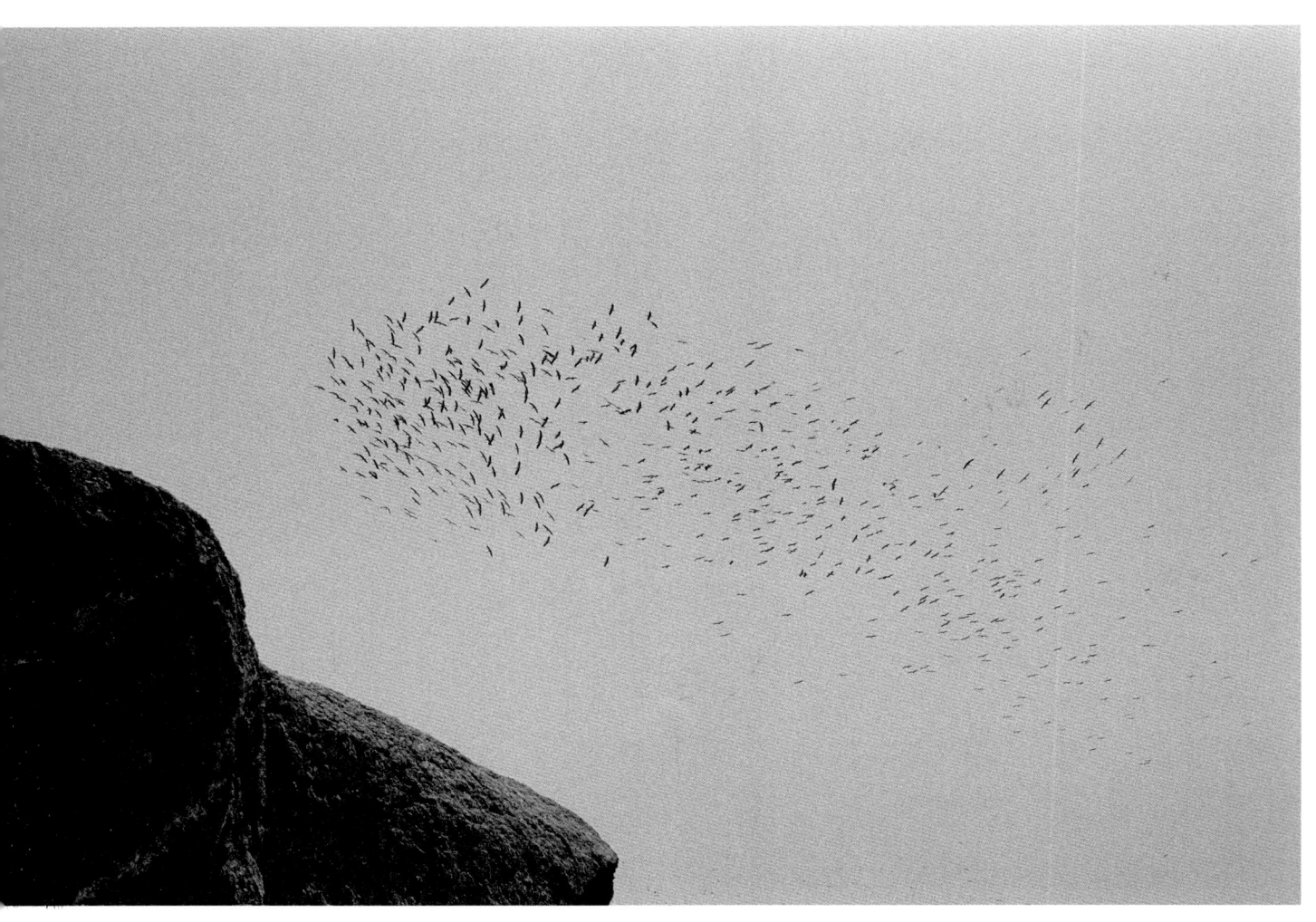

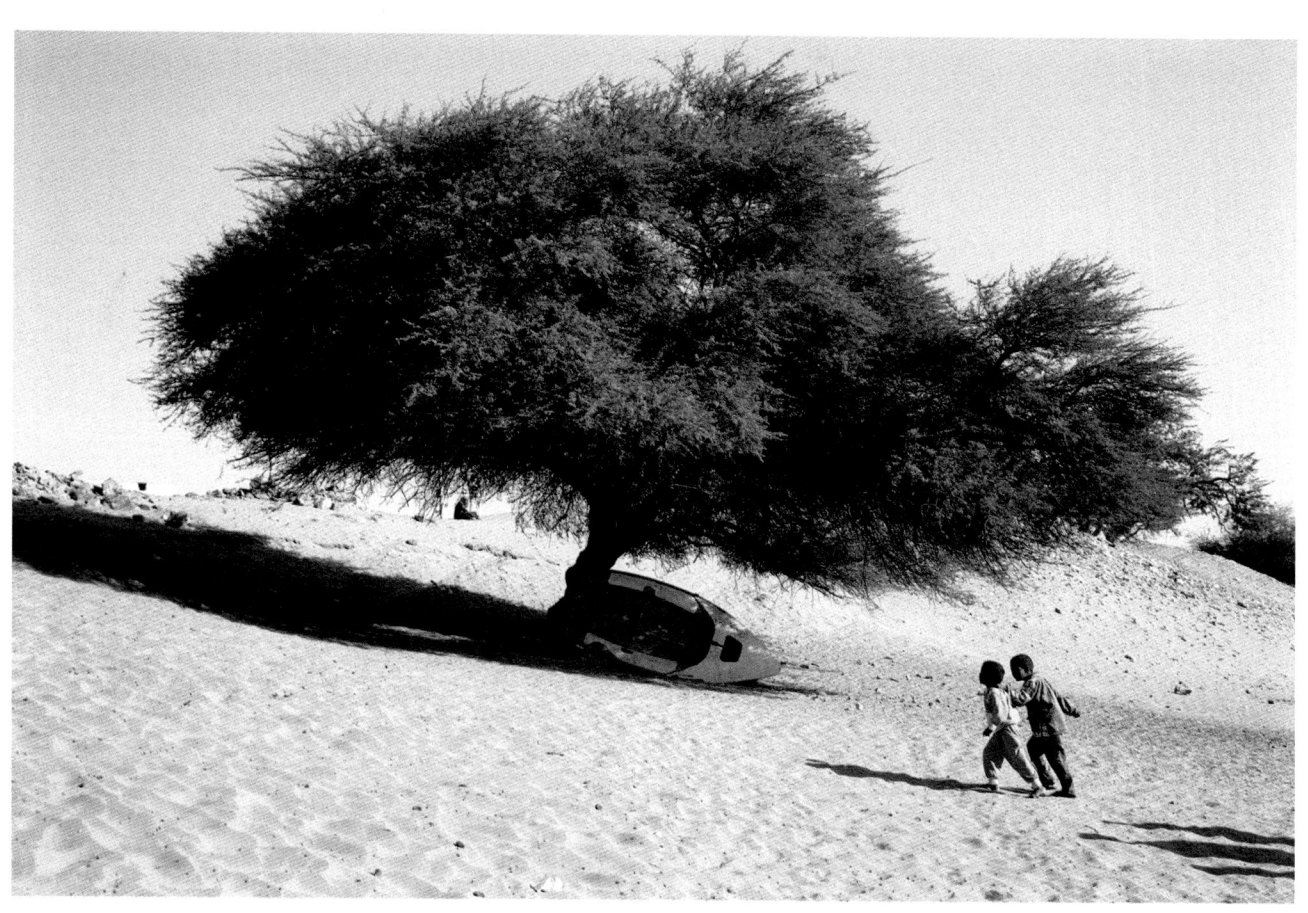

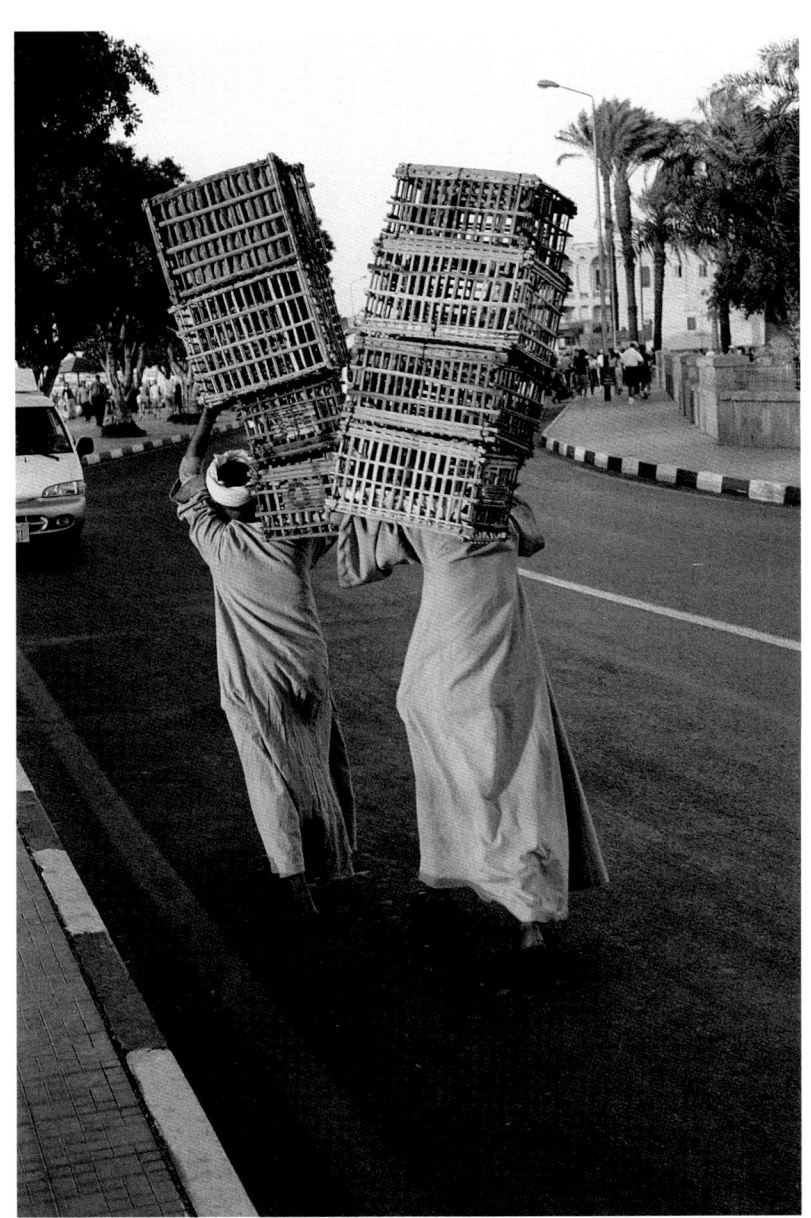

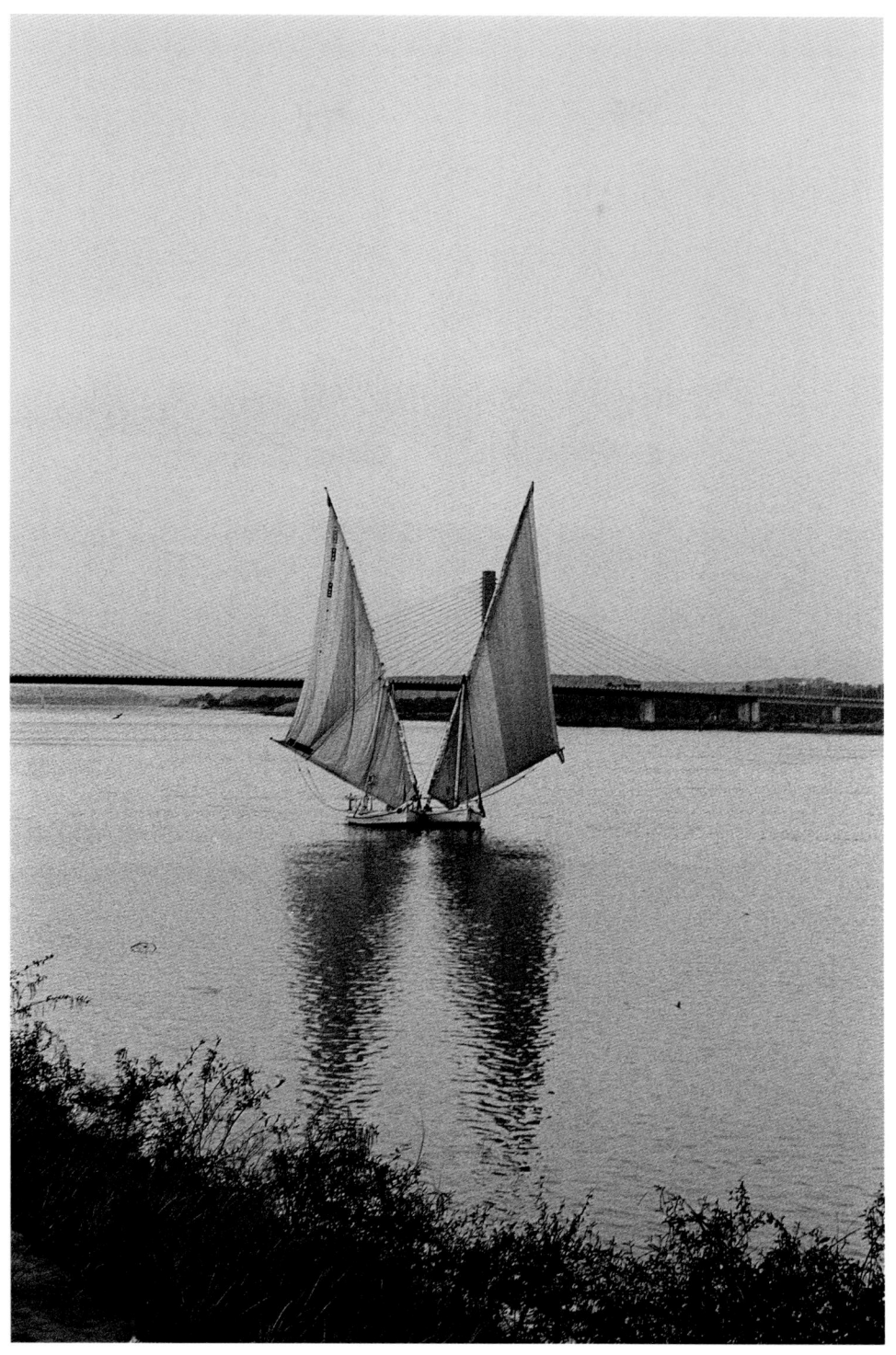

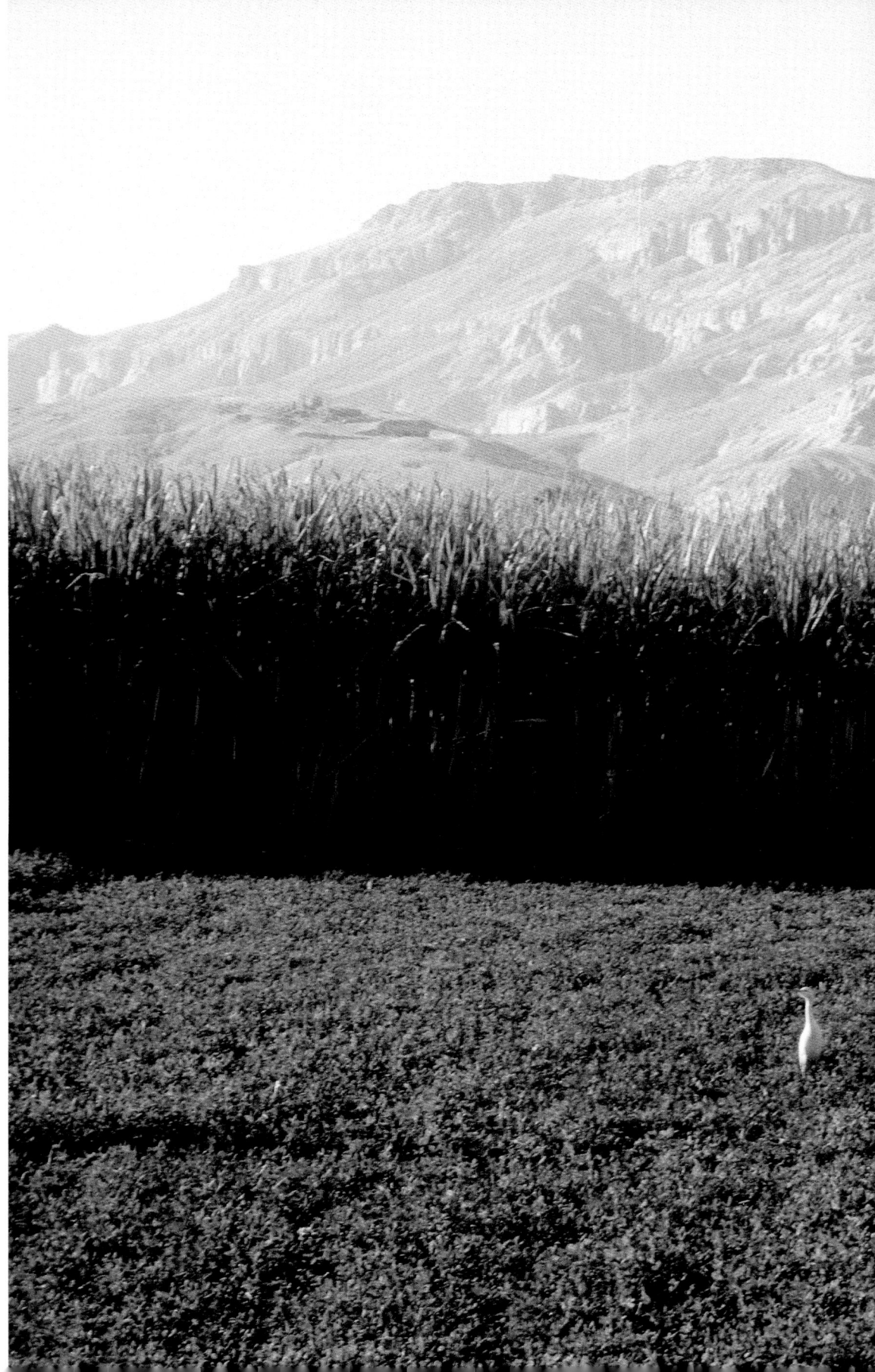

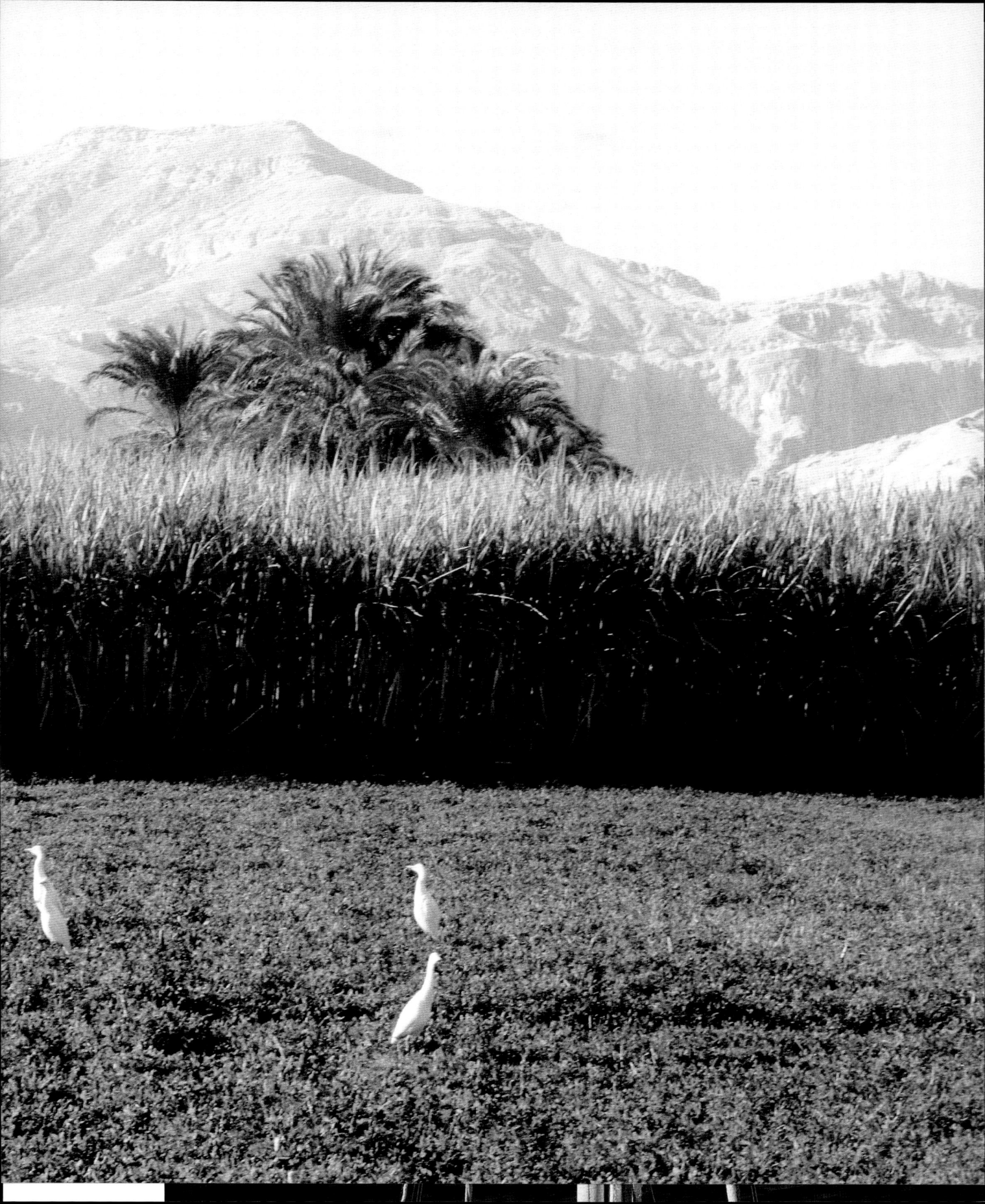

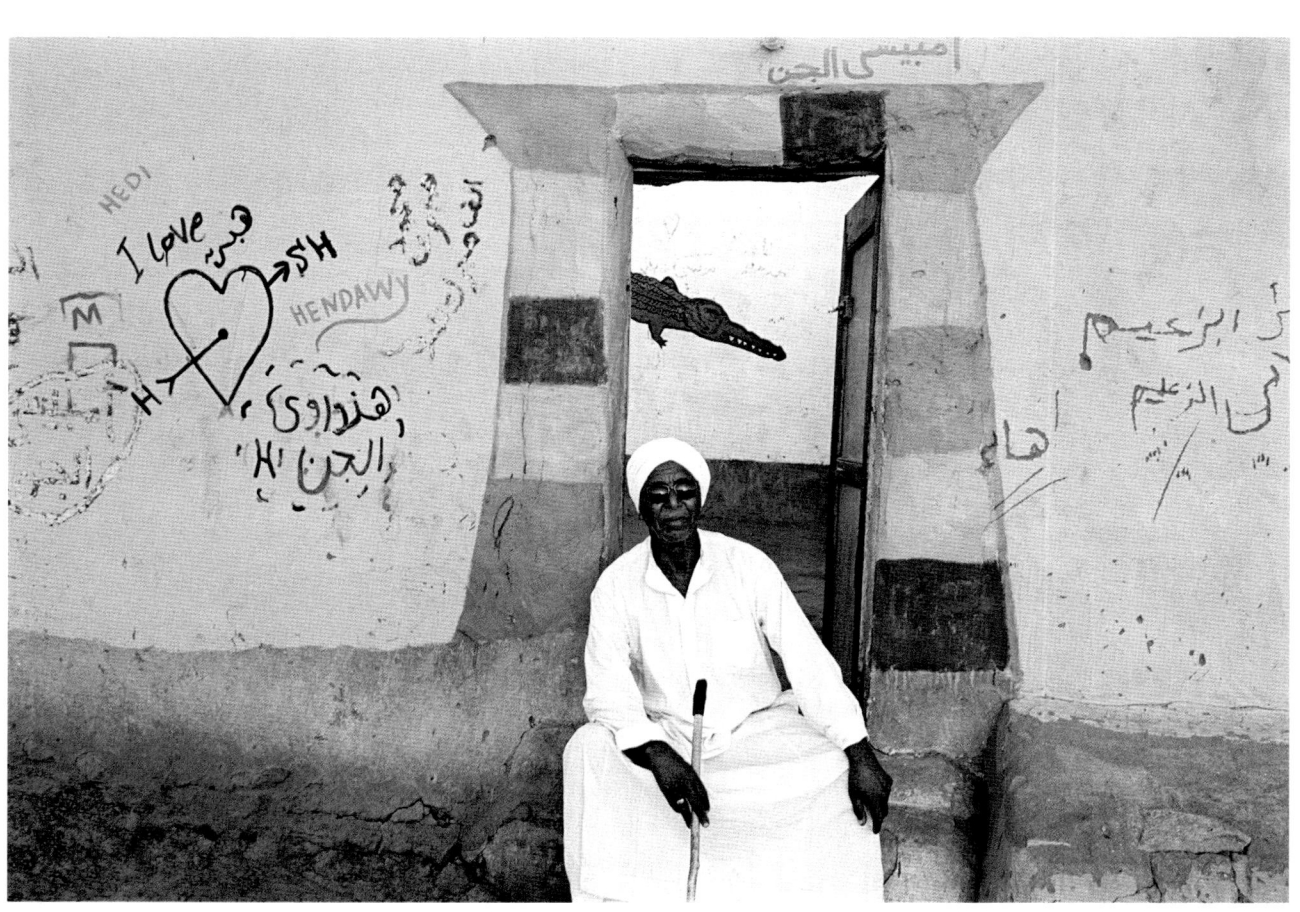

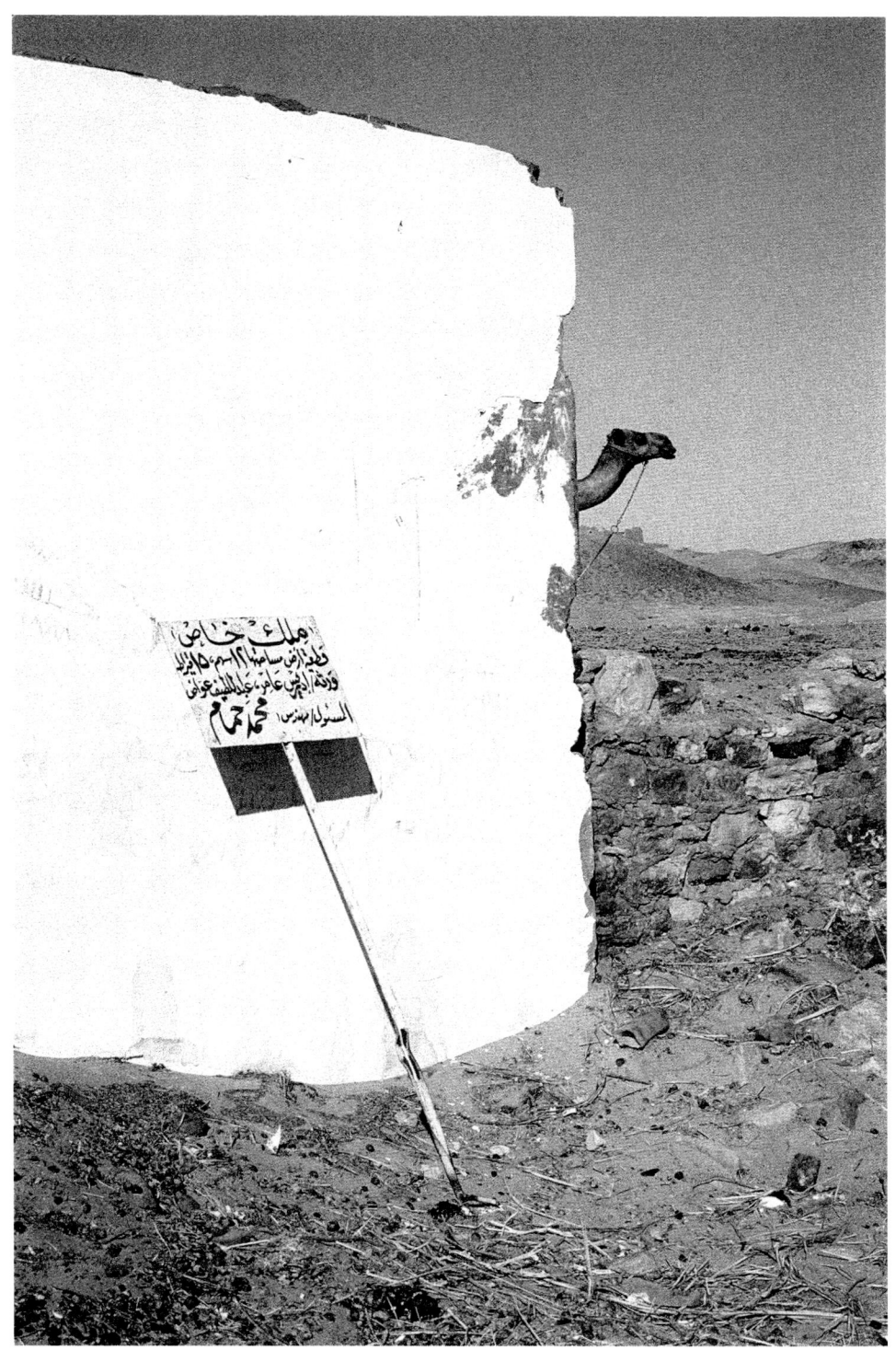

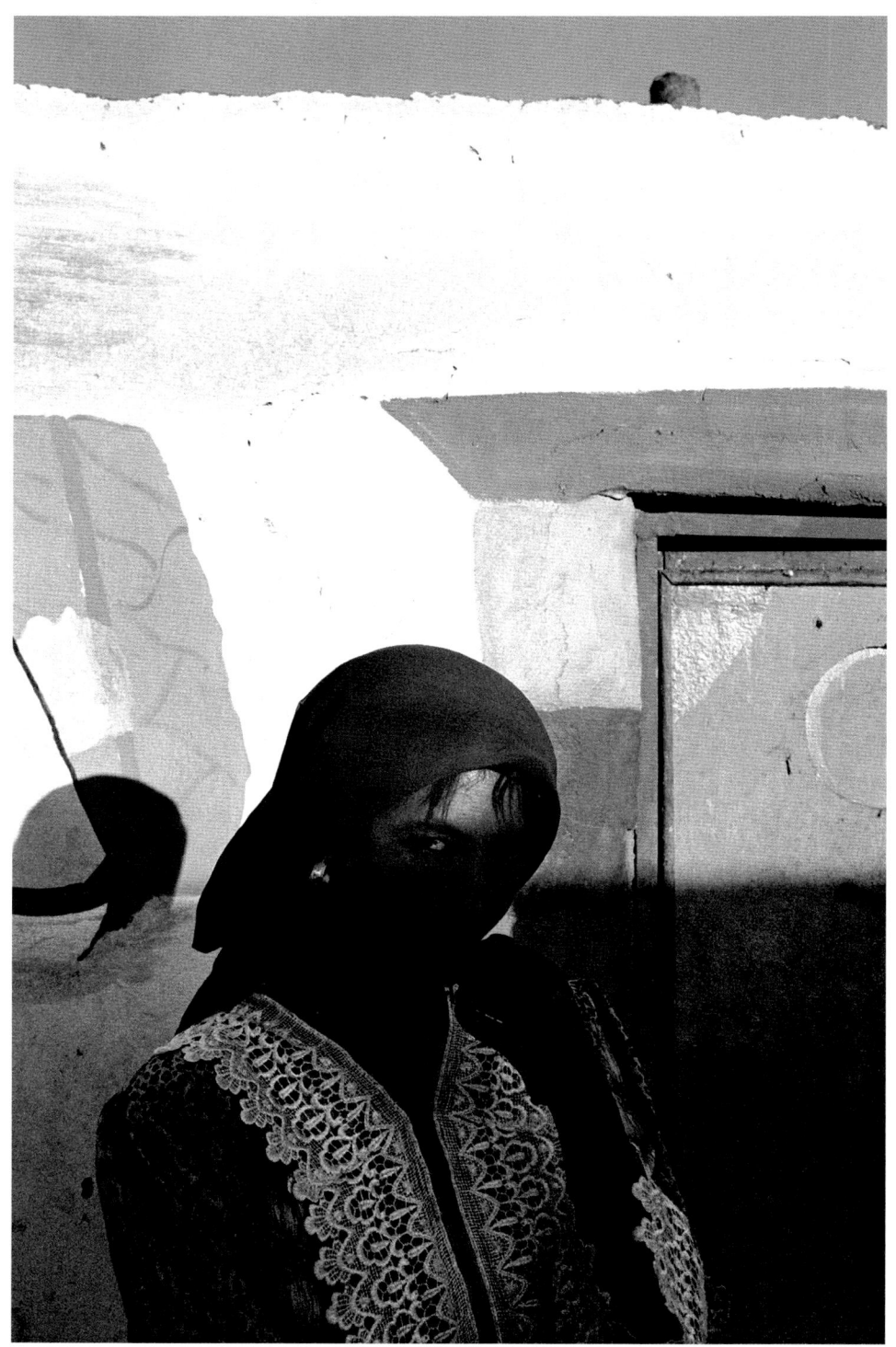

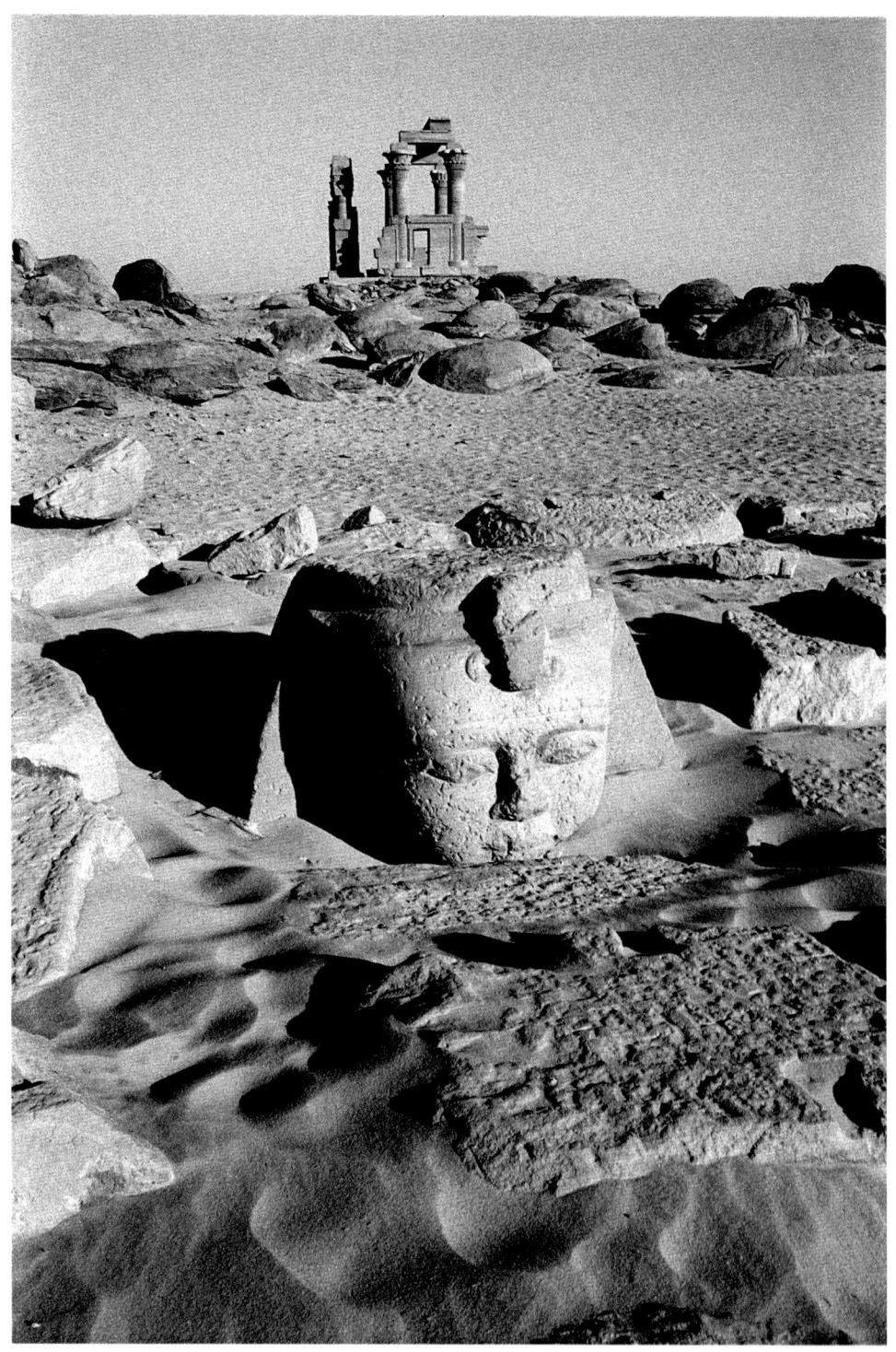

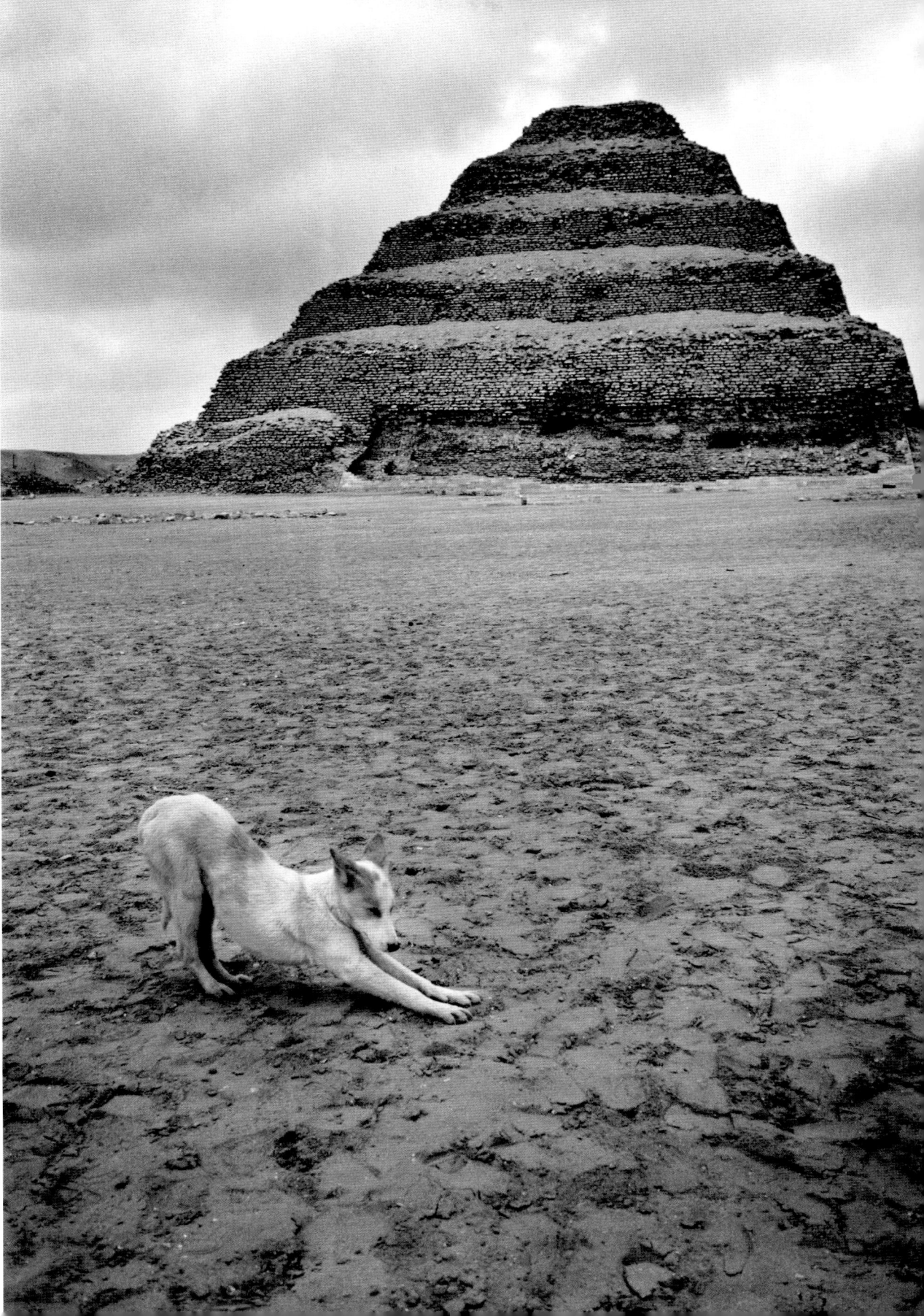

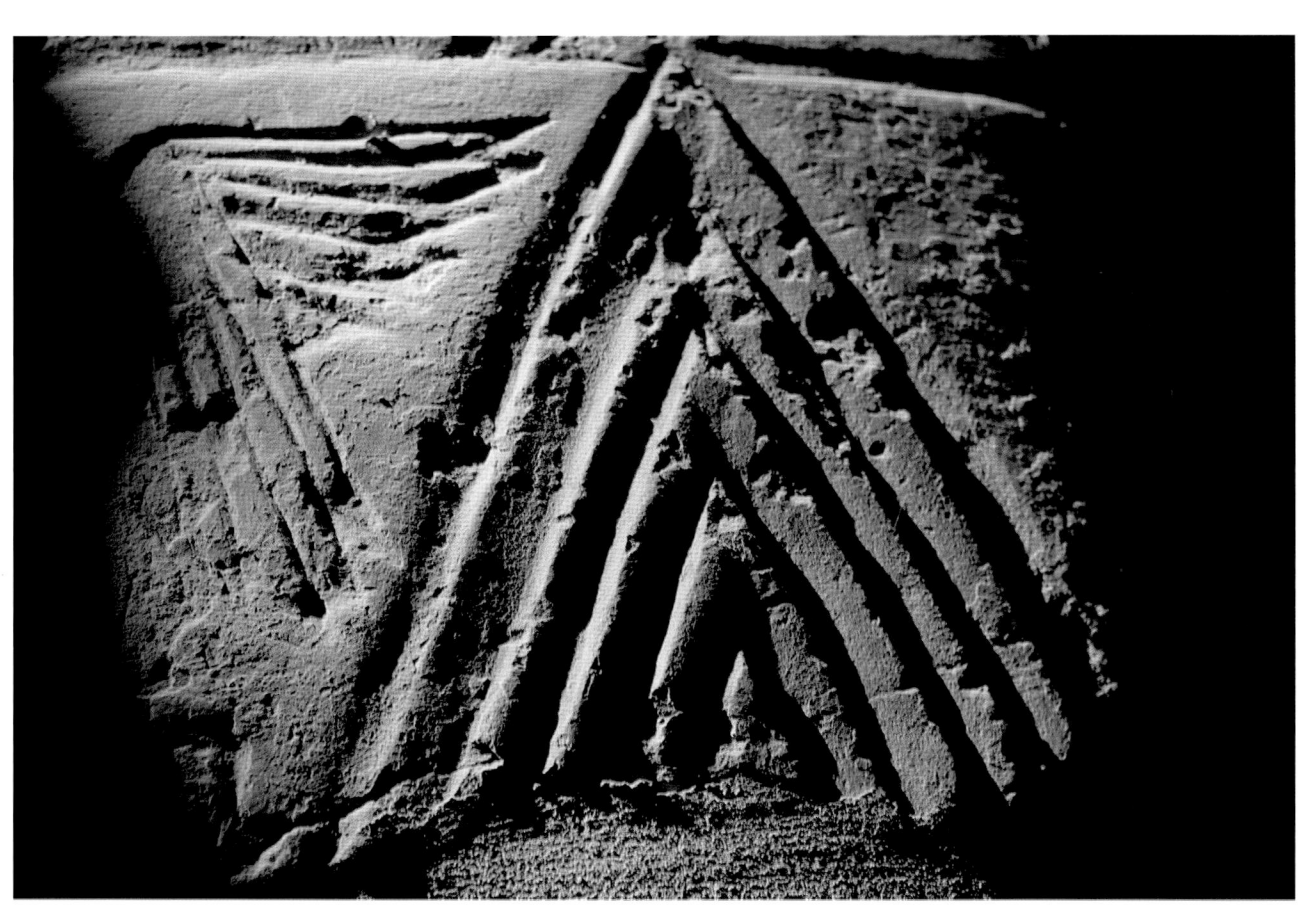

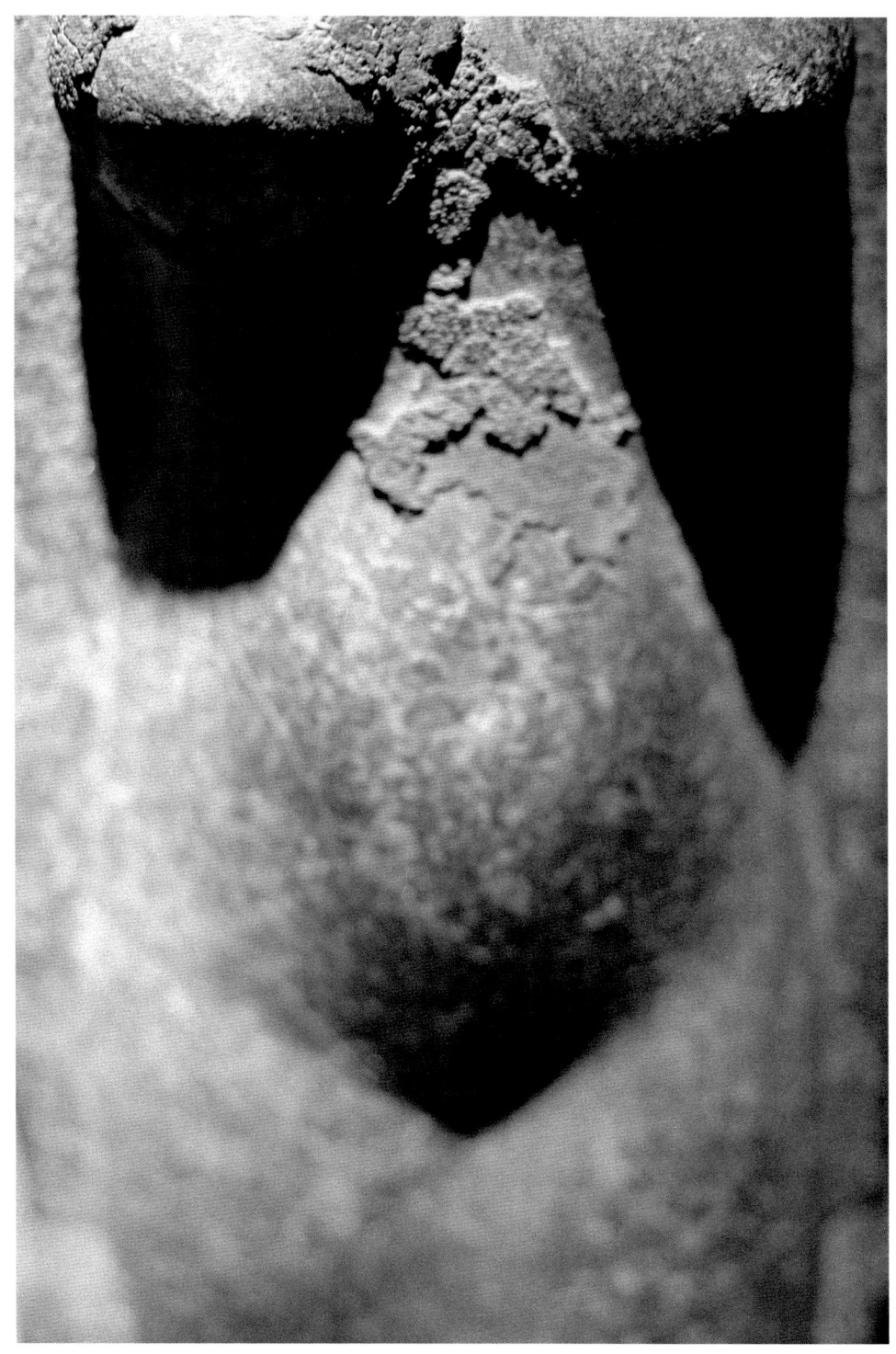

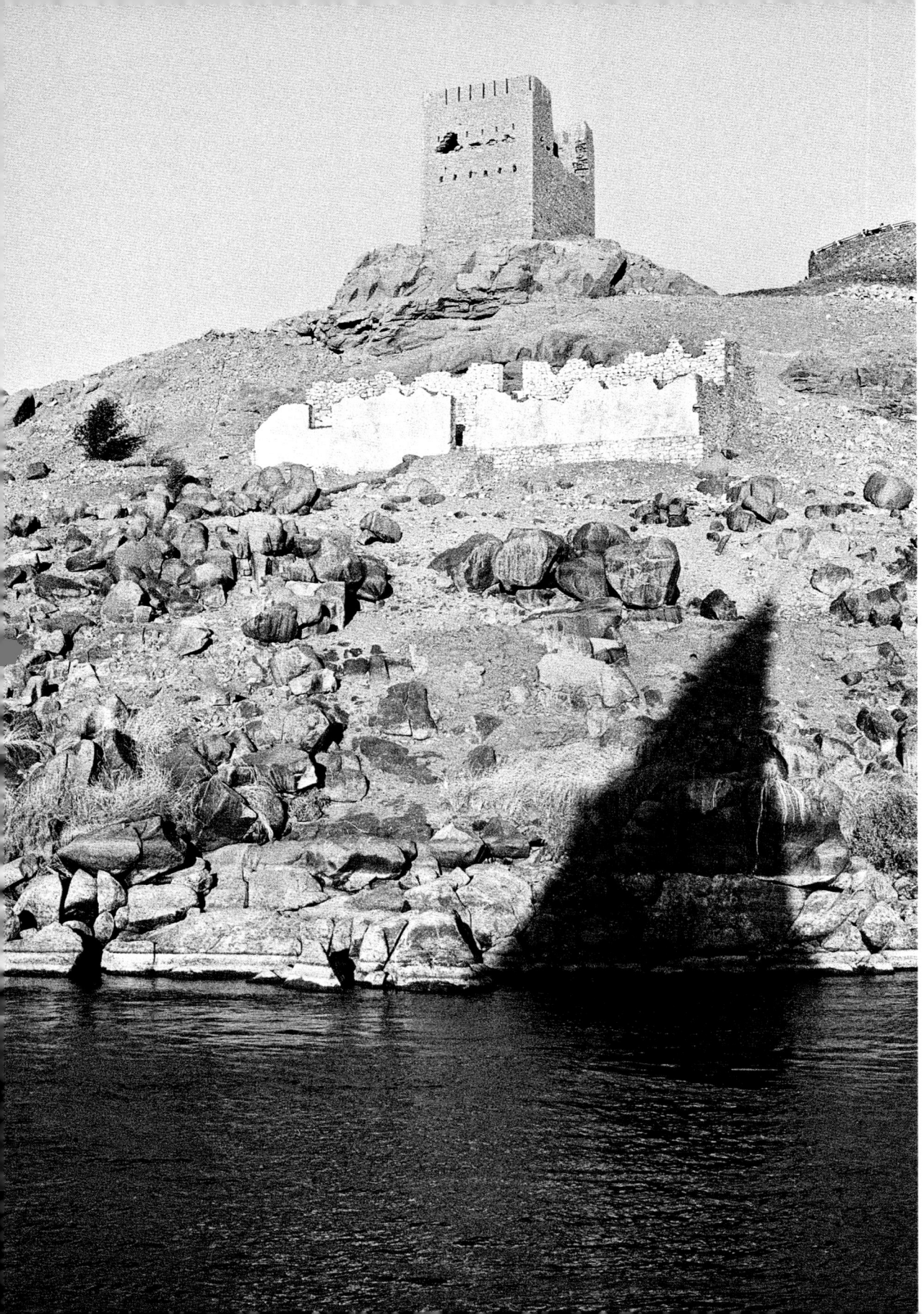

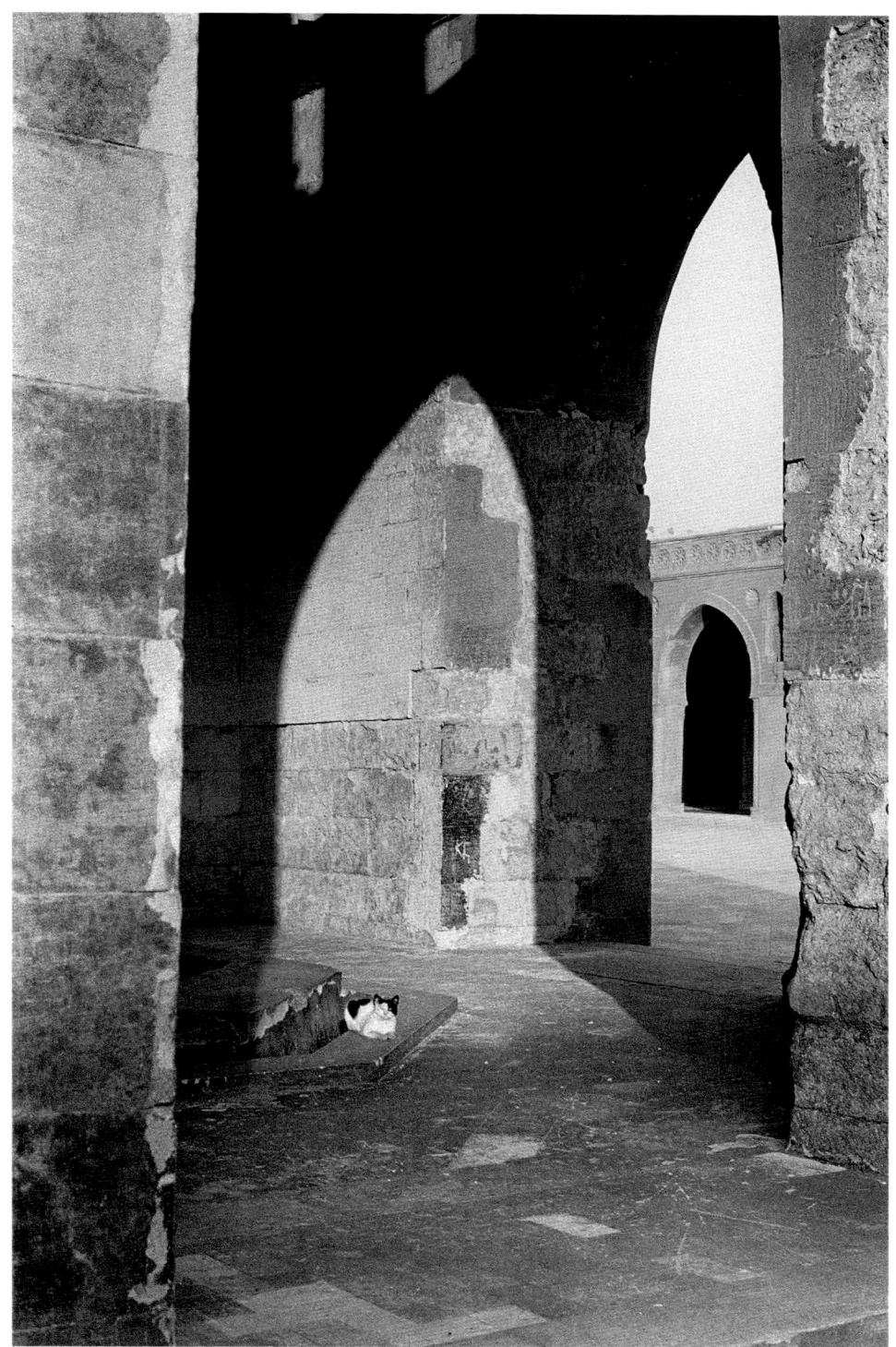

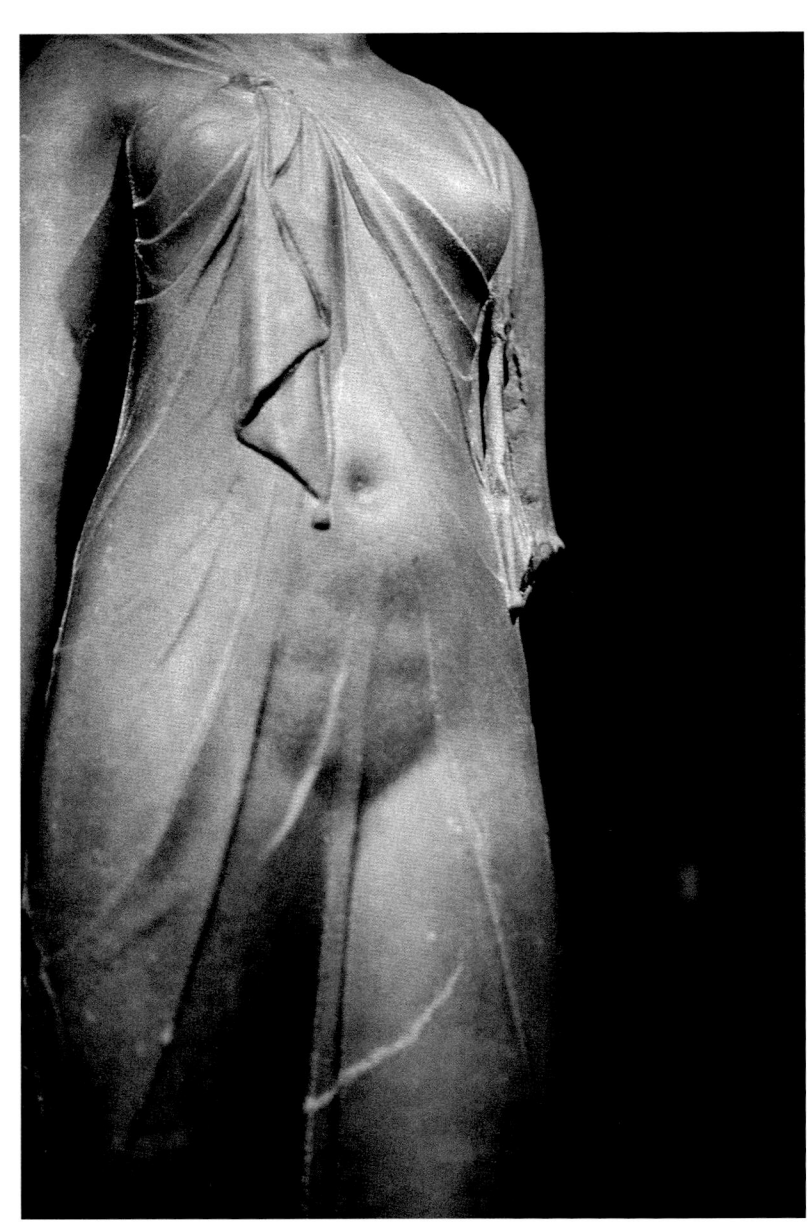

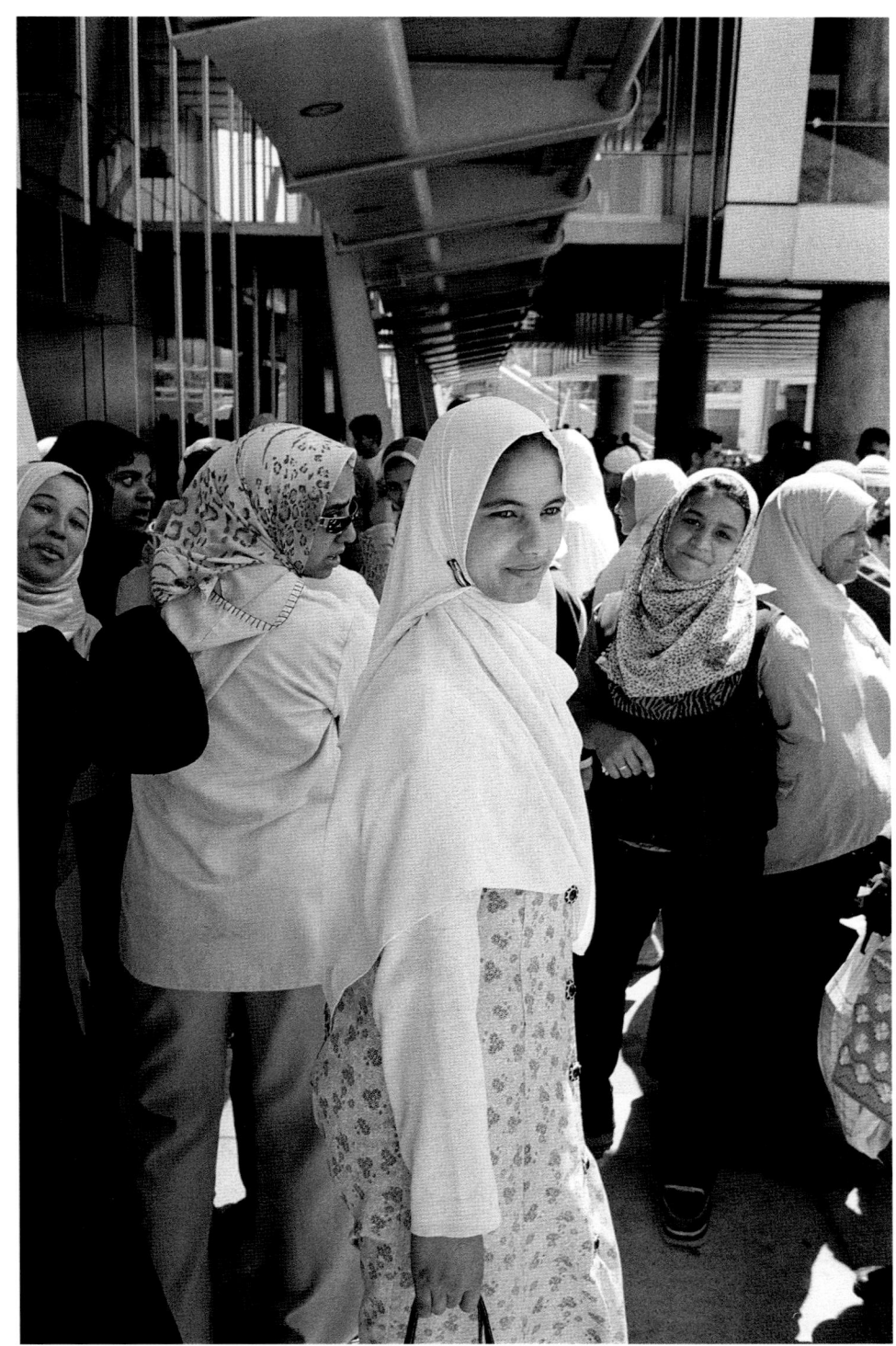

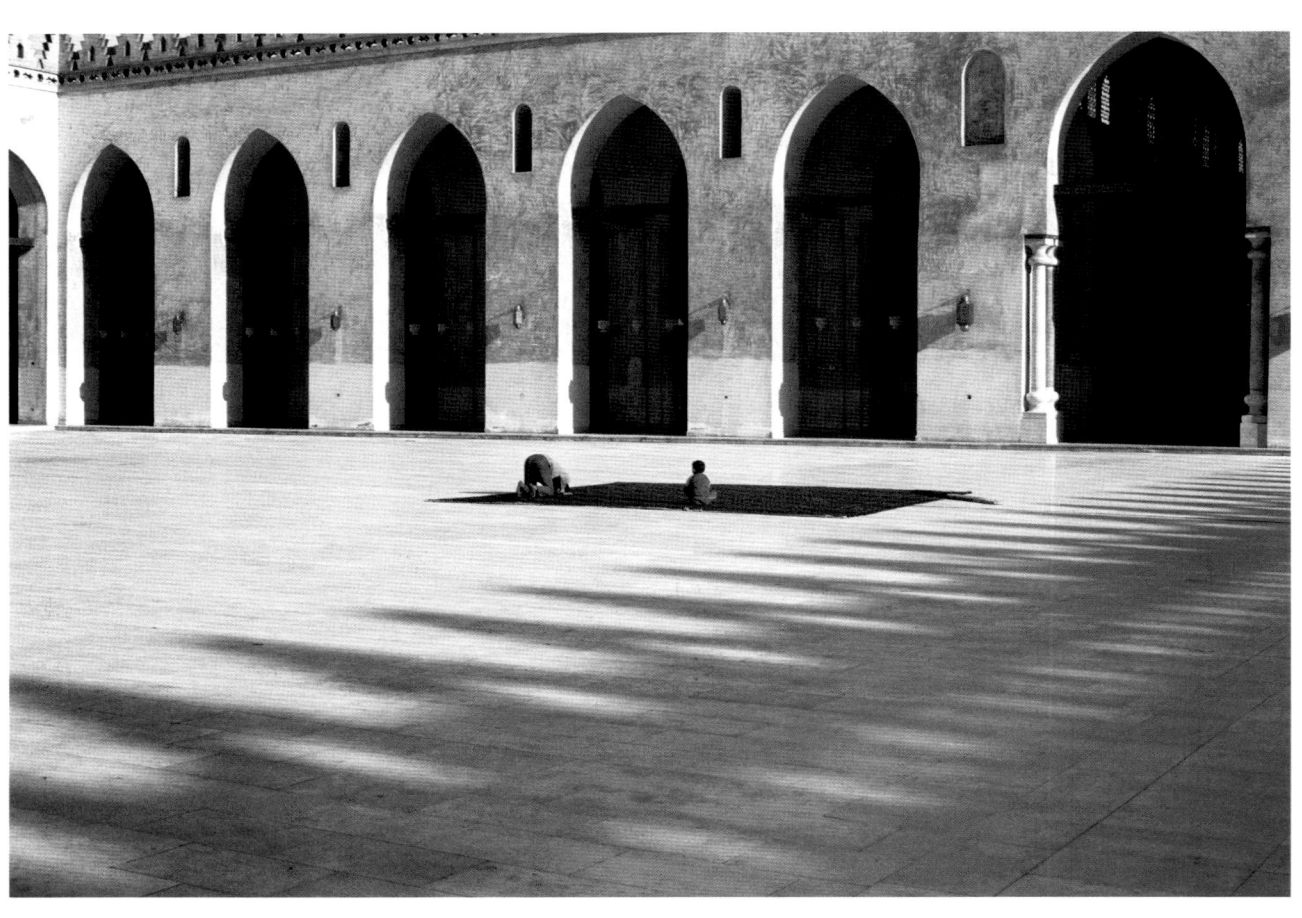

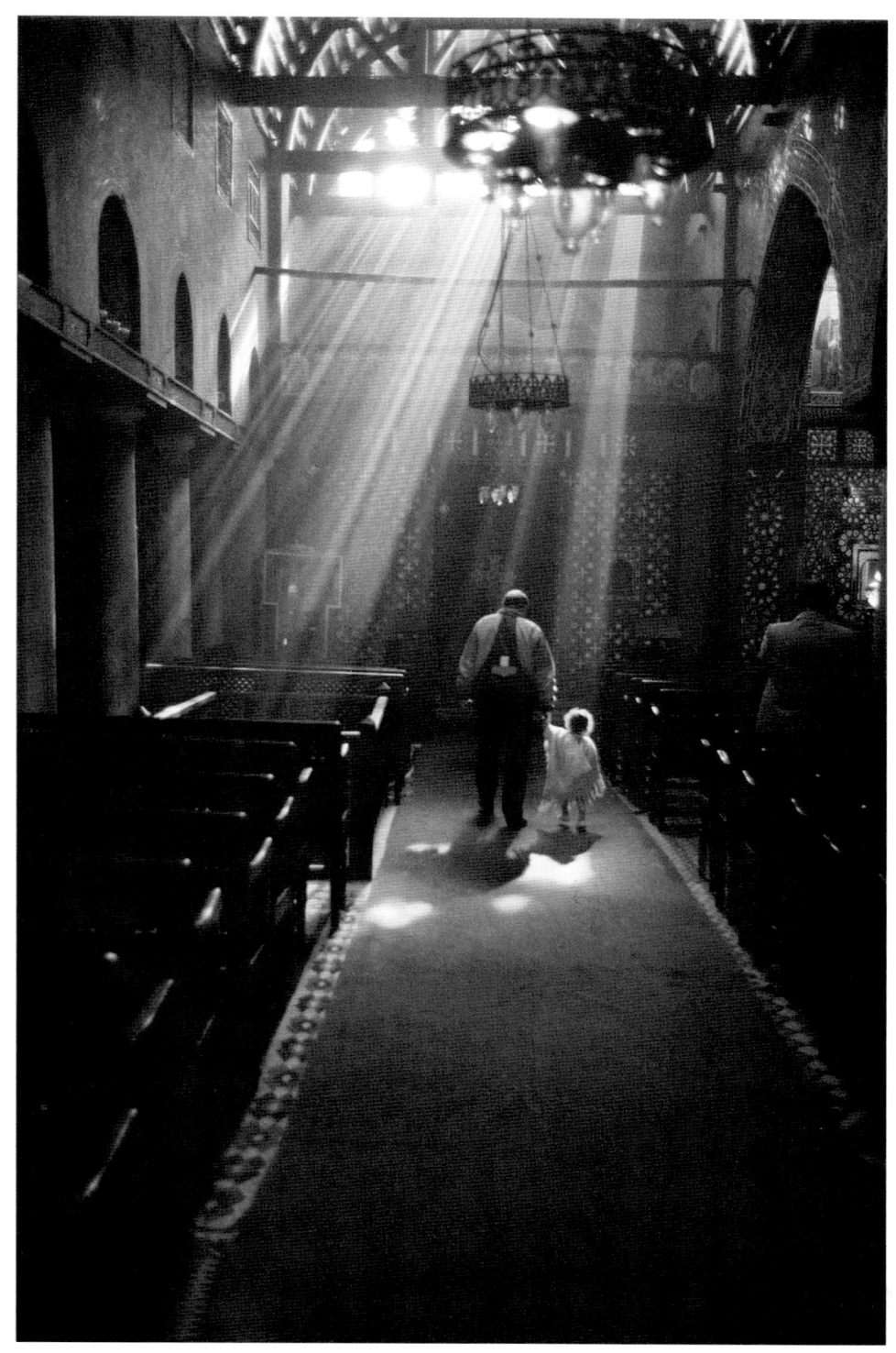

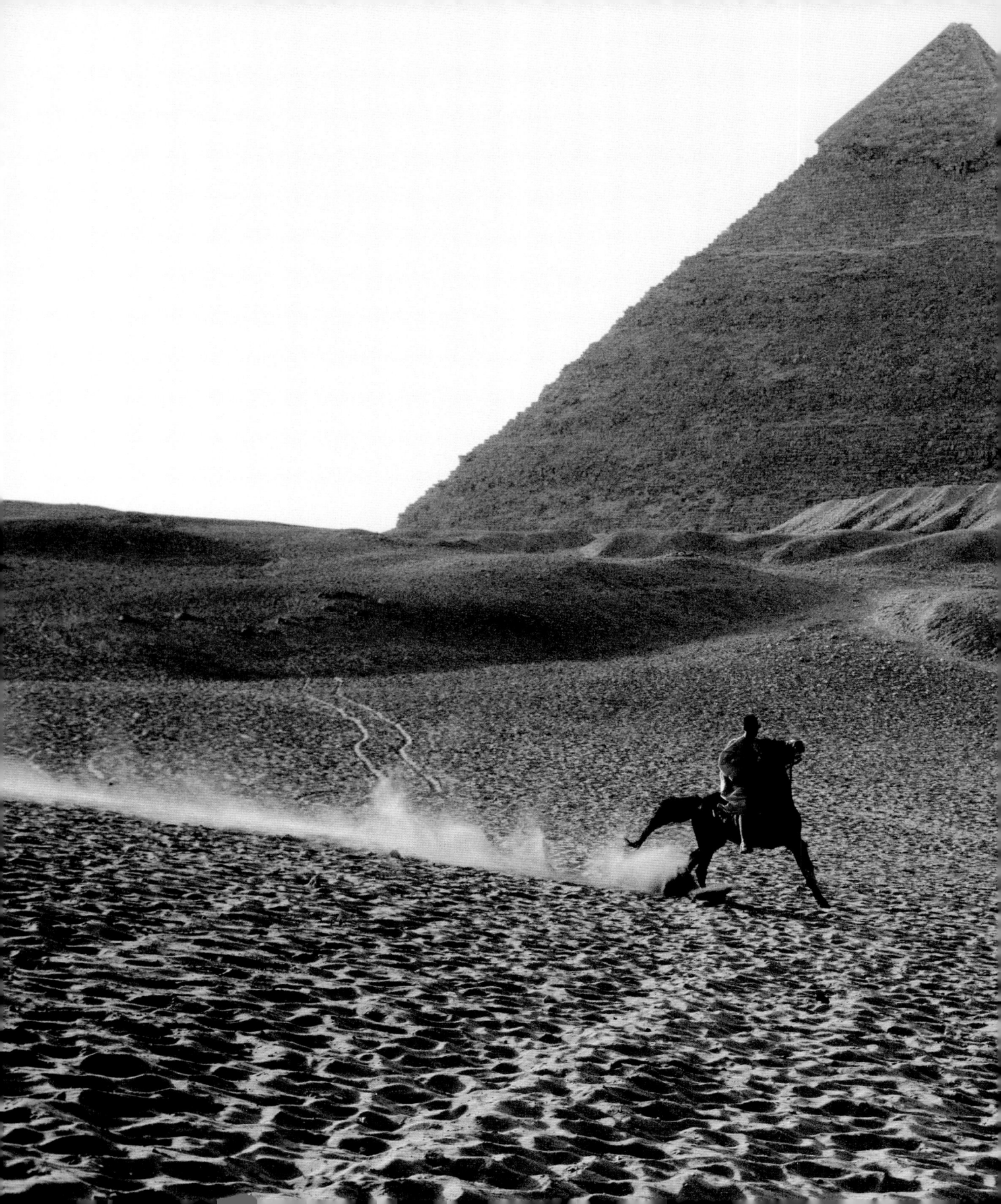

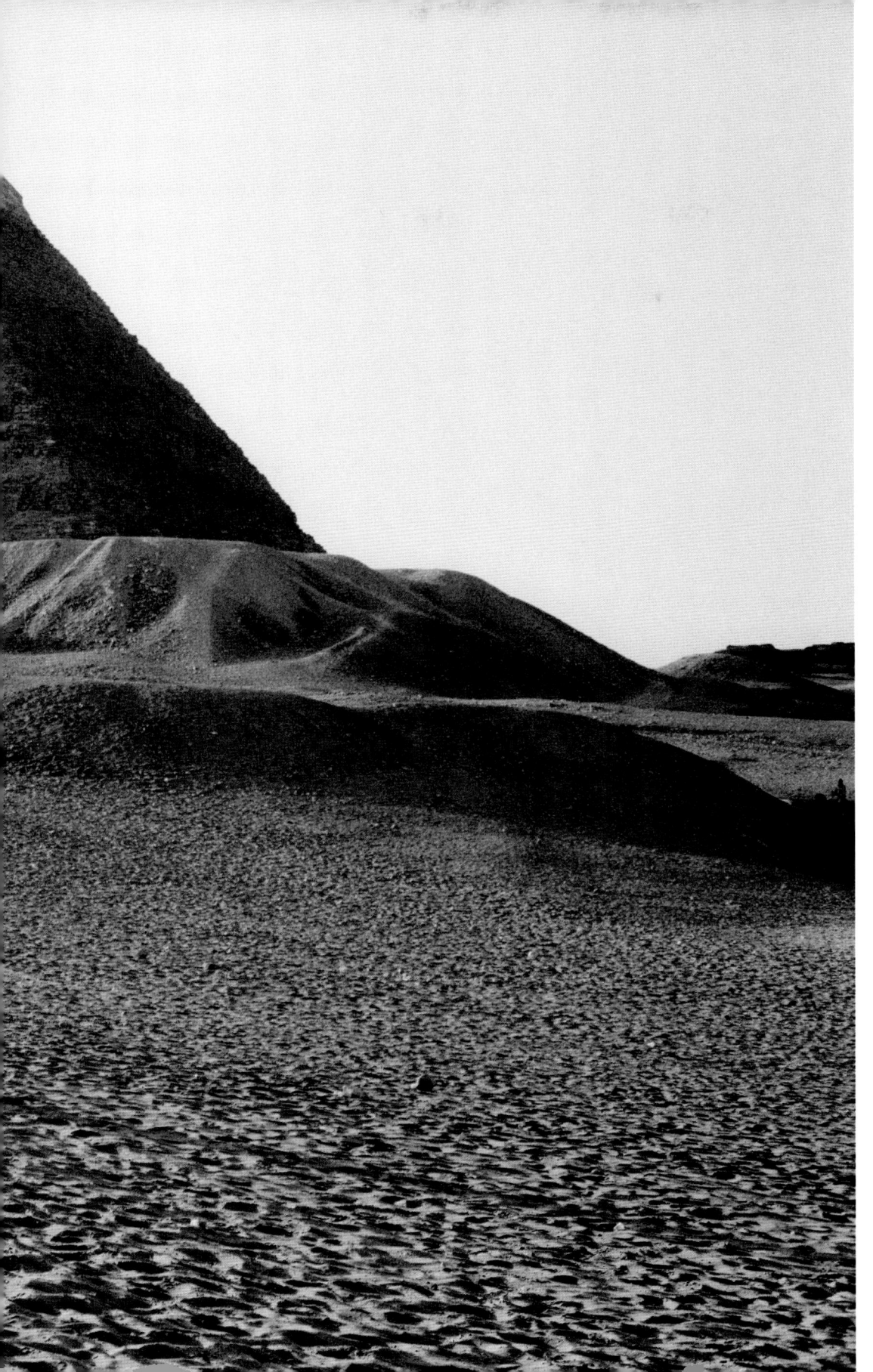

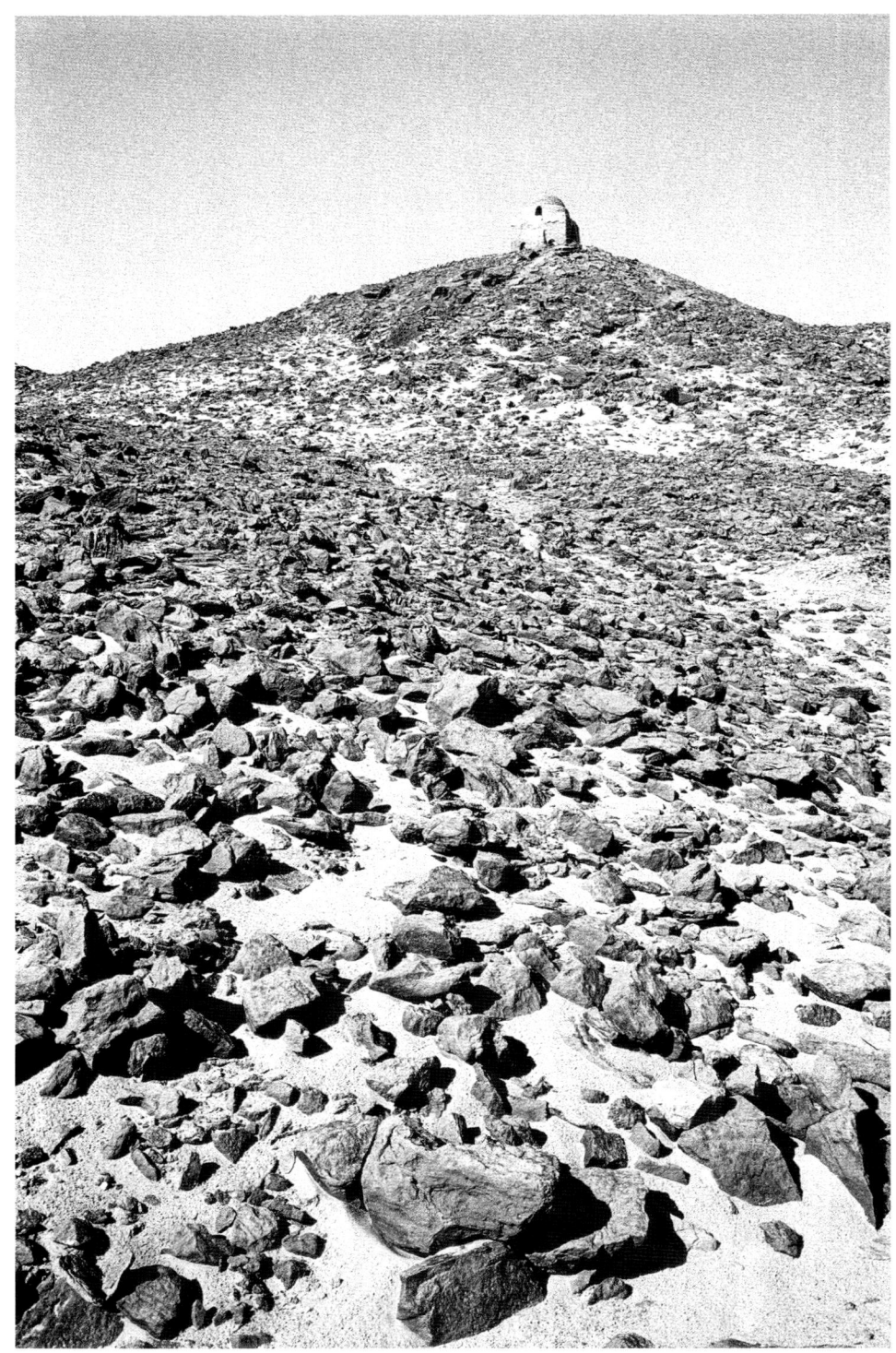

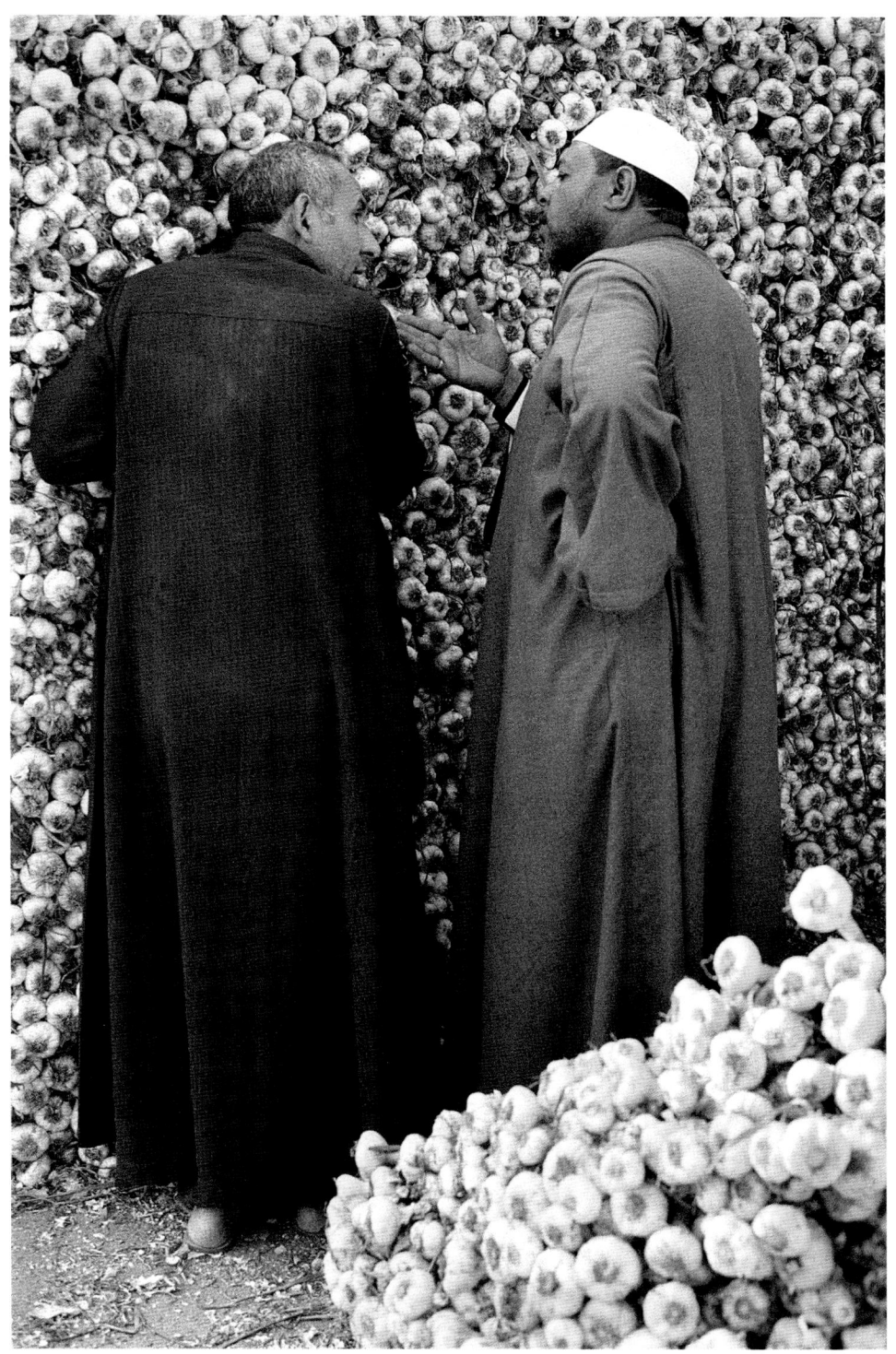

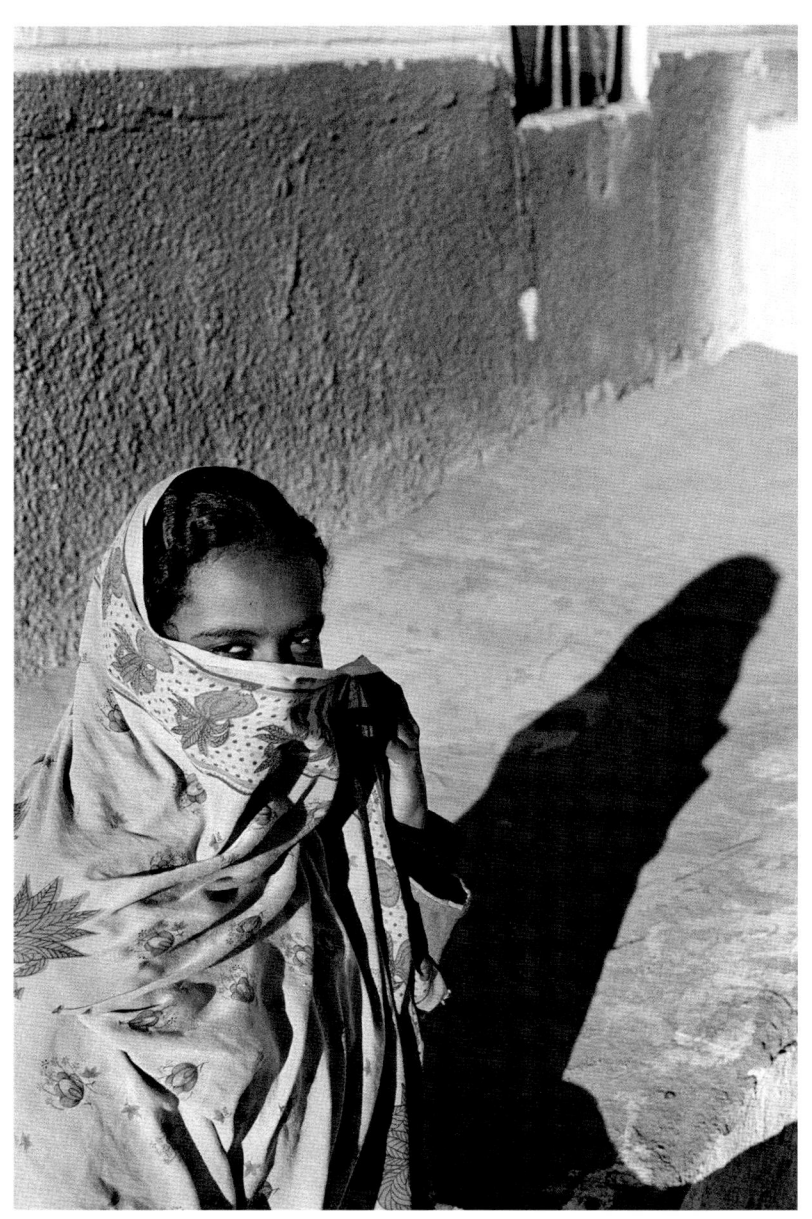

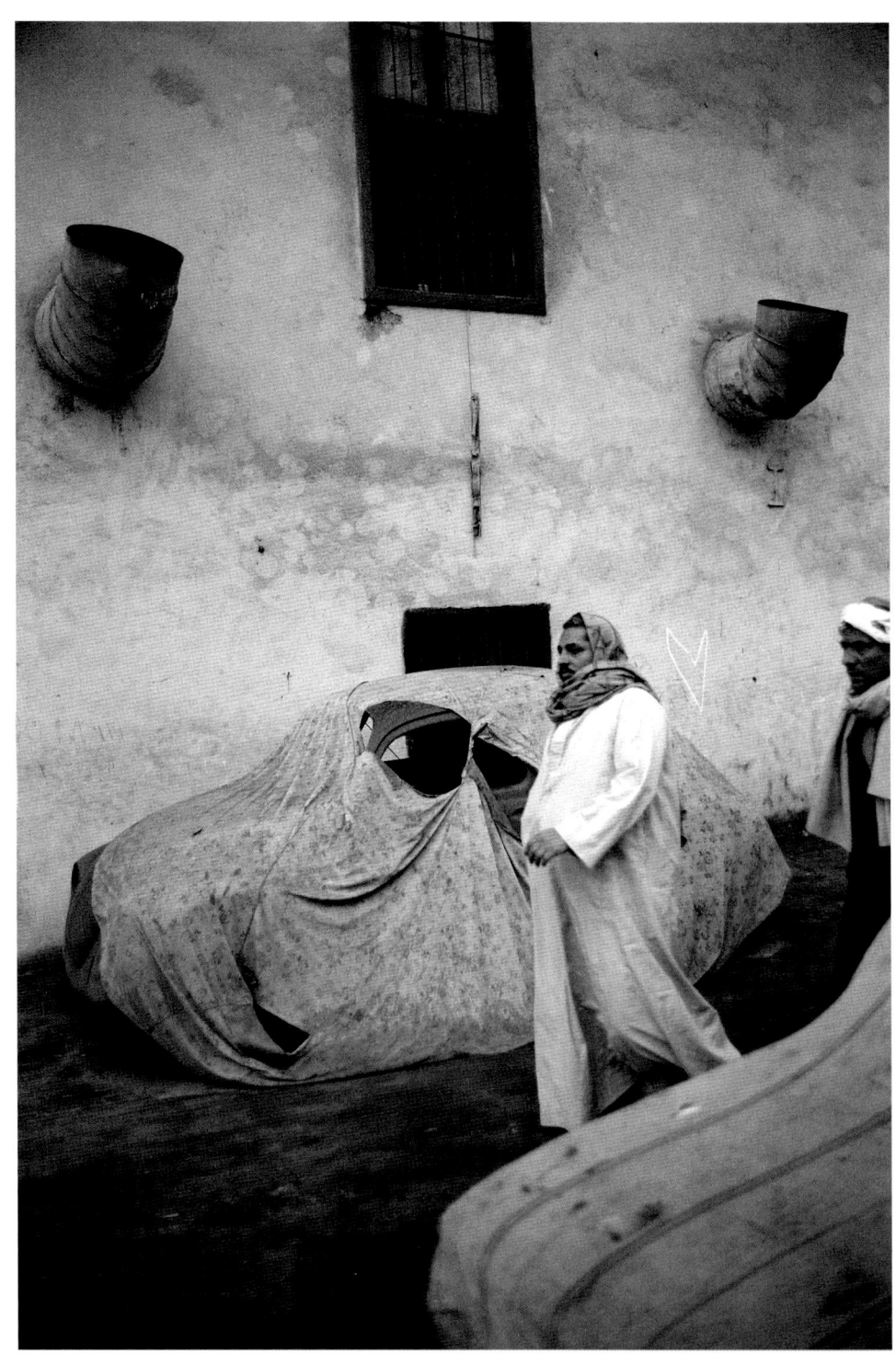

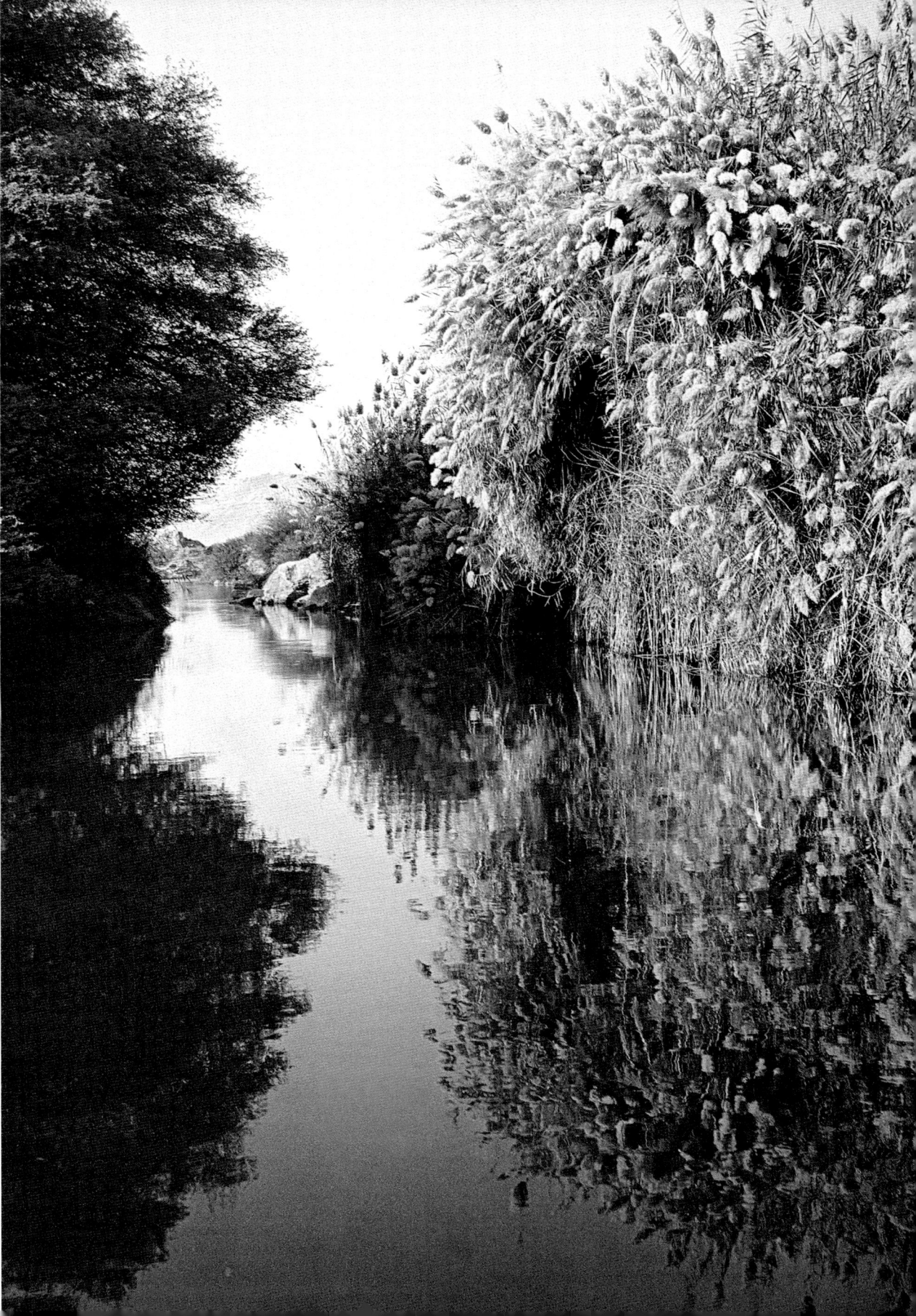

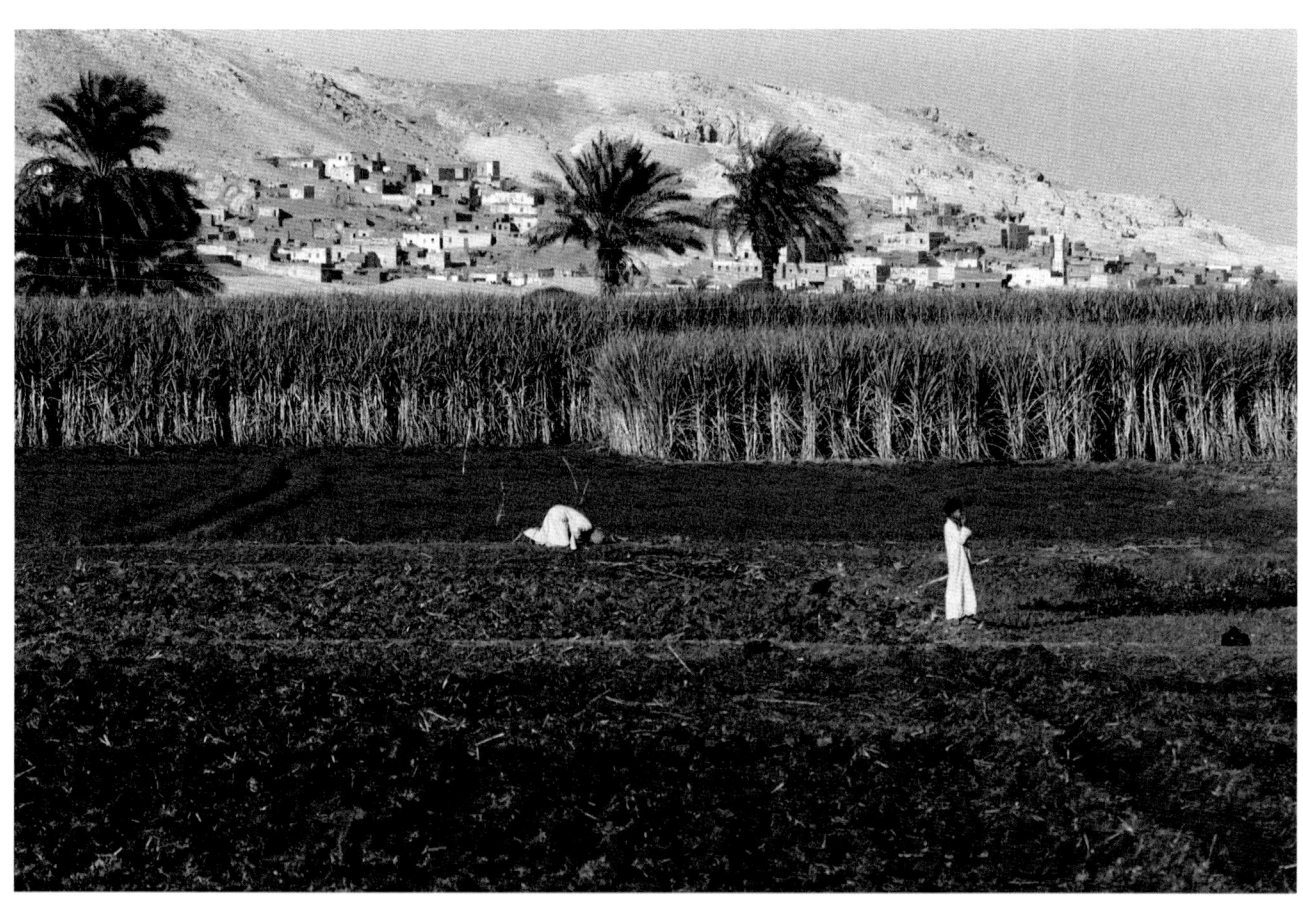

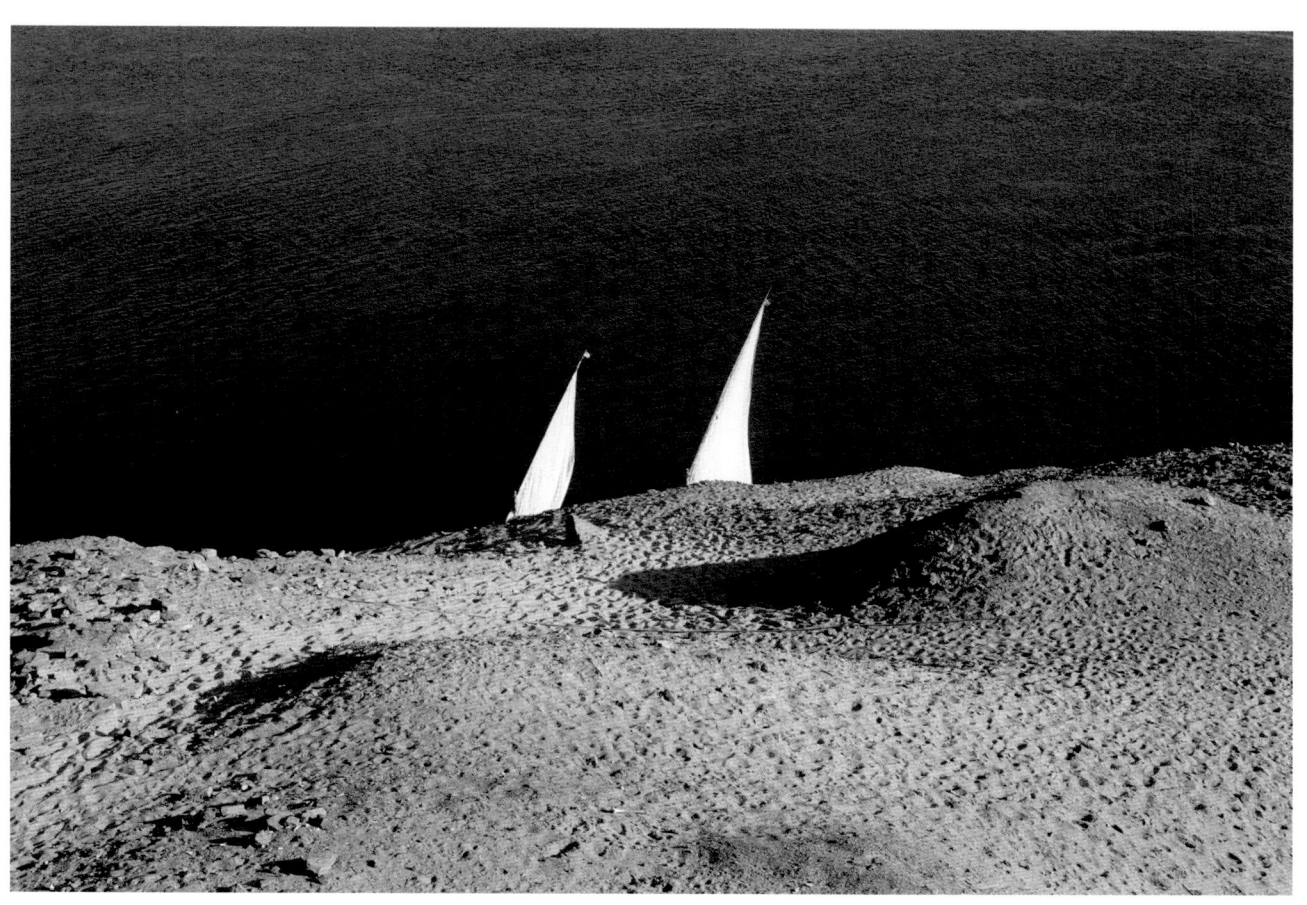

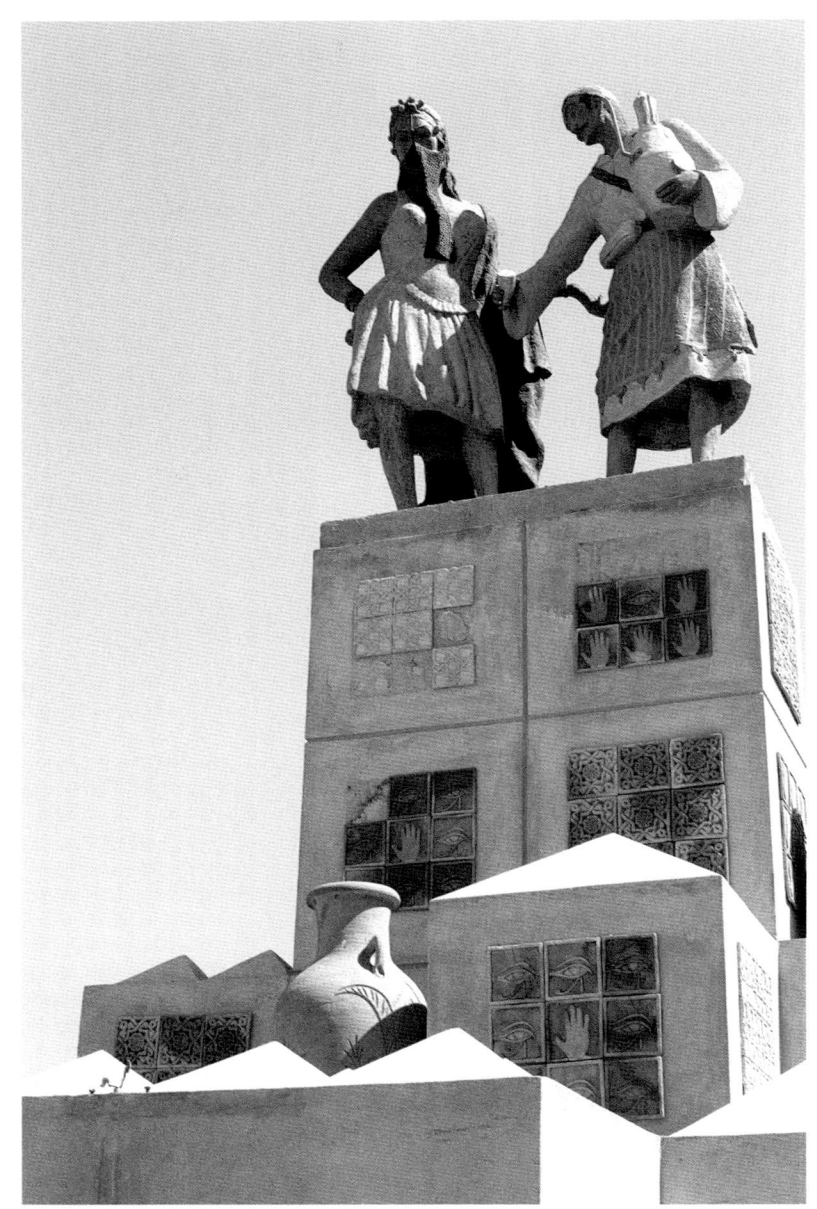

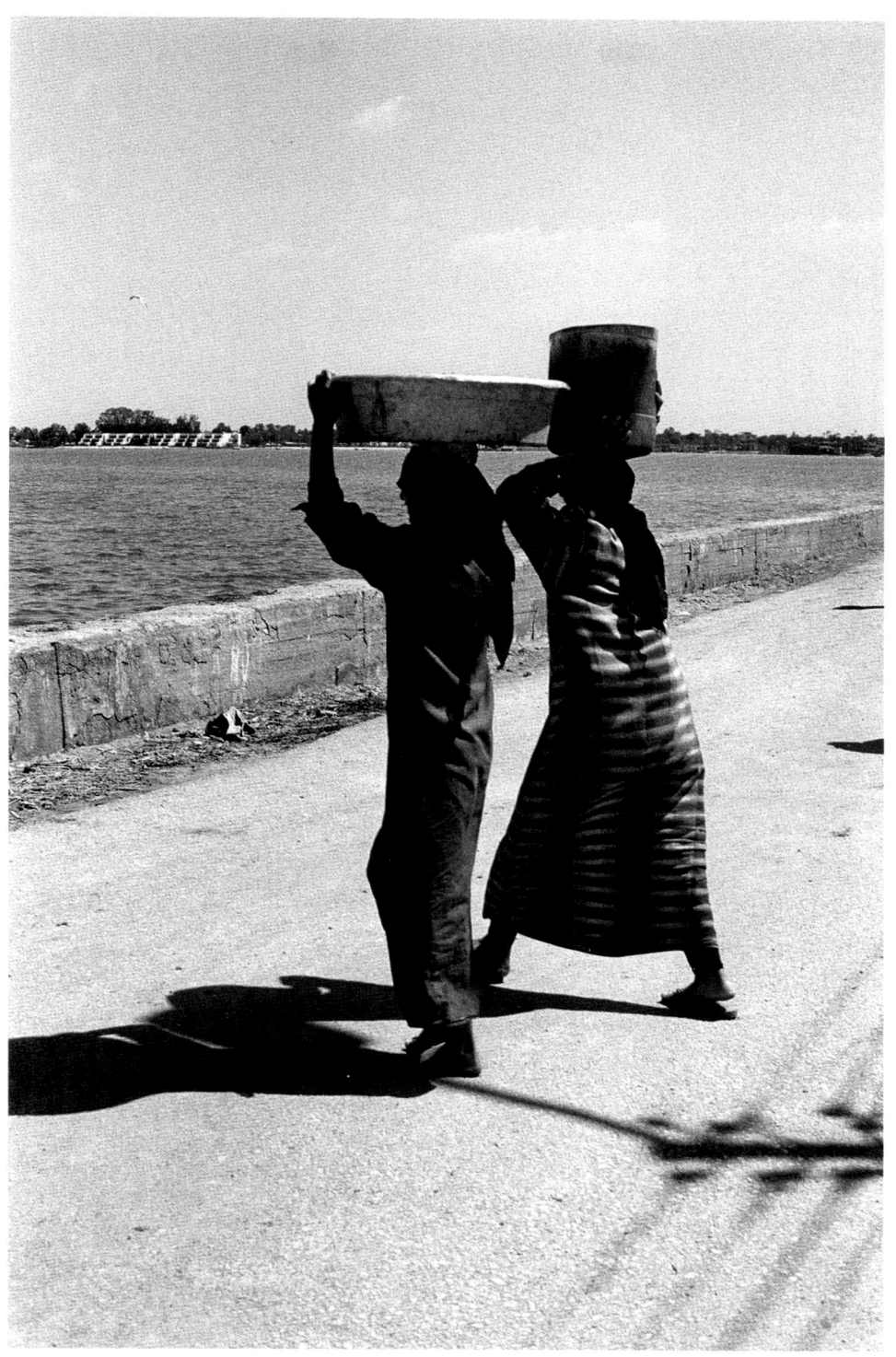

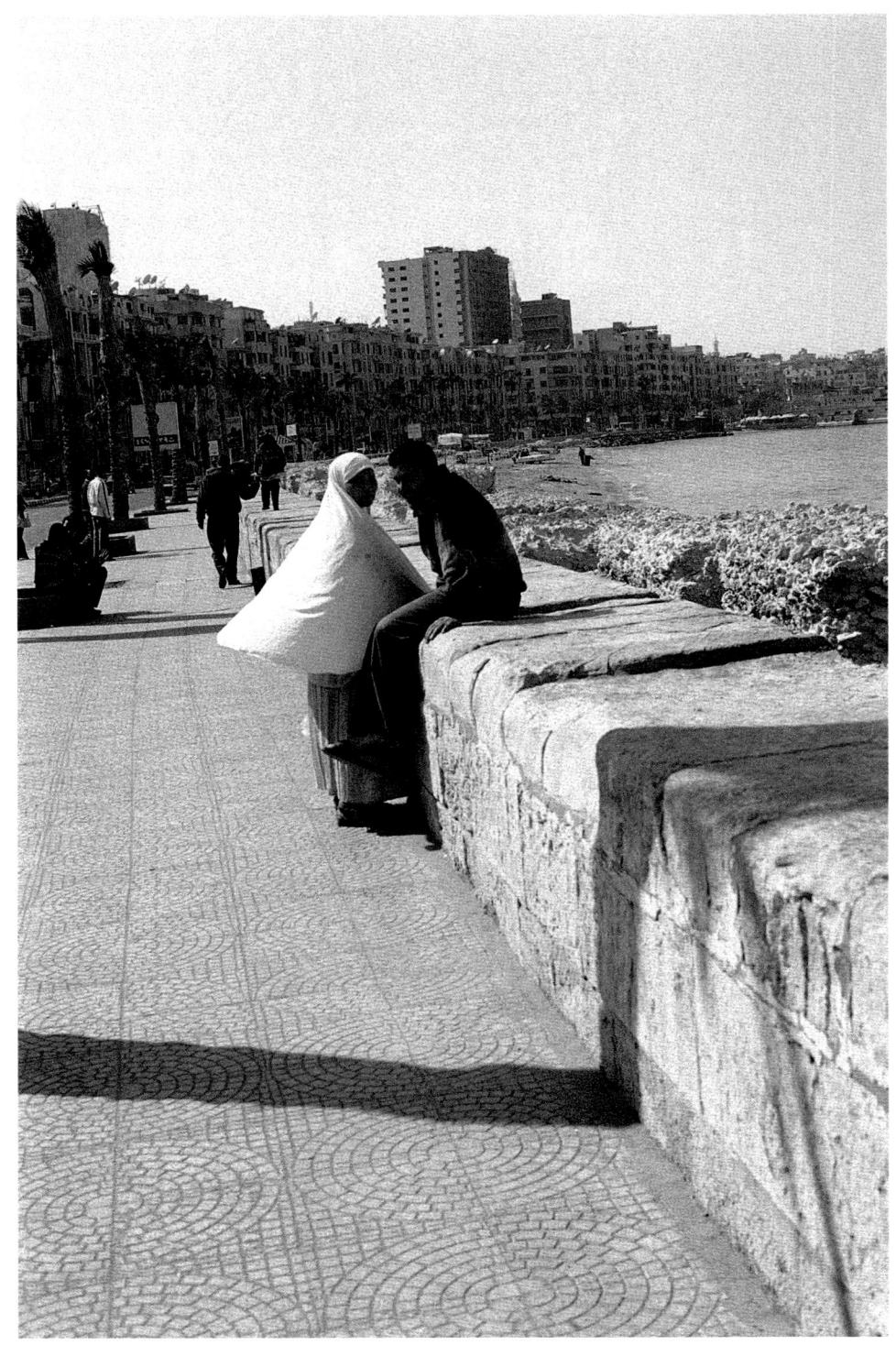

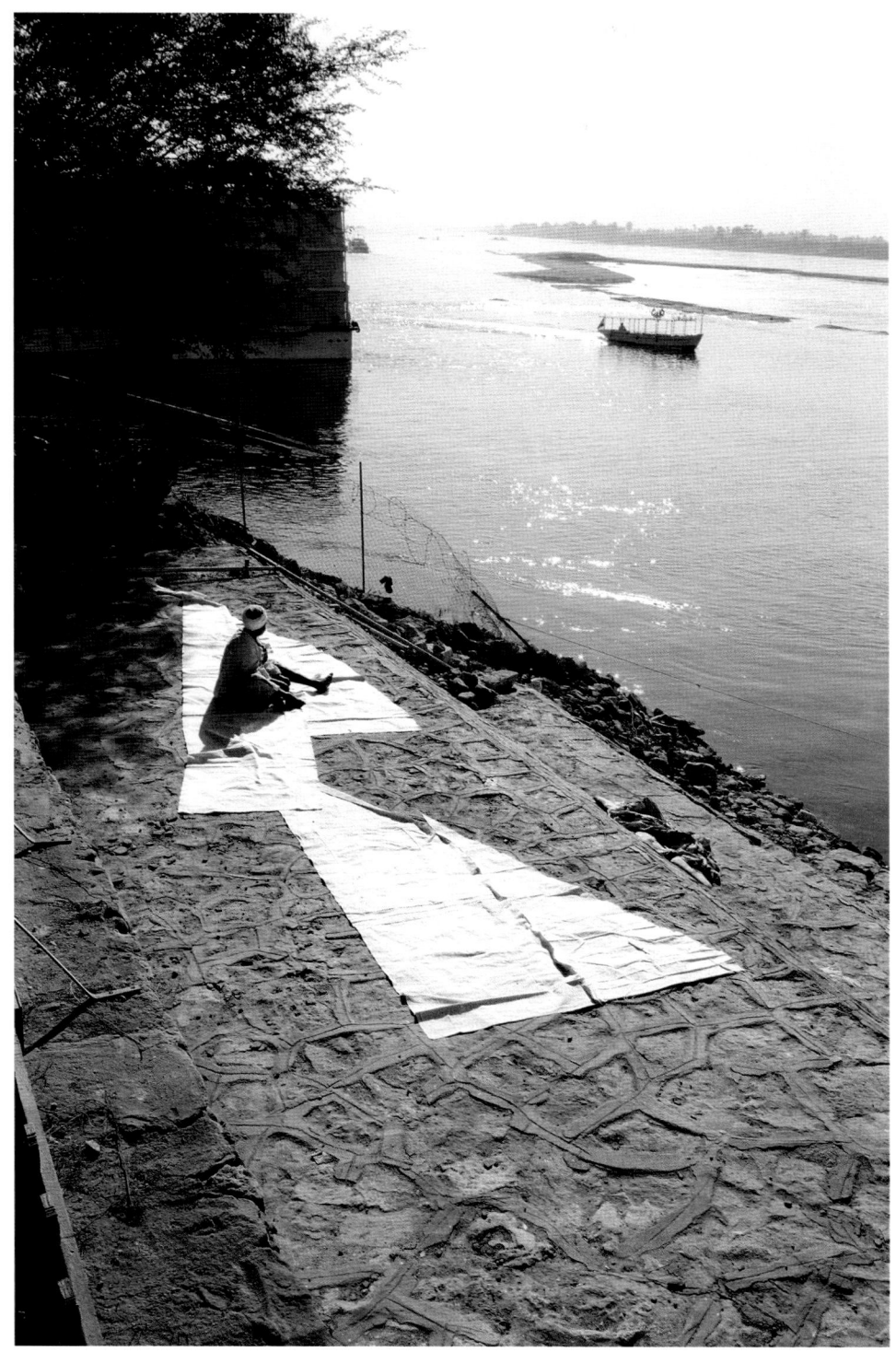

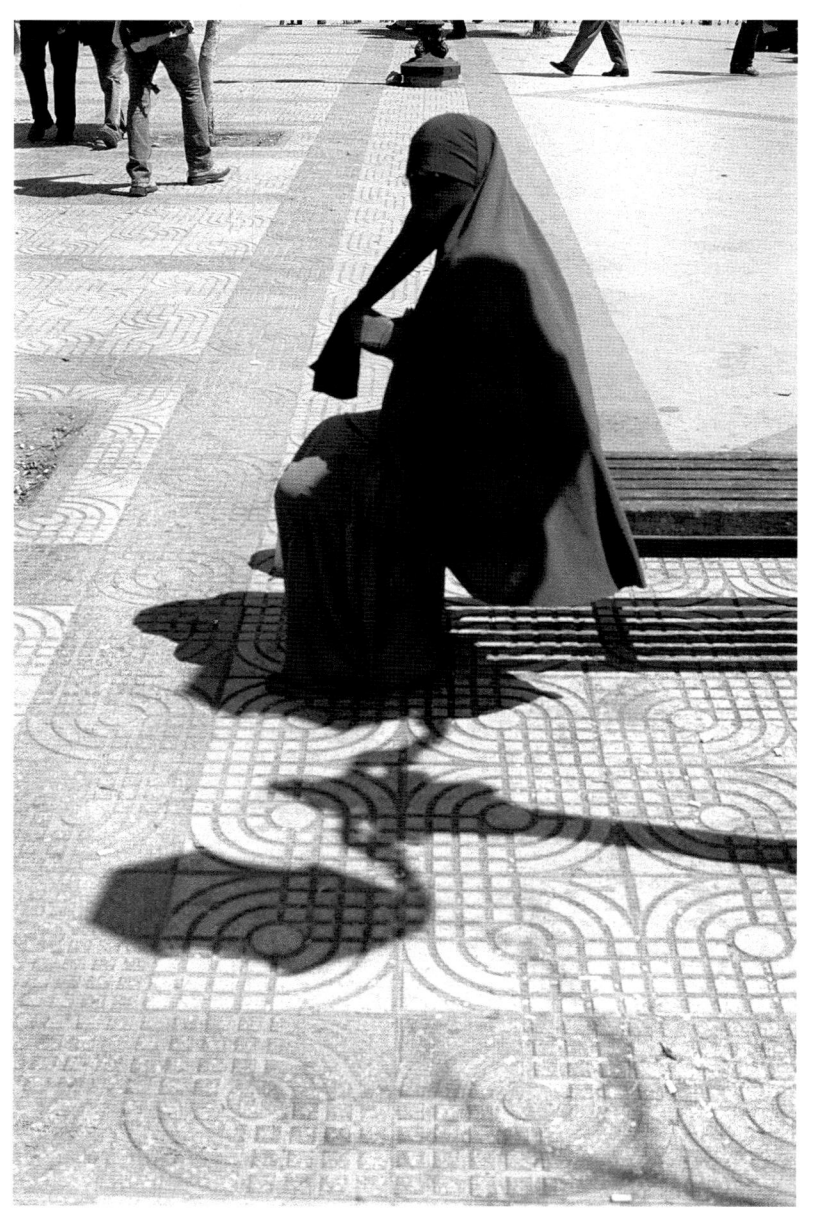

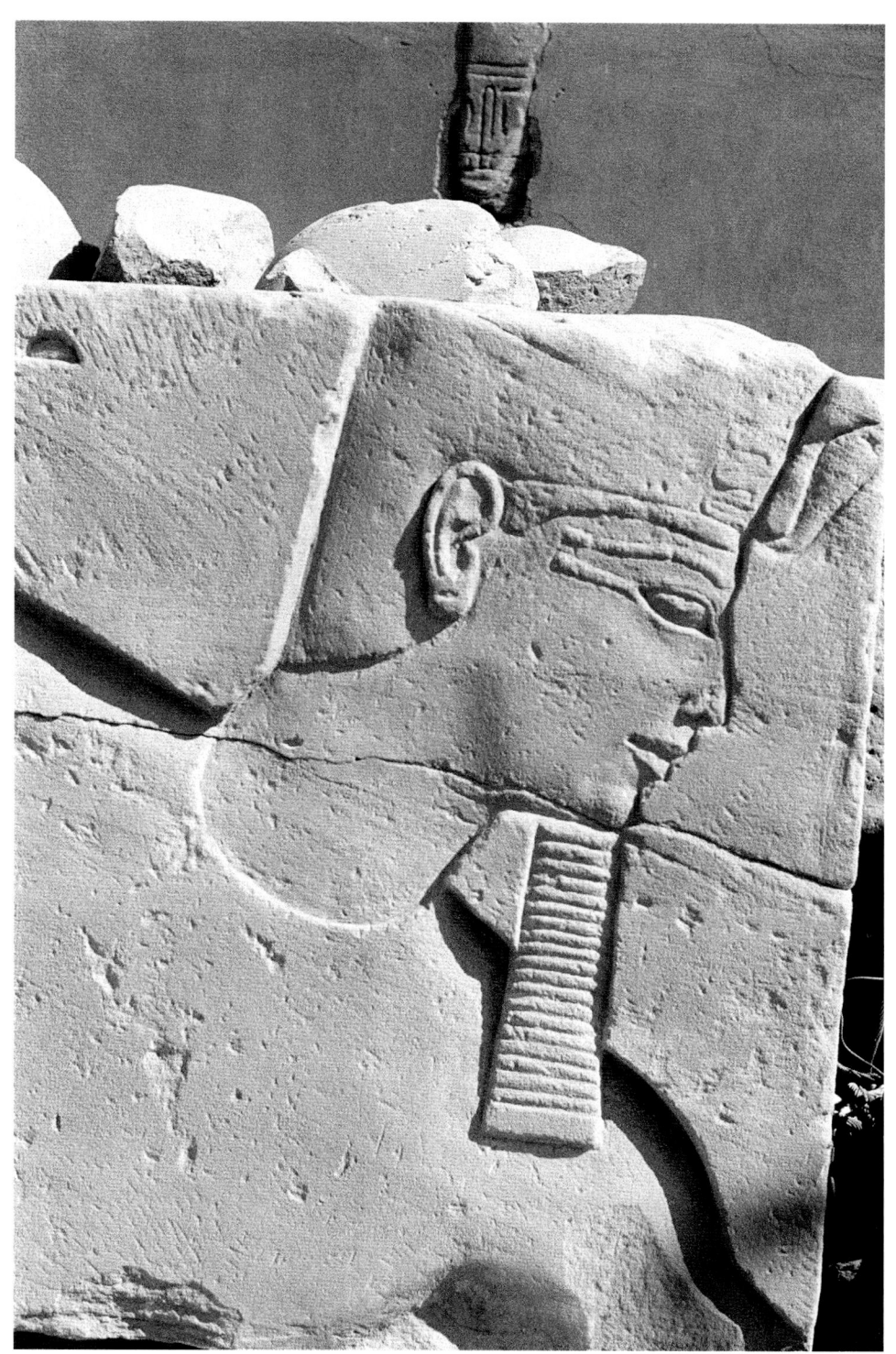

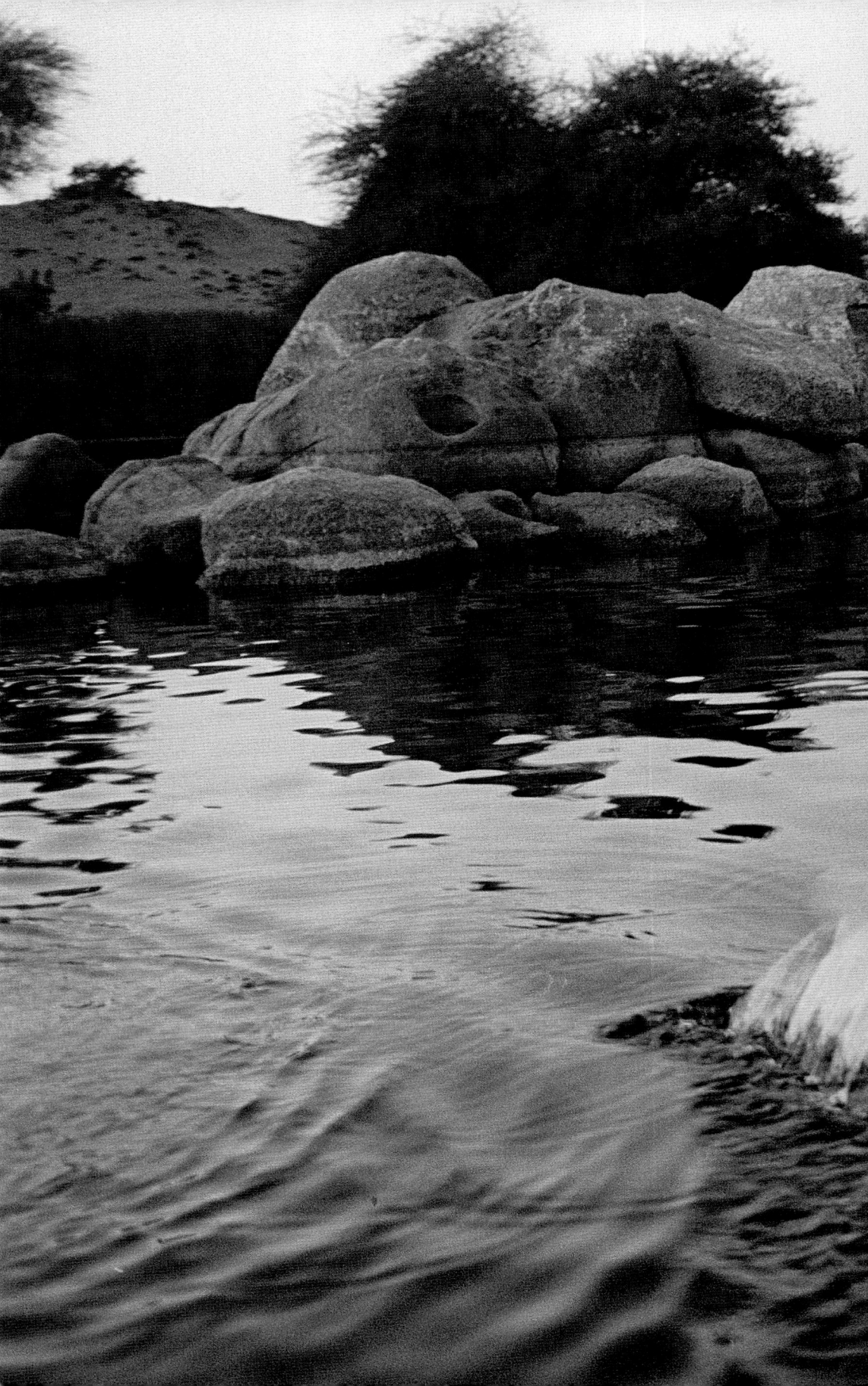

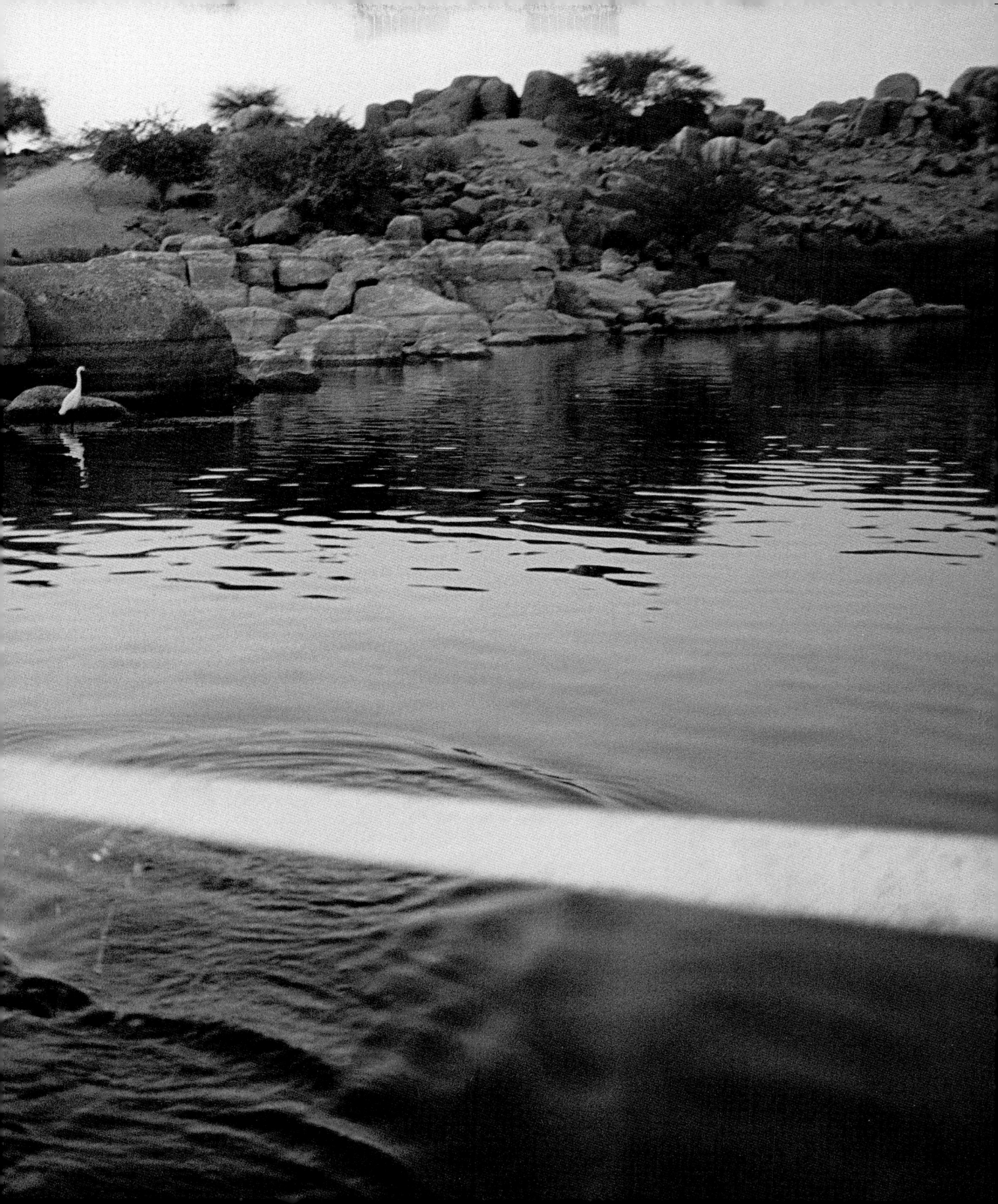

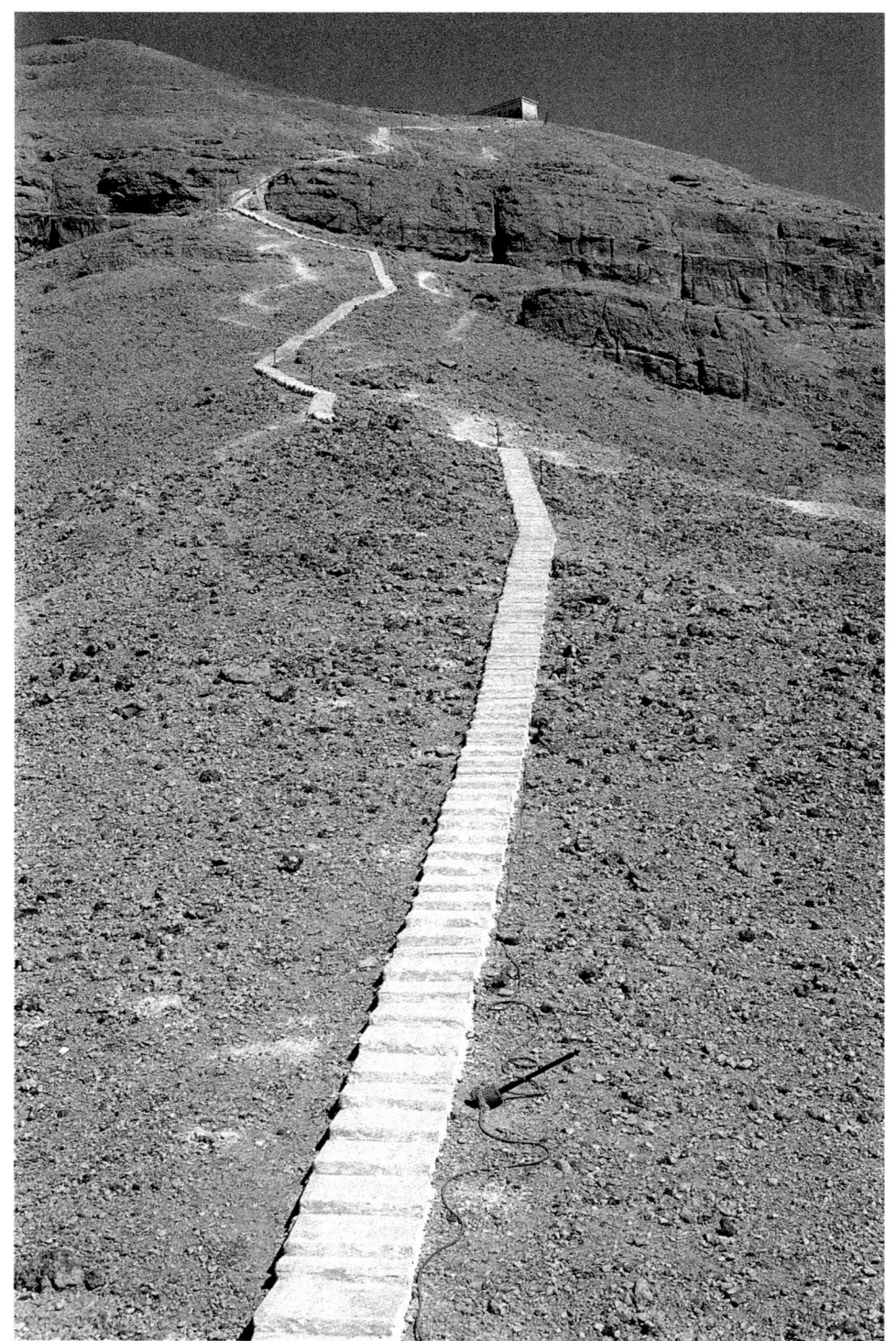

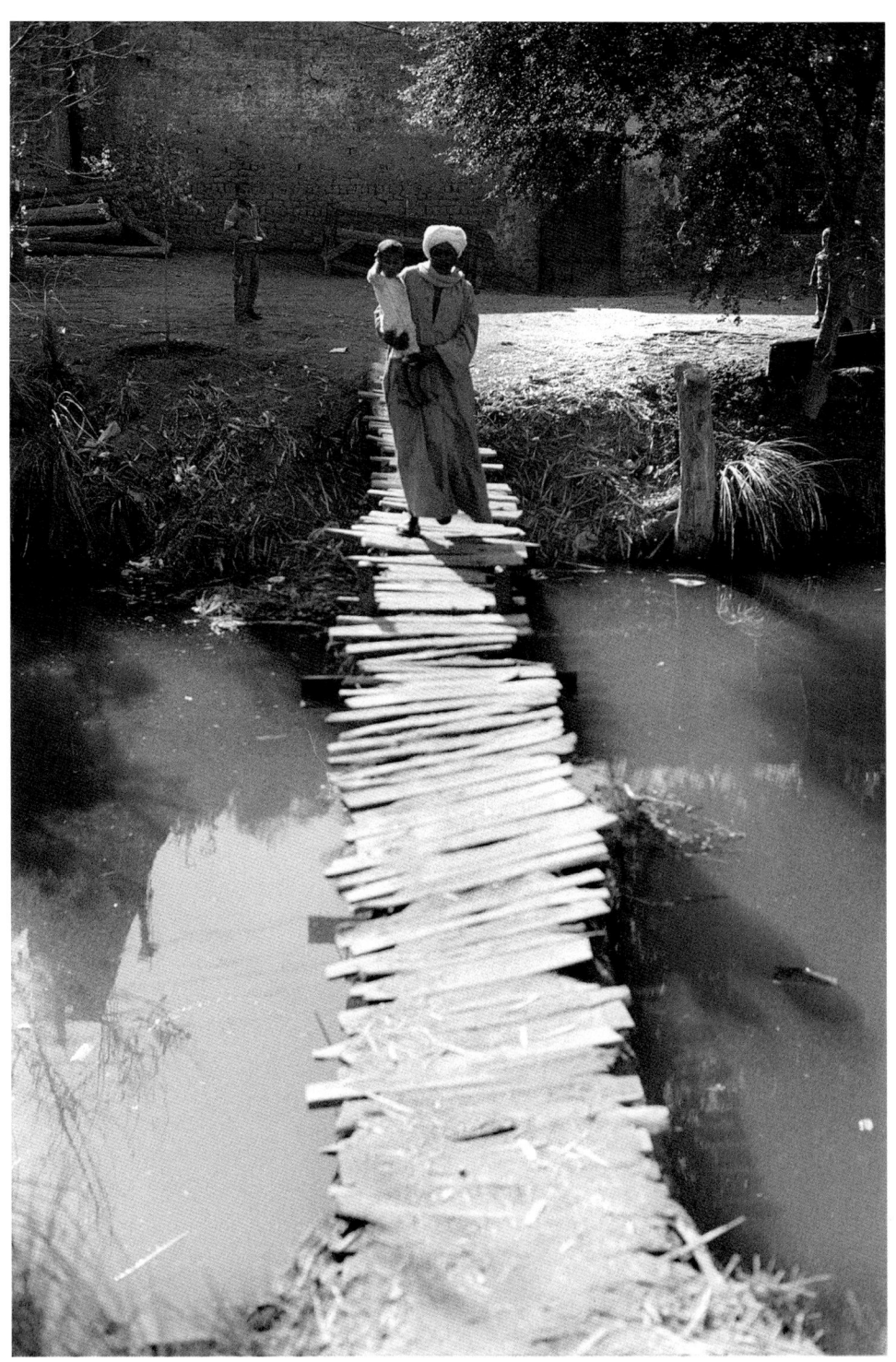

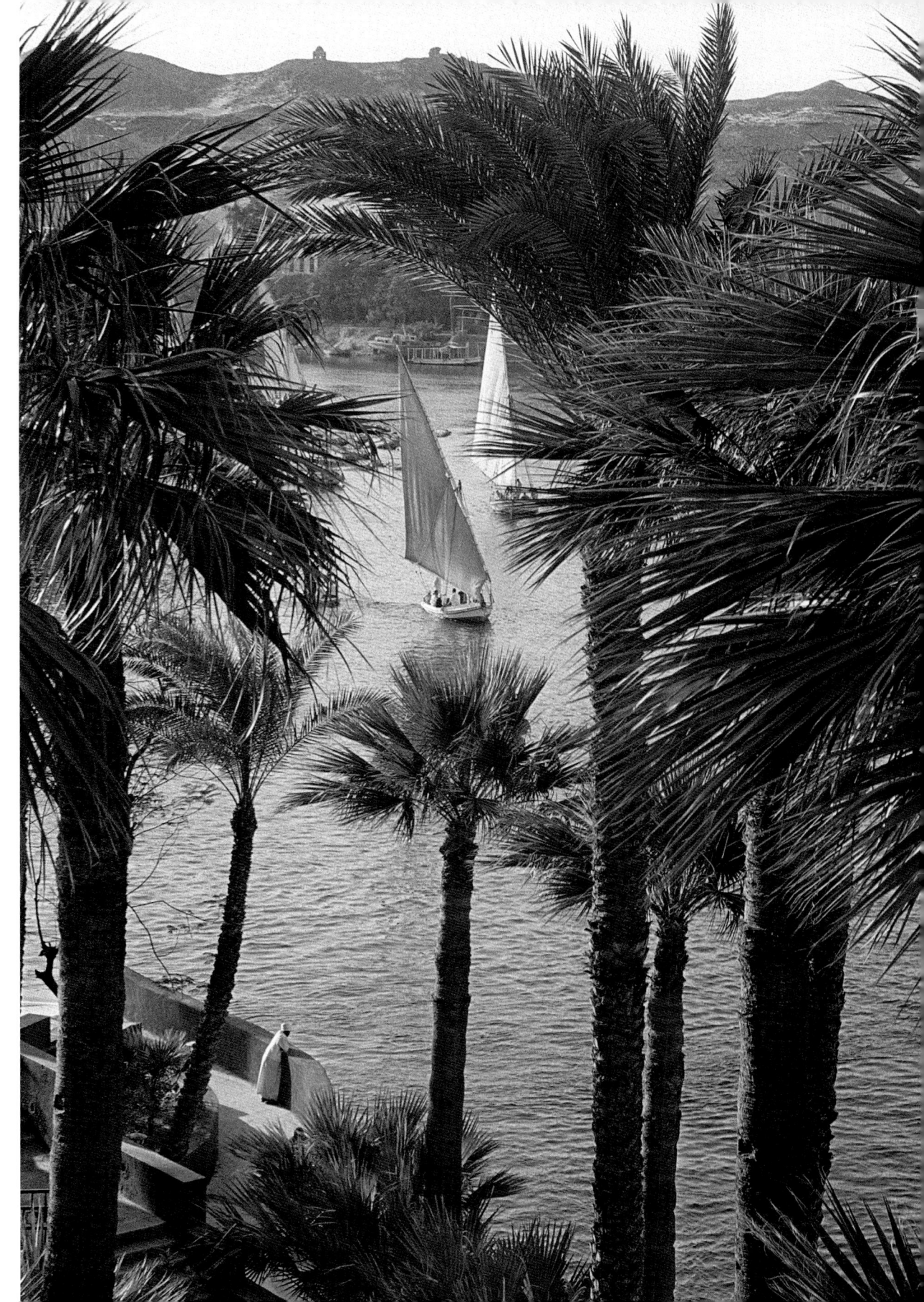

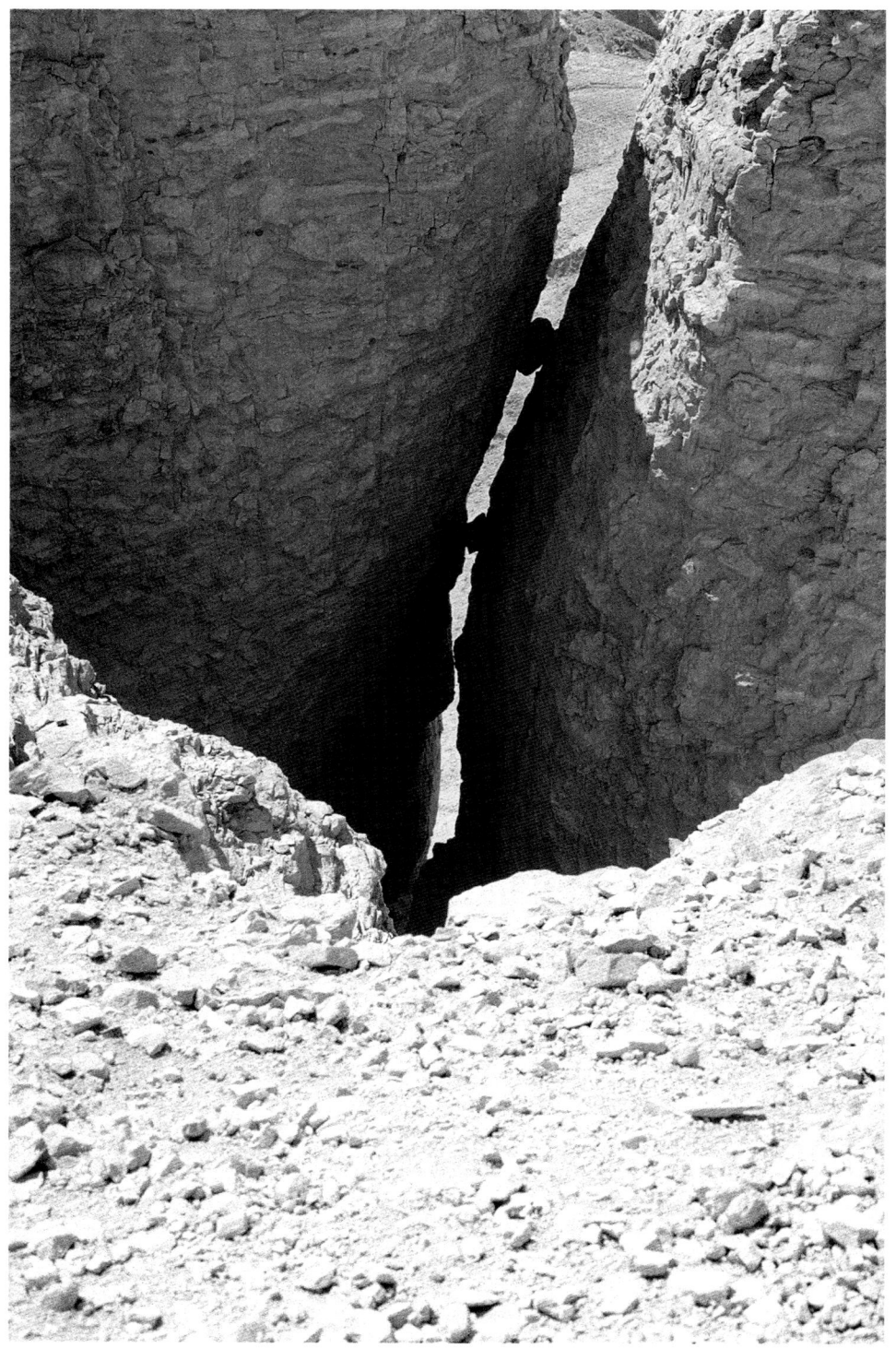

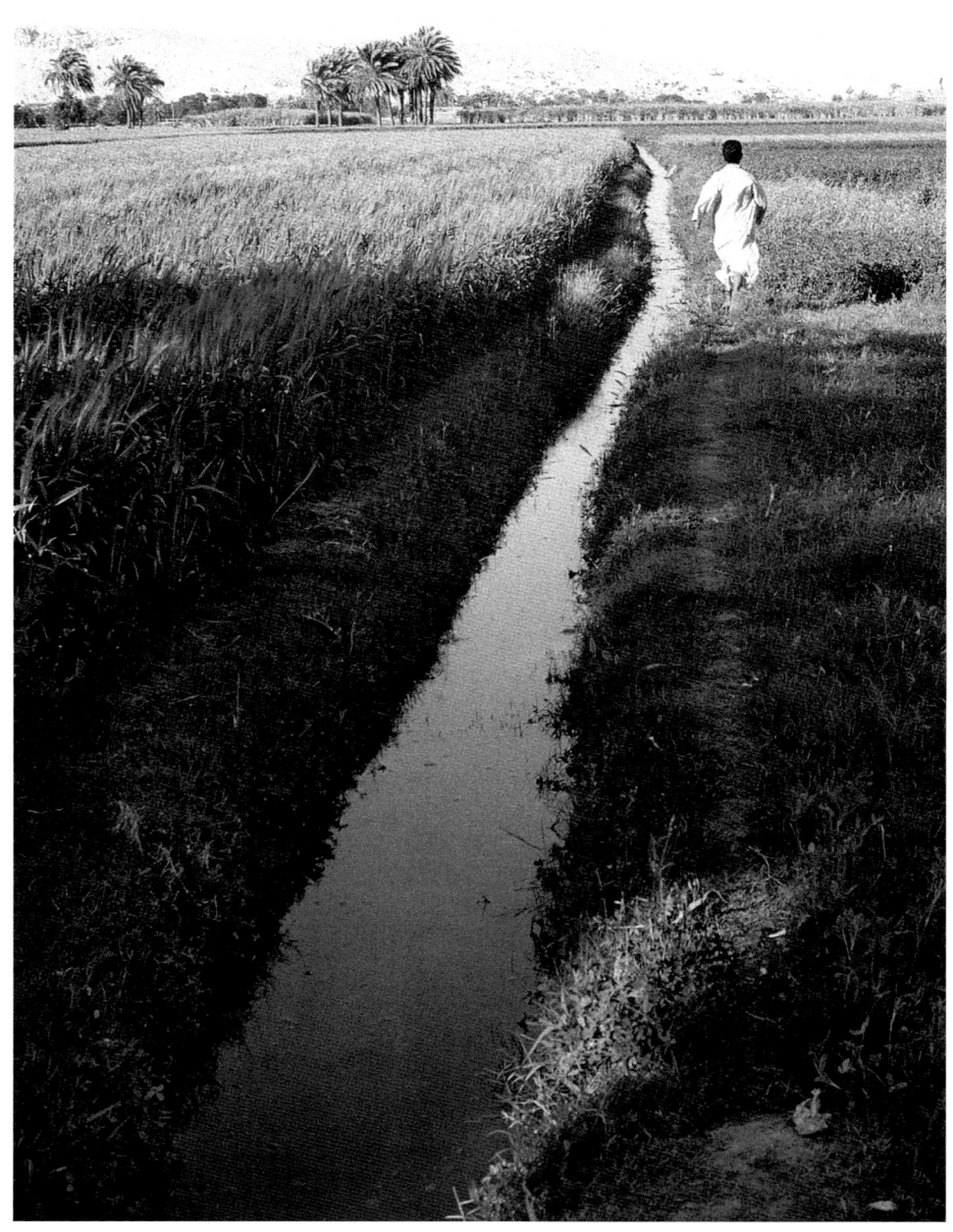

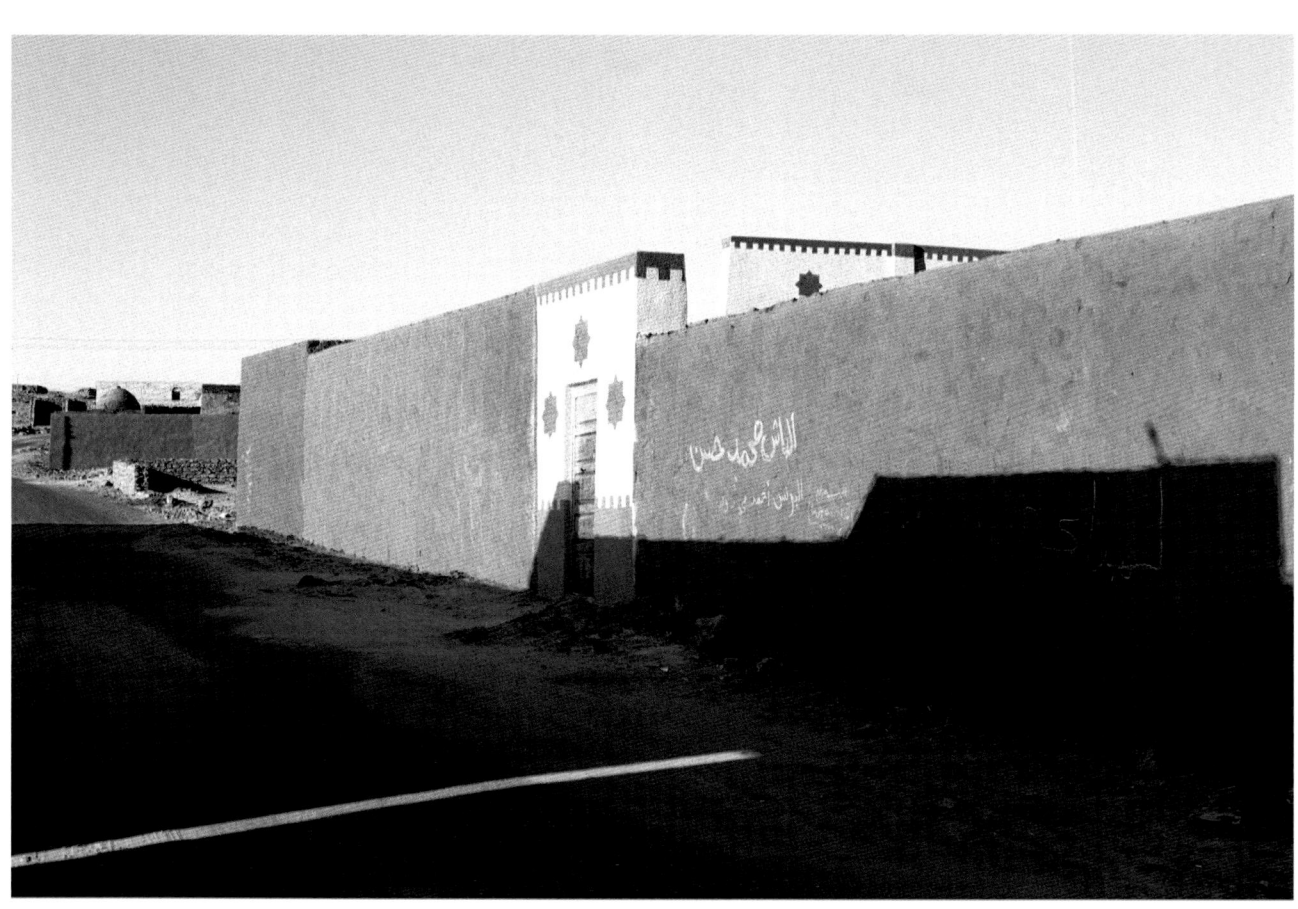

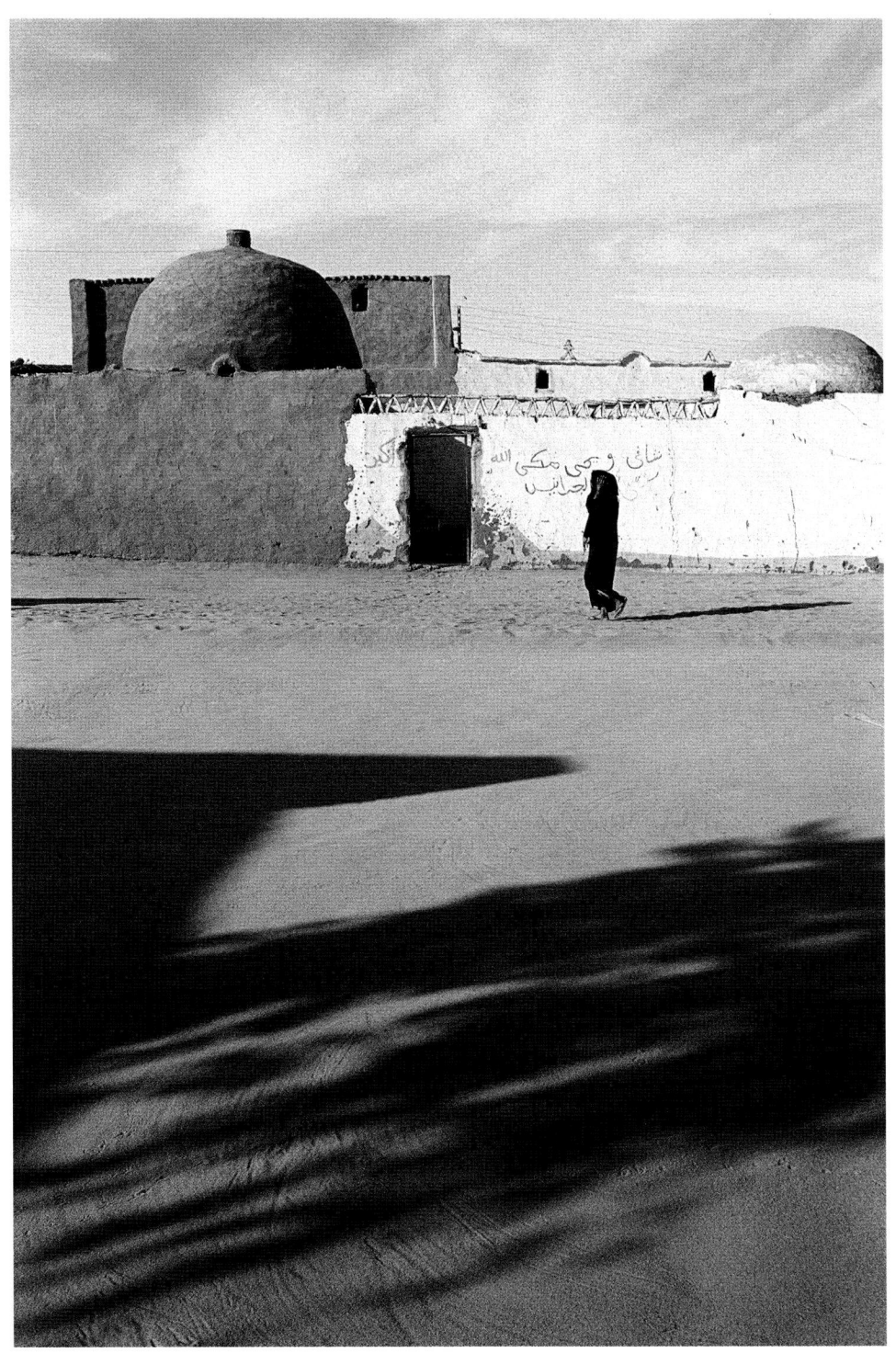

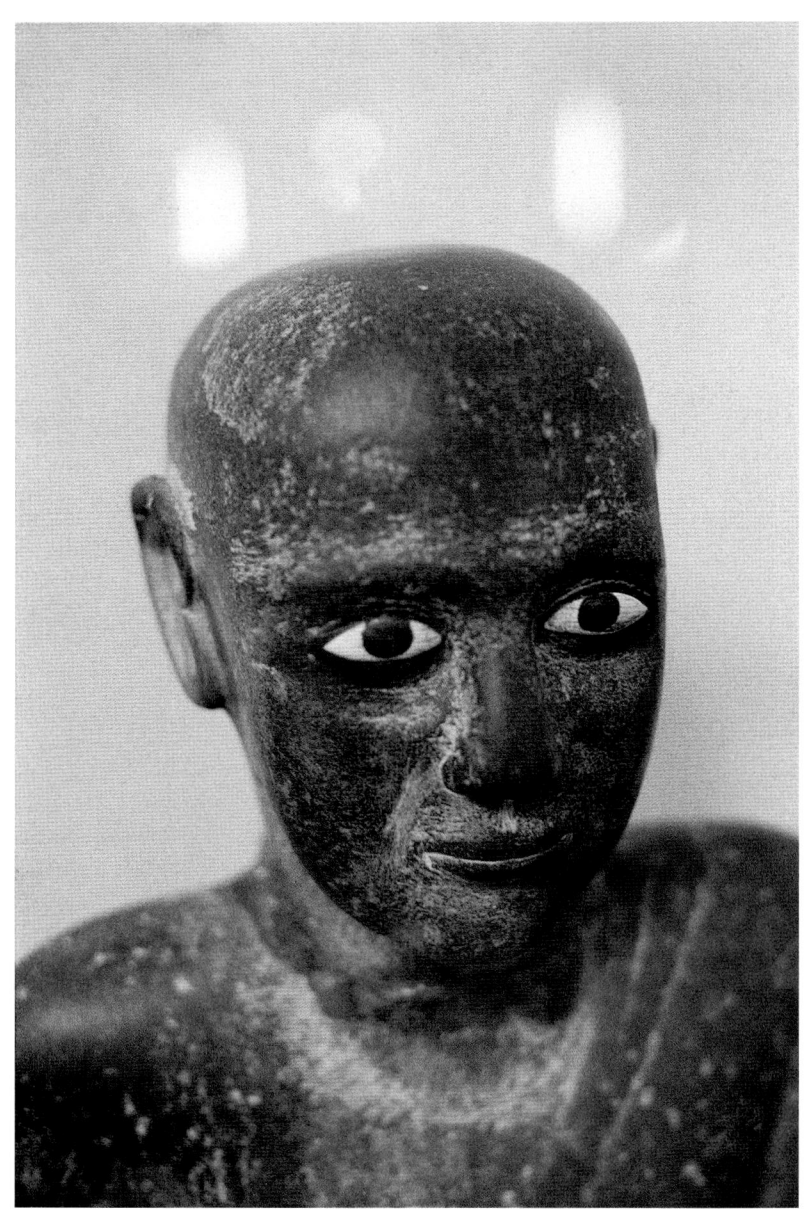

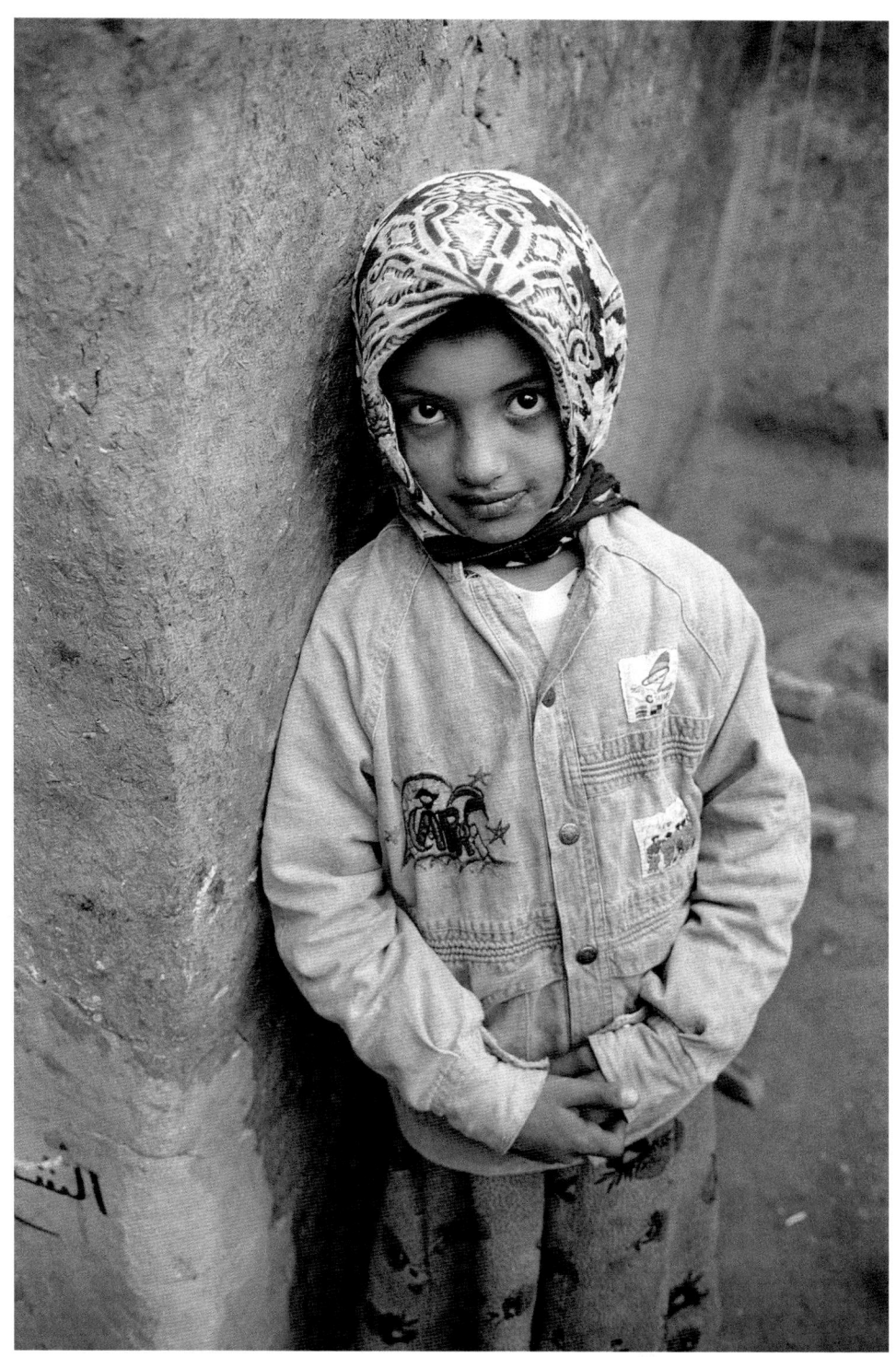

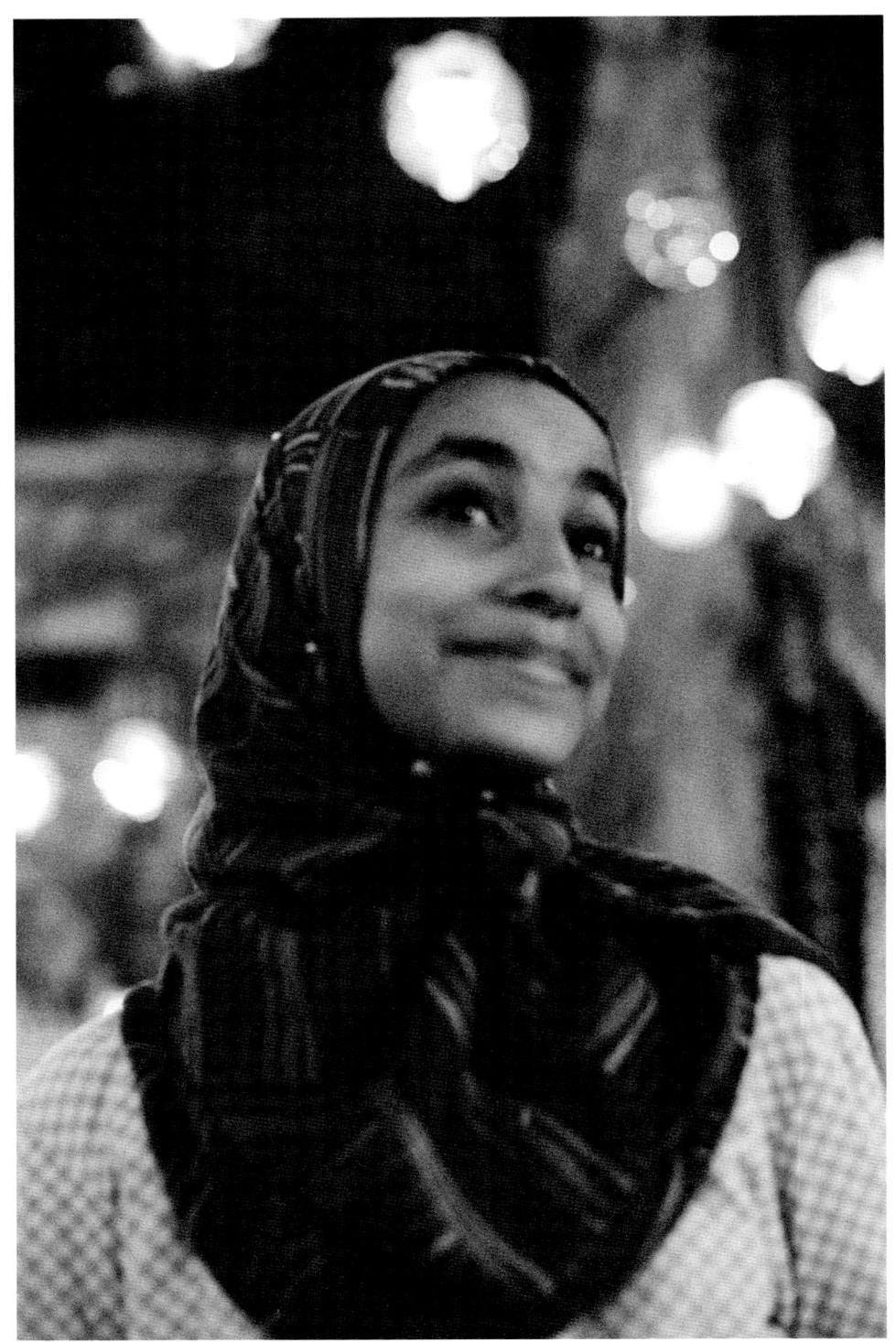

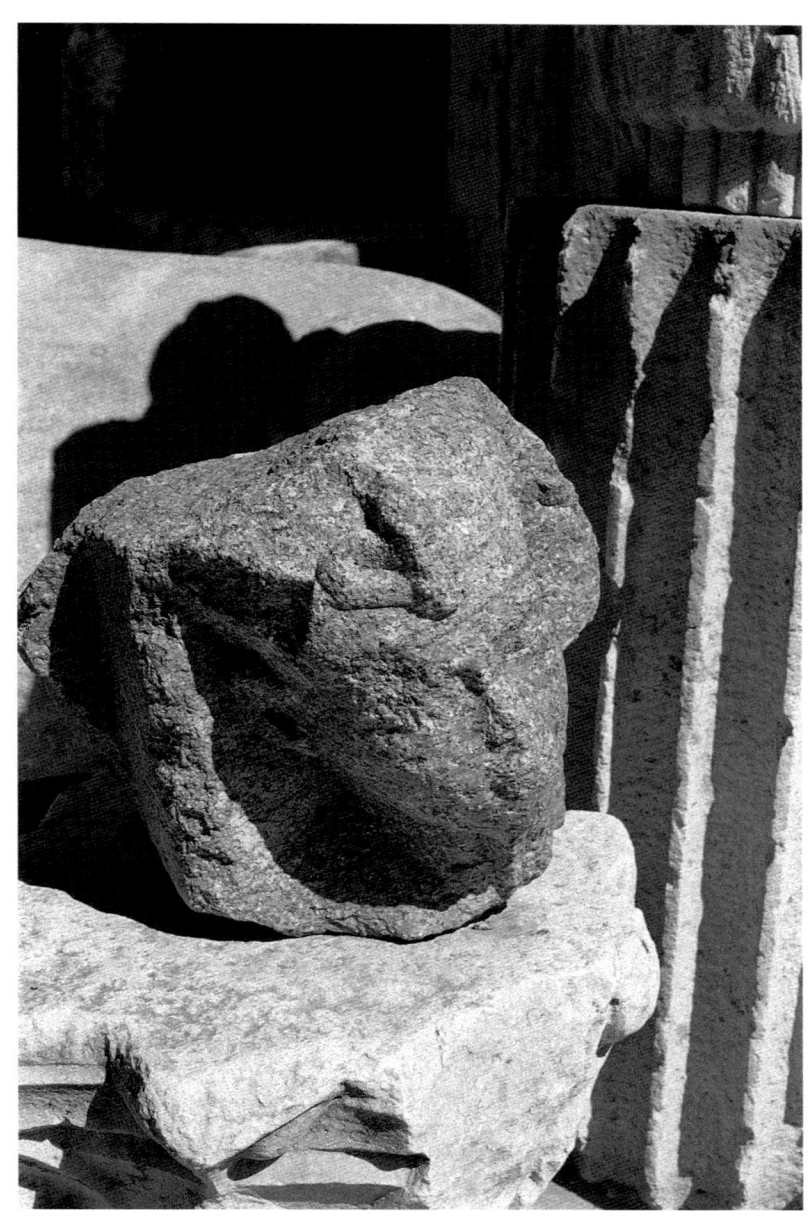

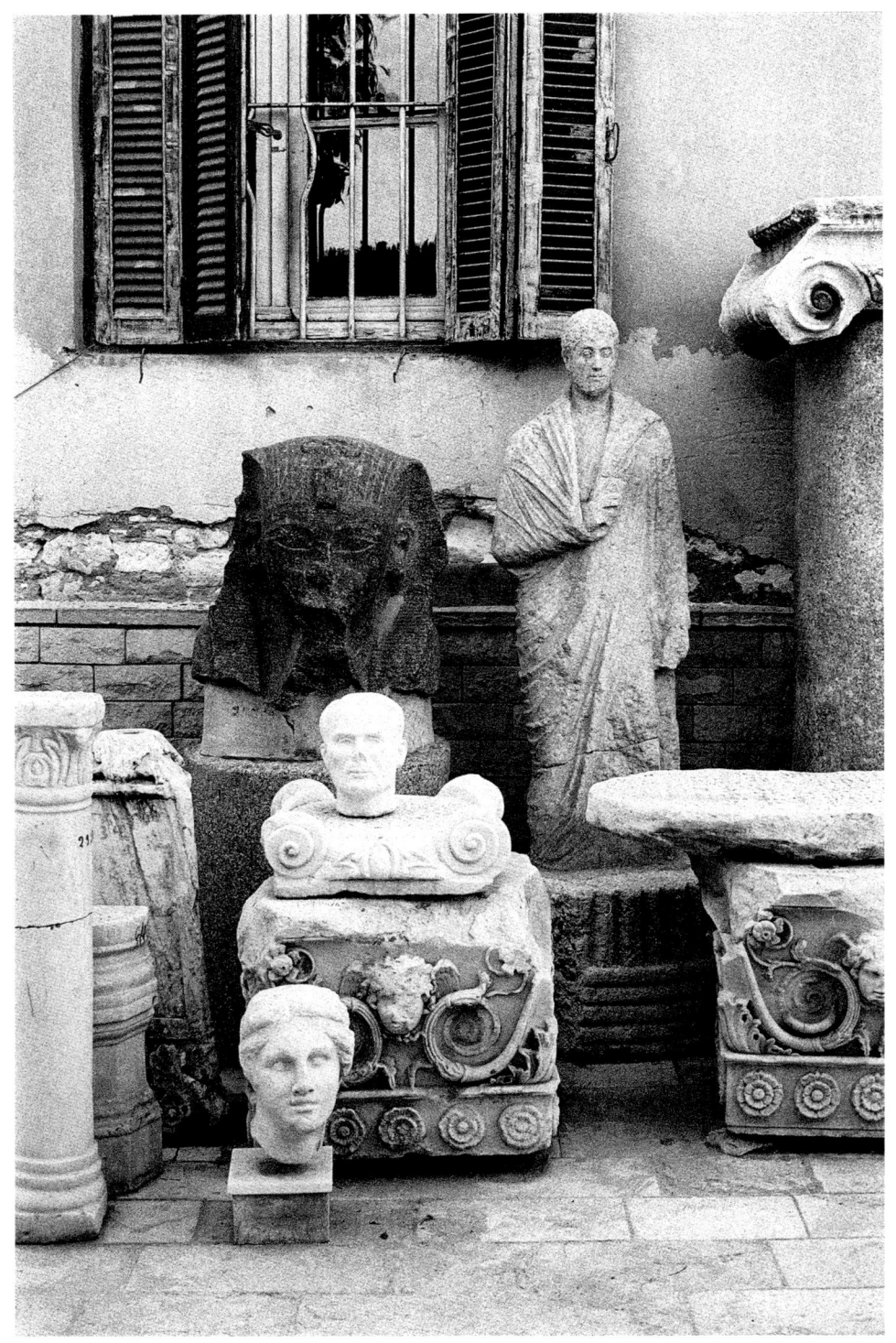

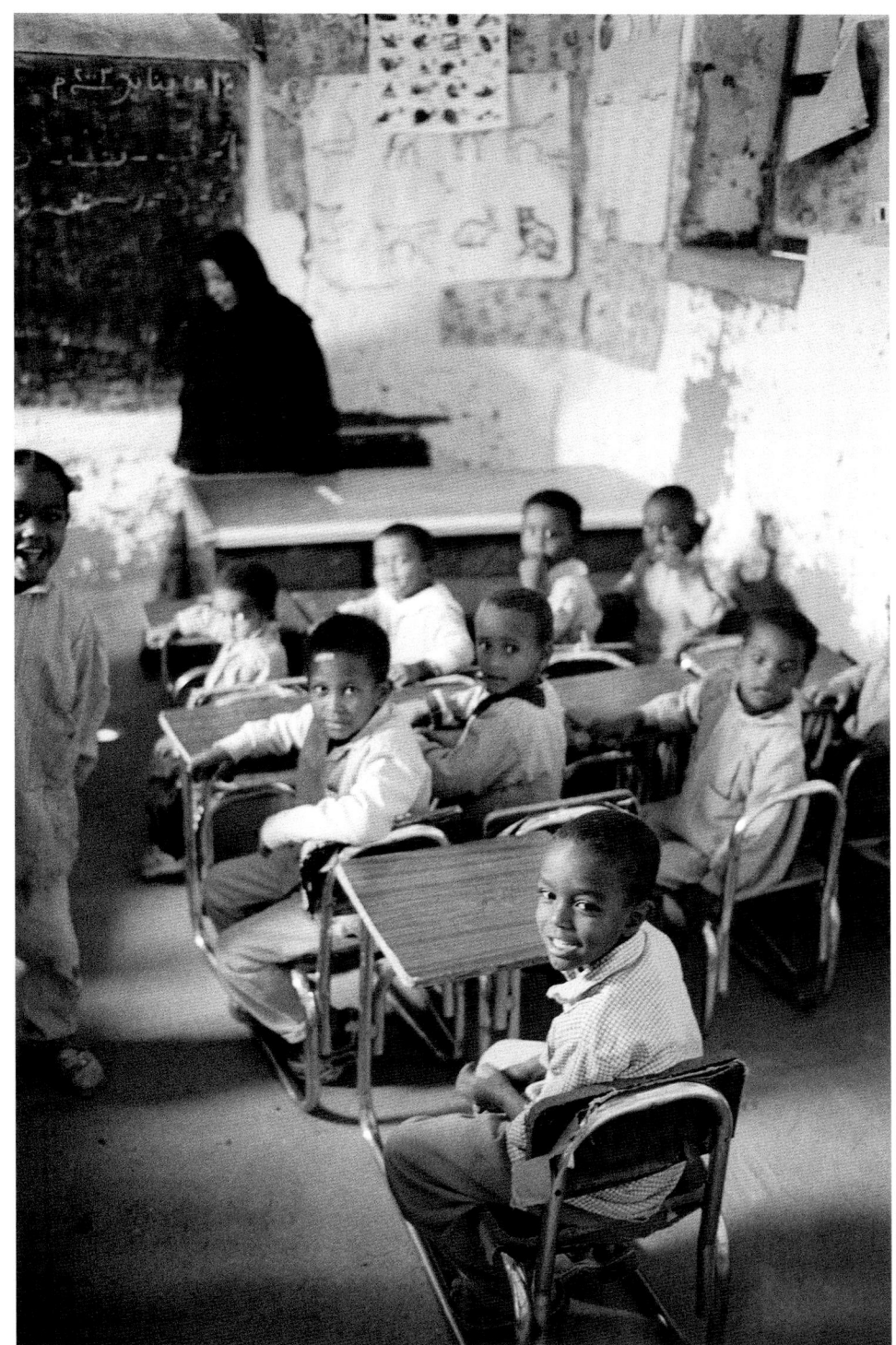

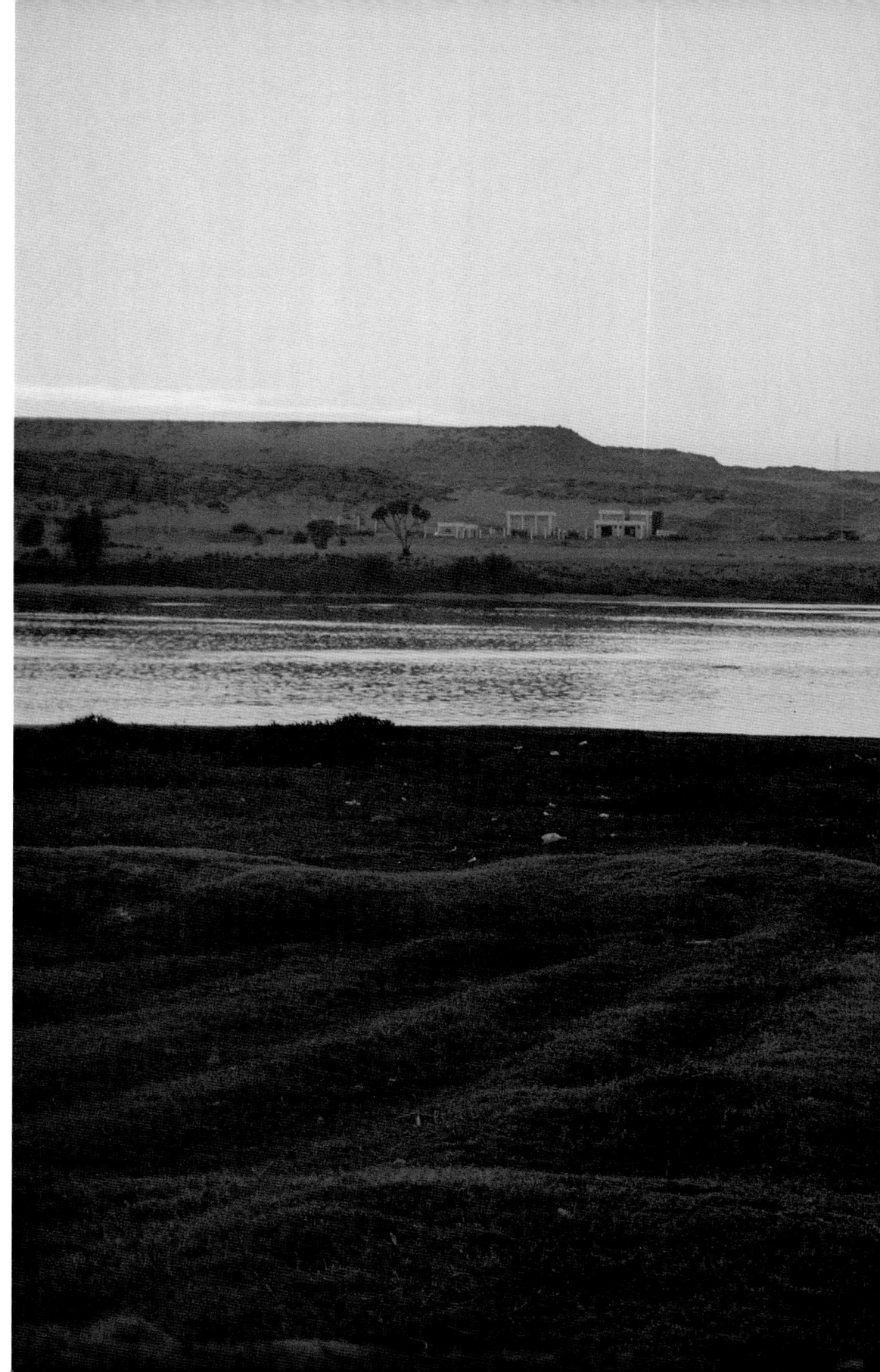

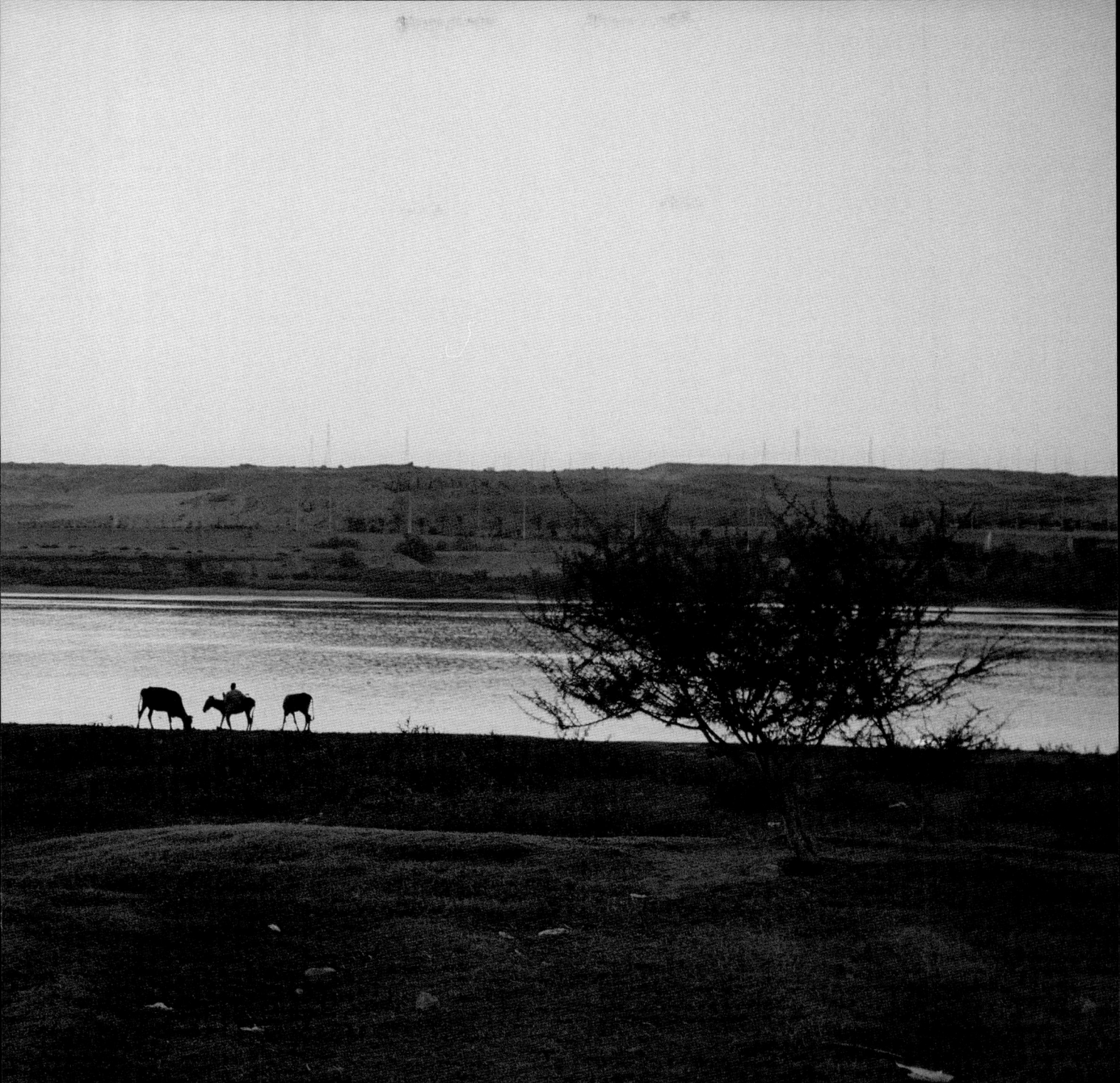

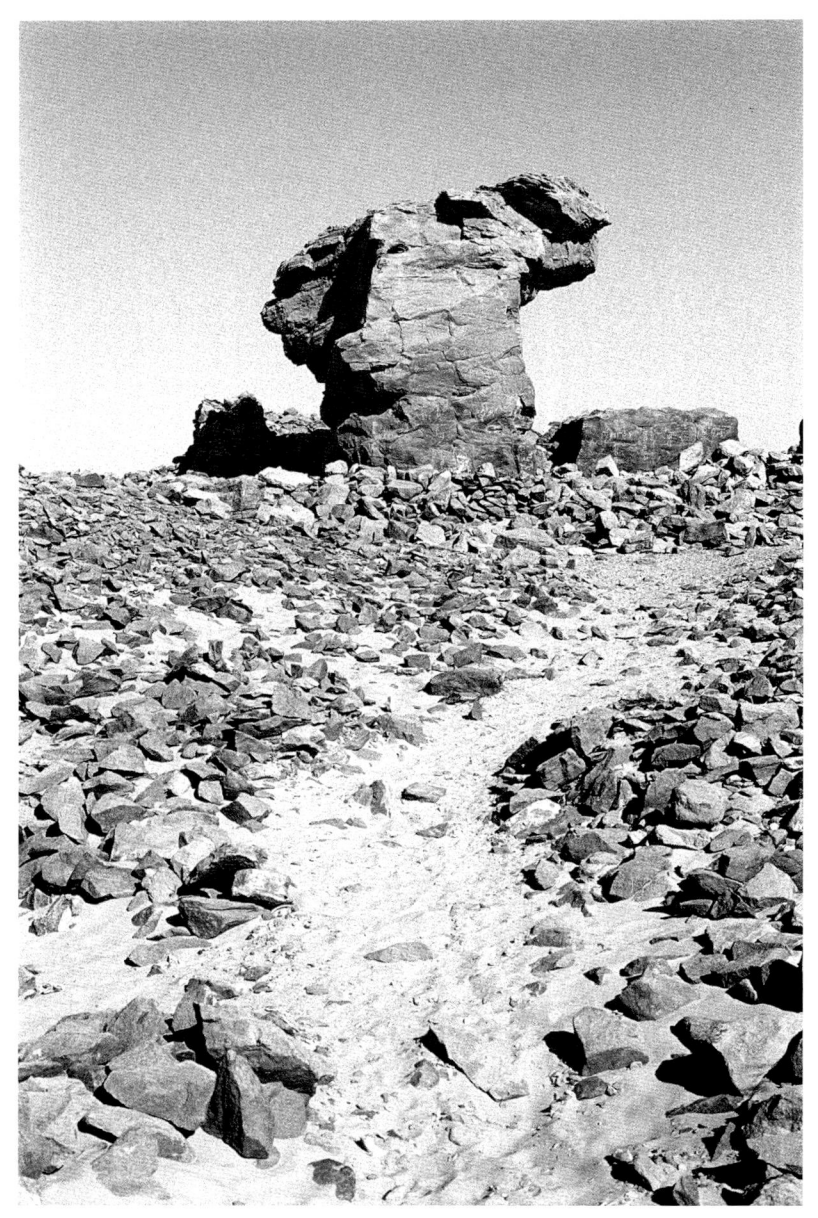

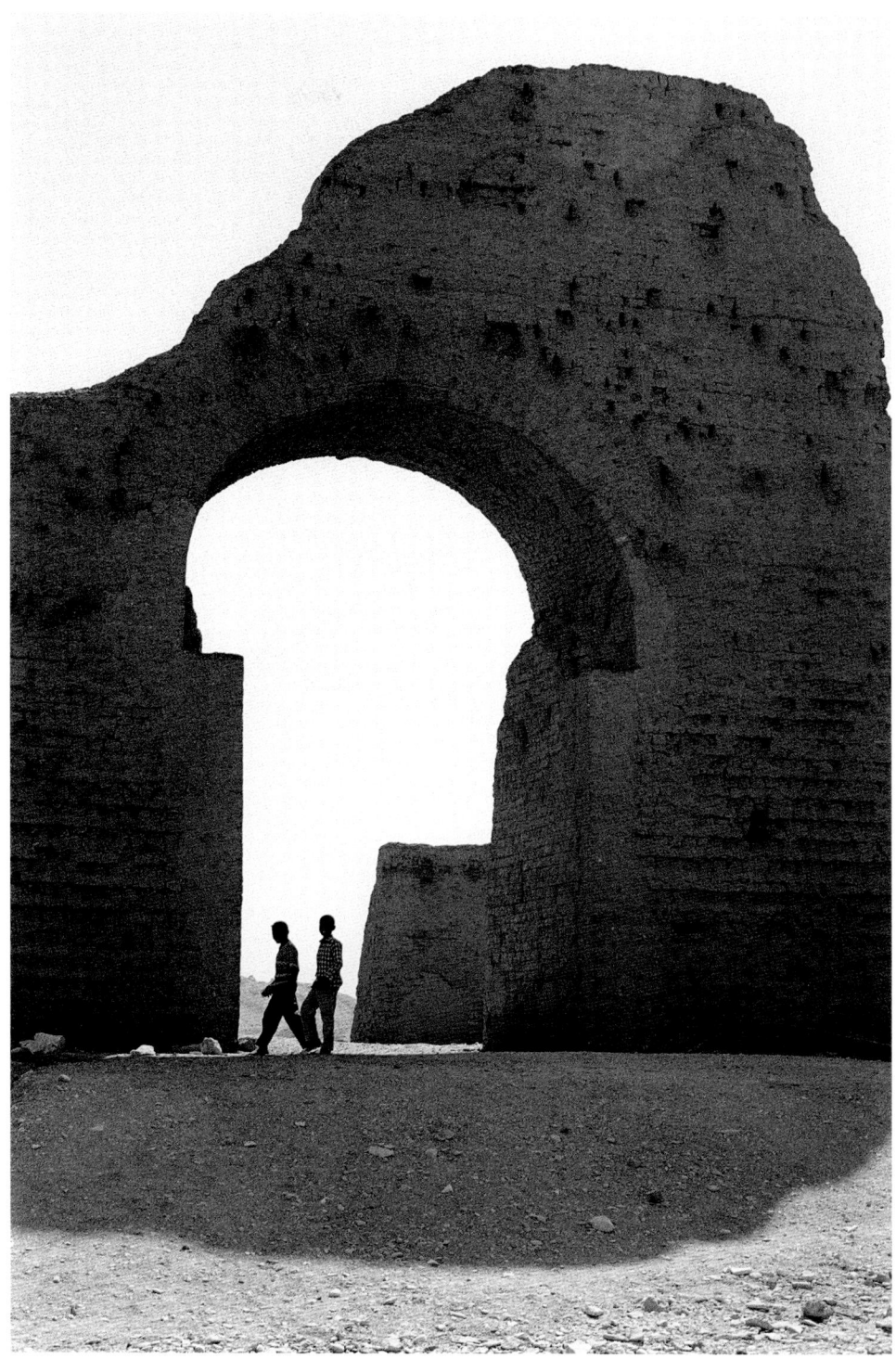

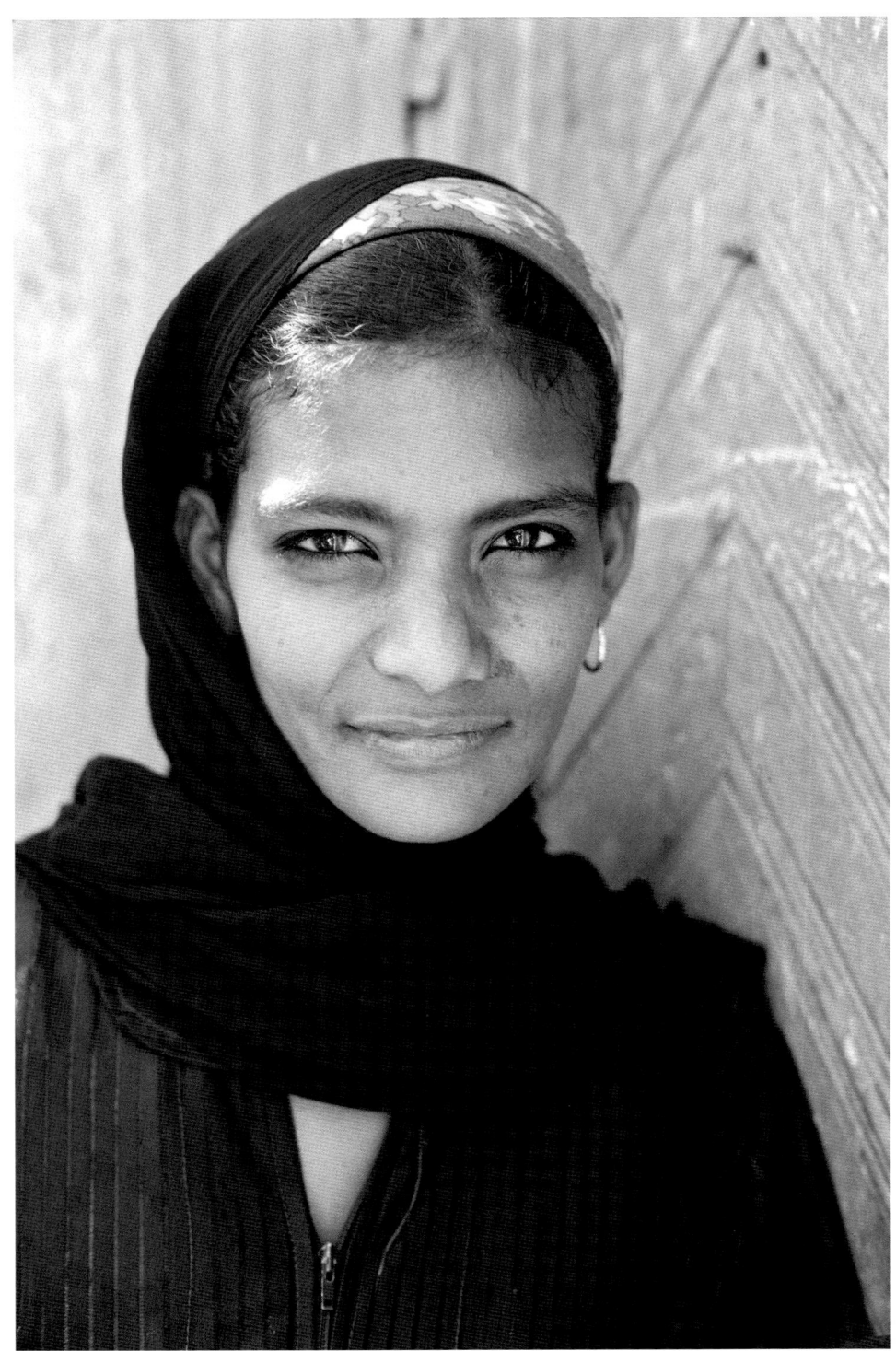

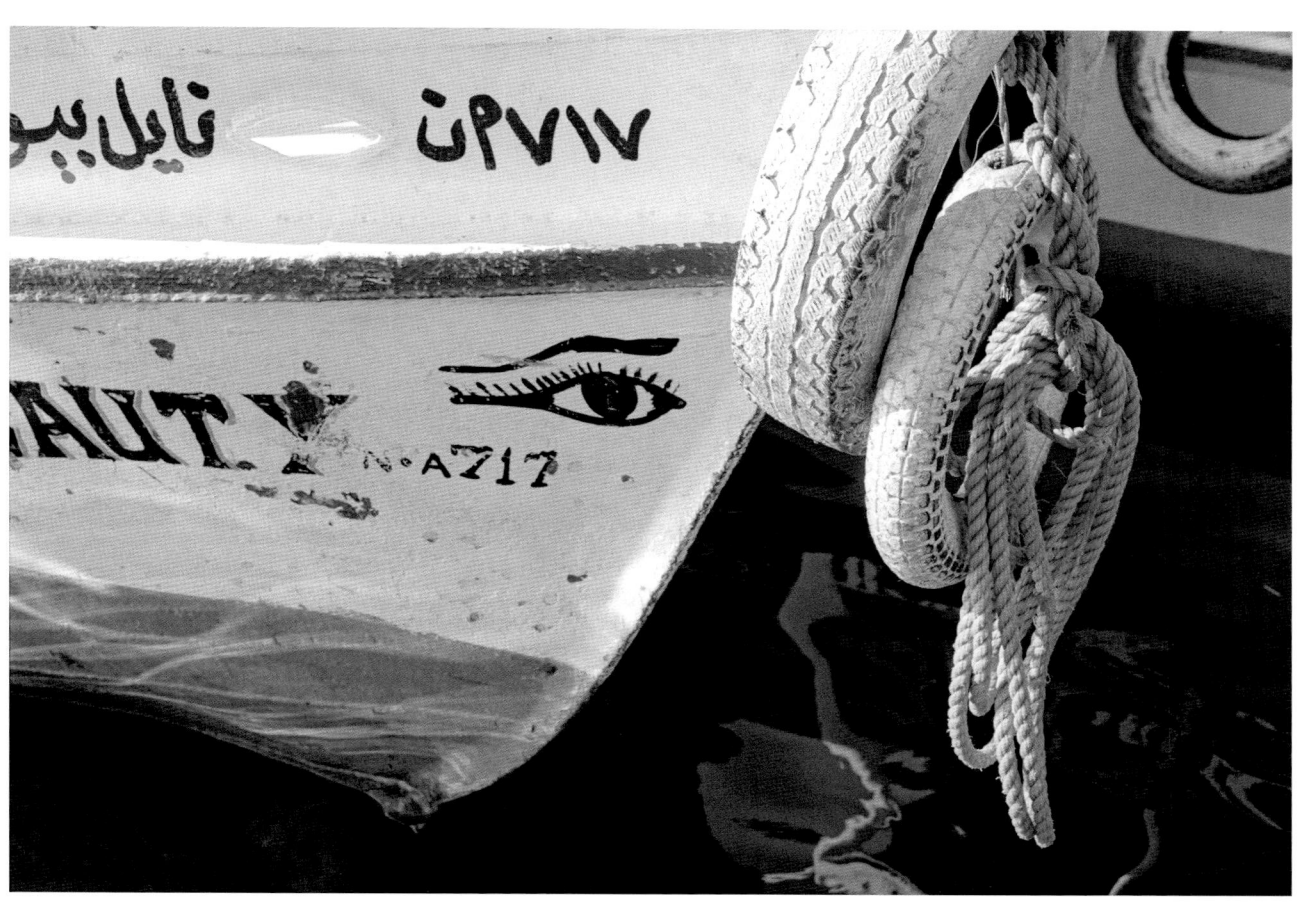

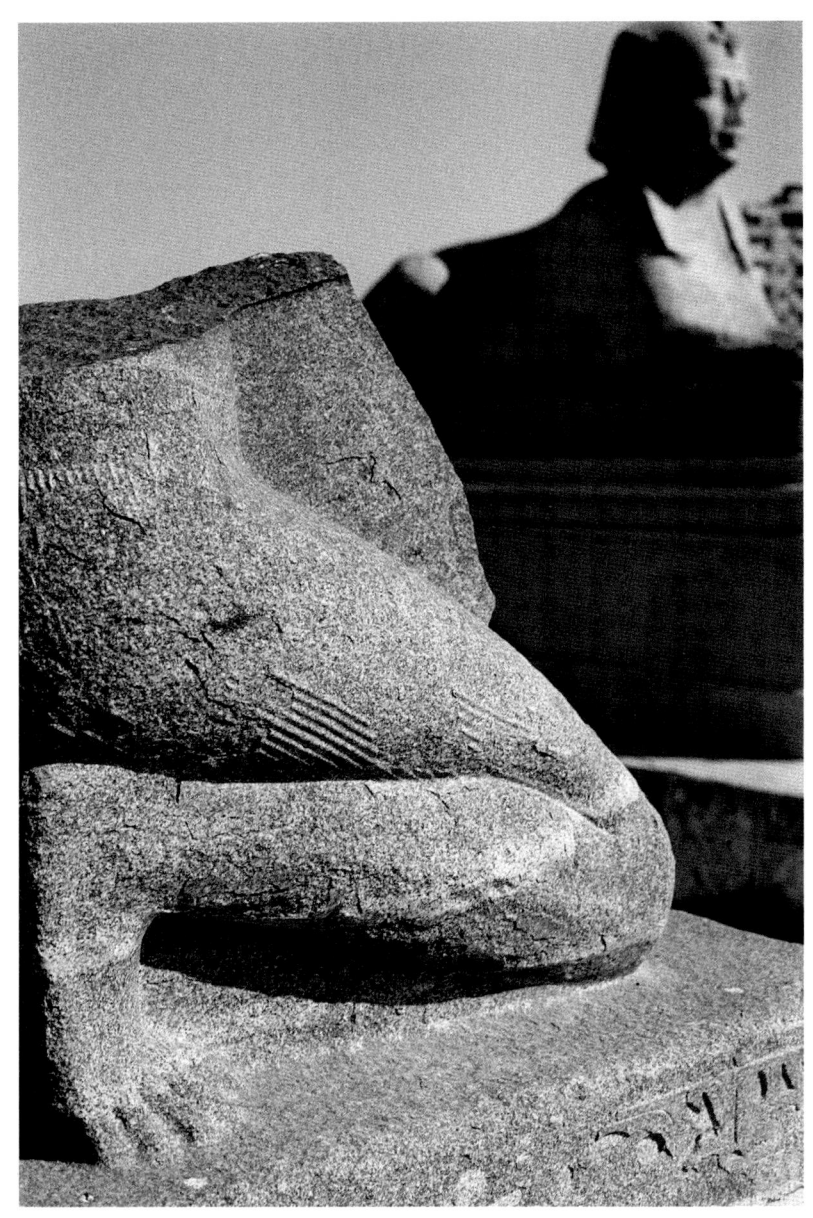

134

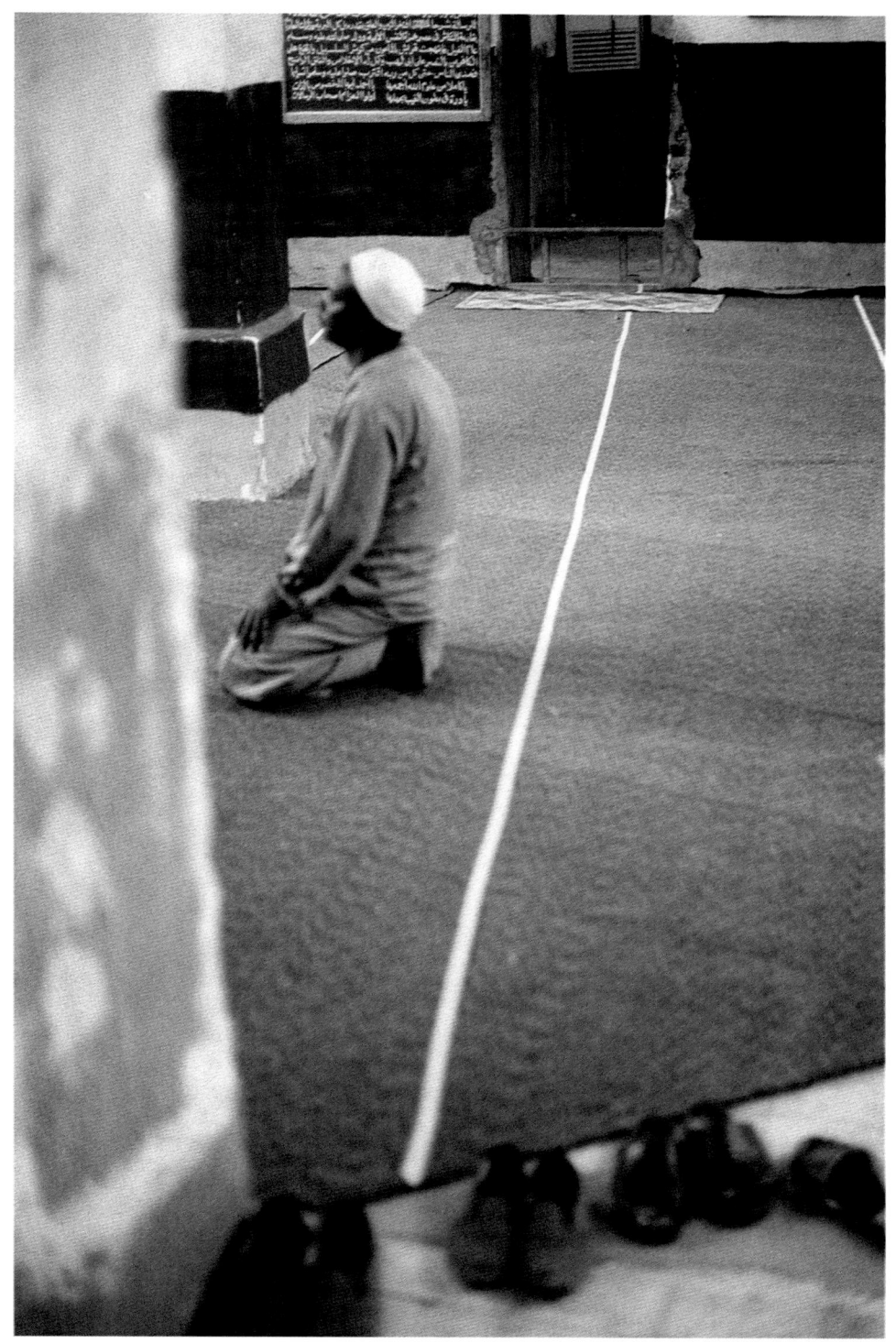

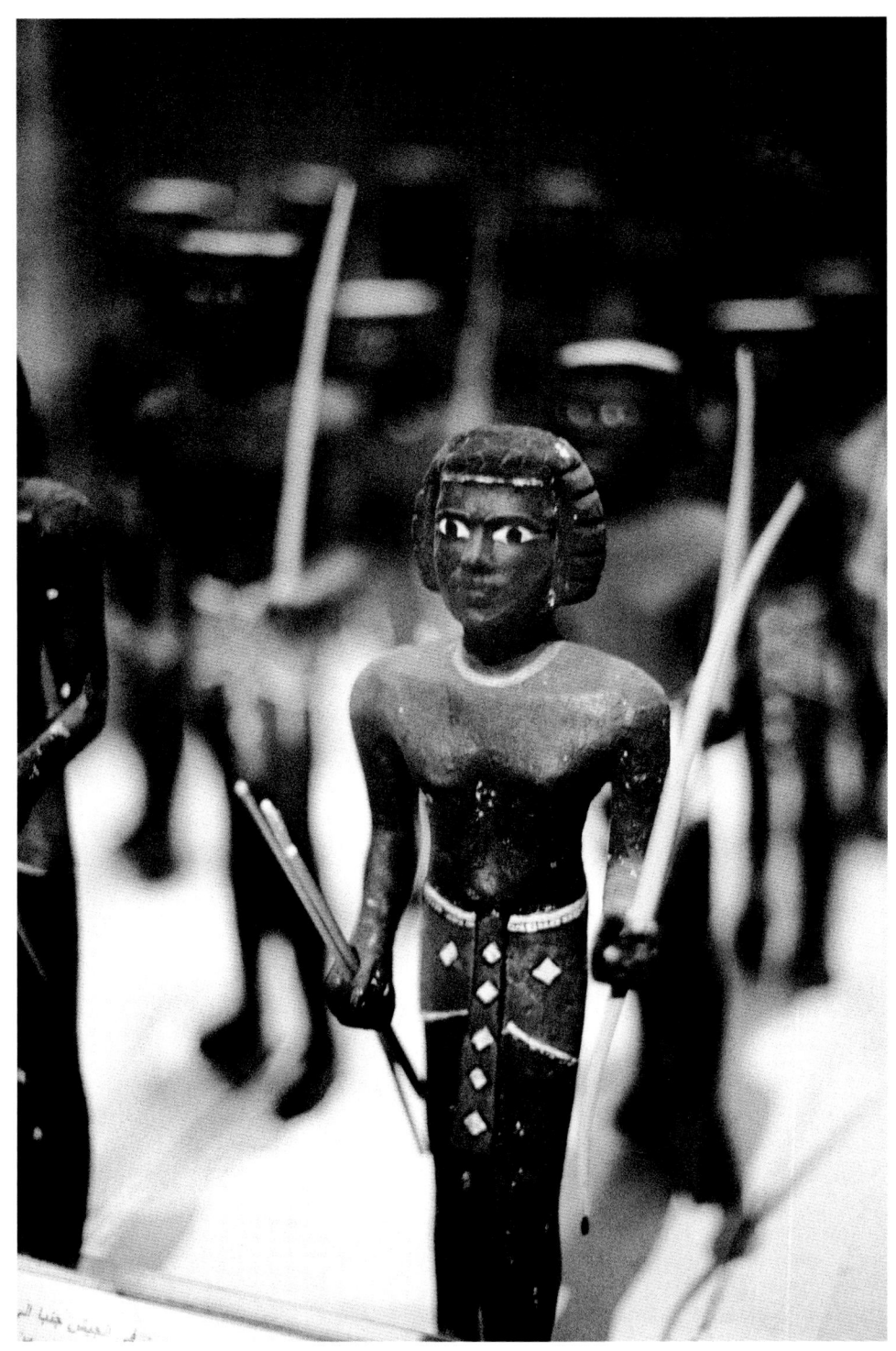

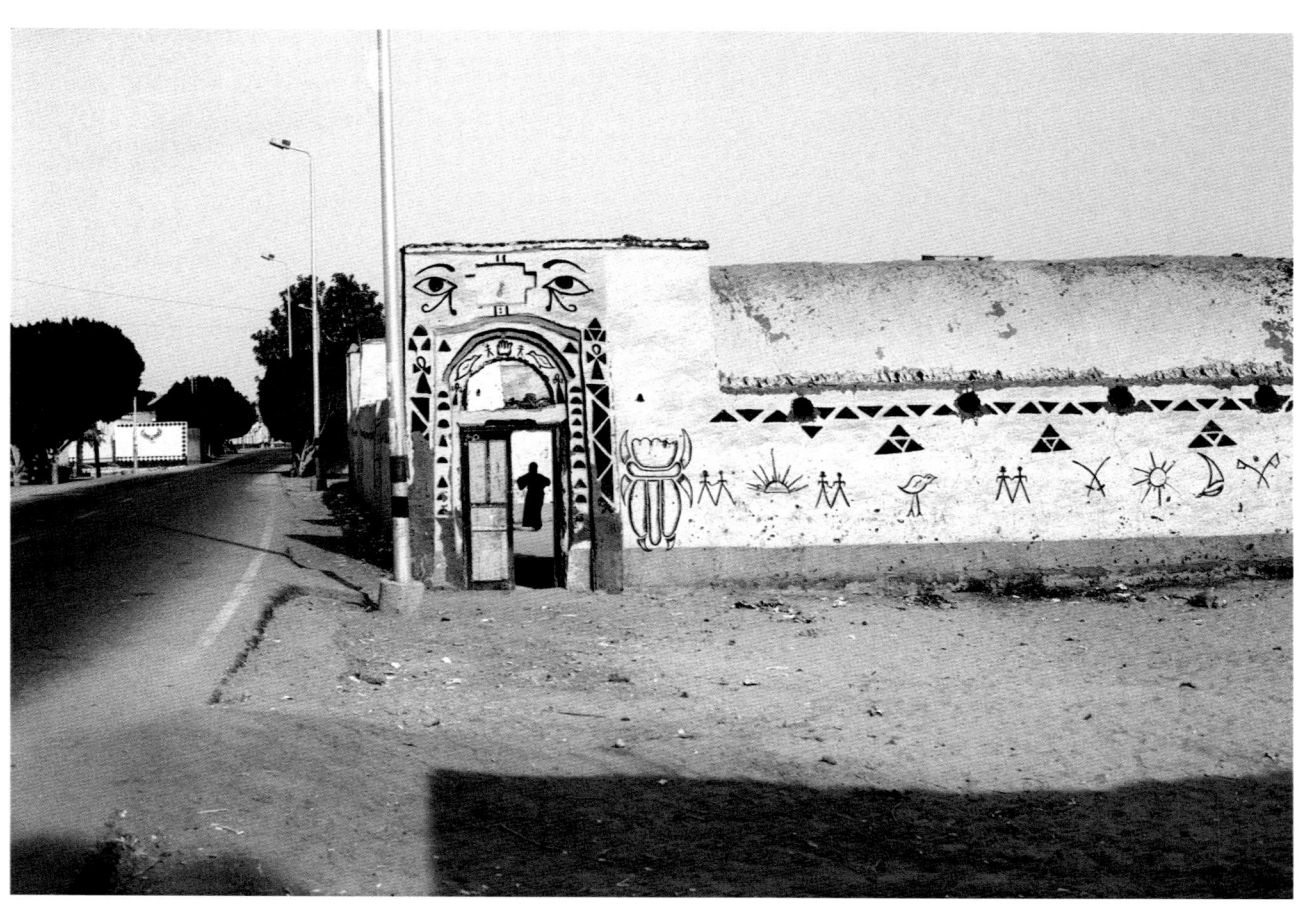

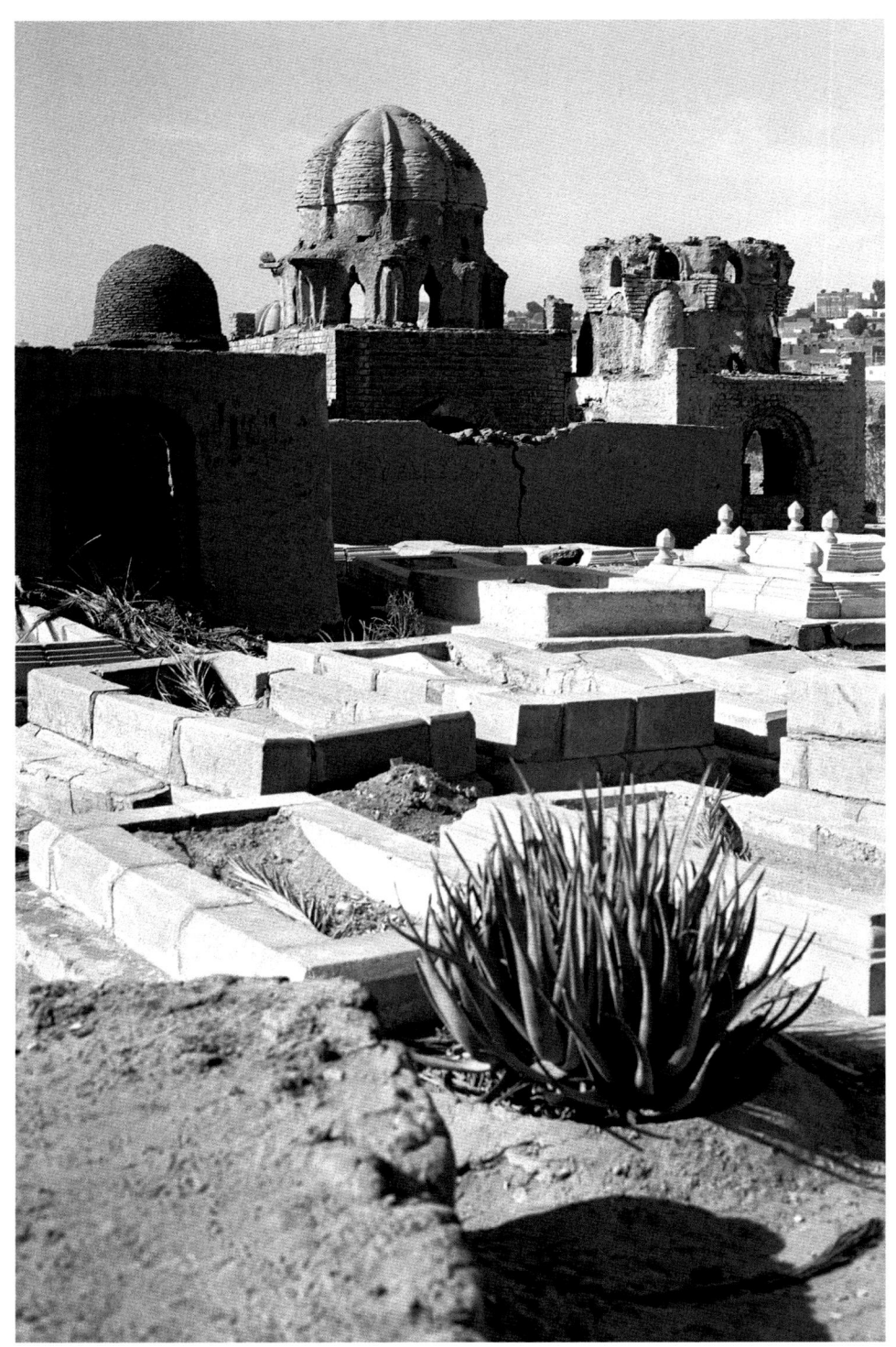

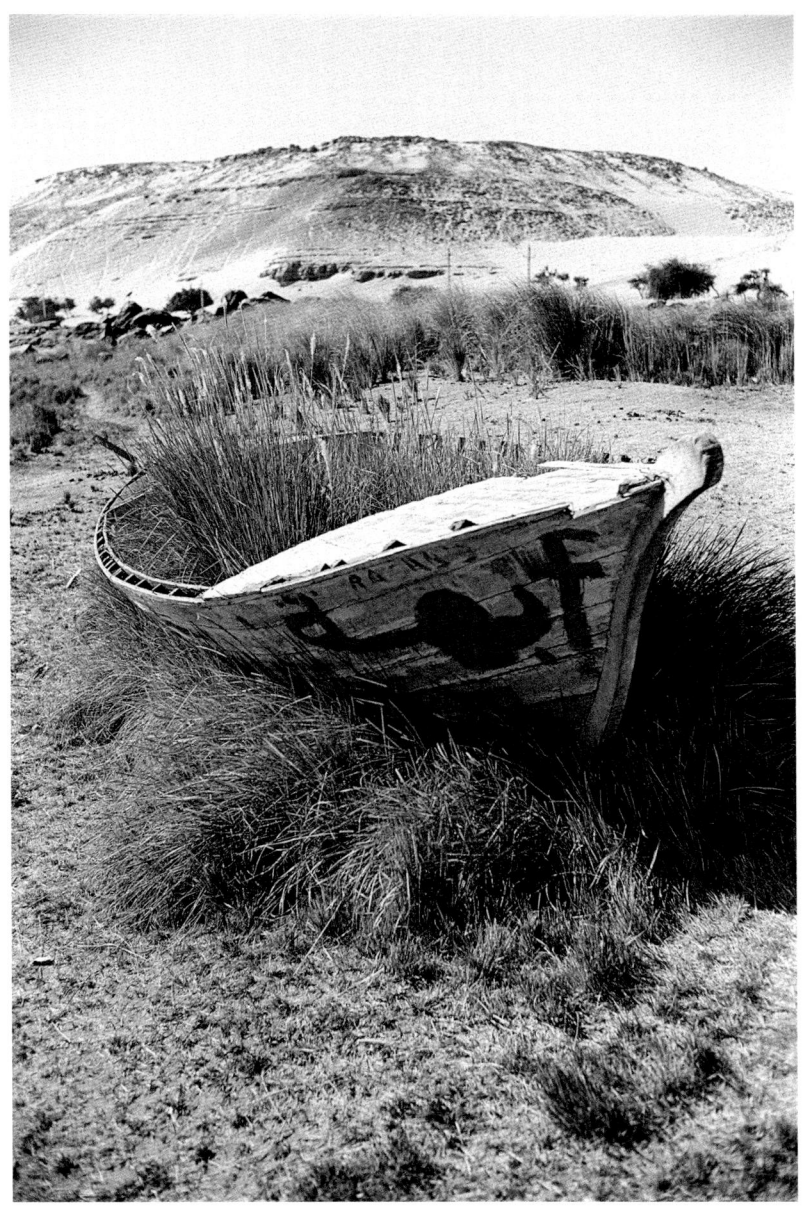

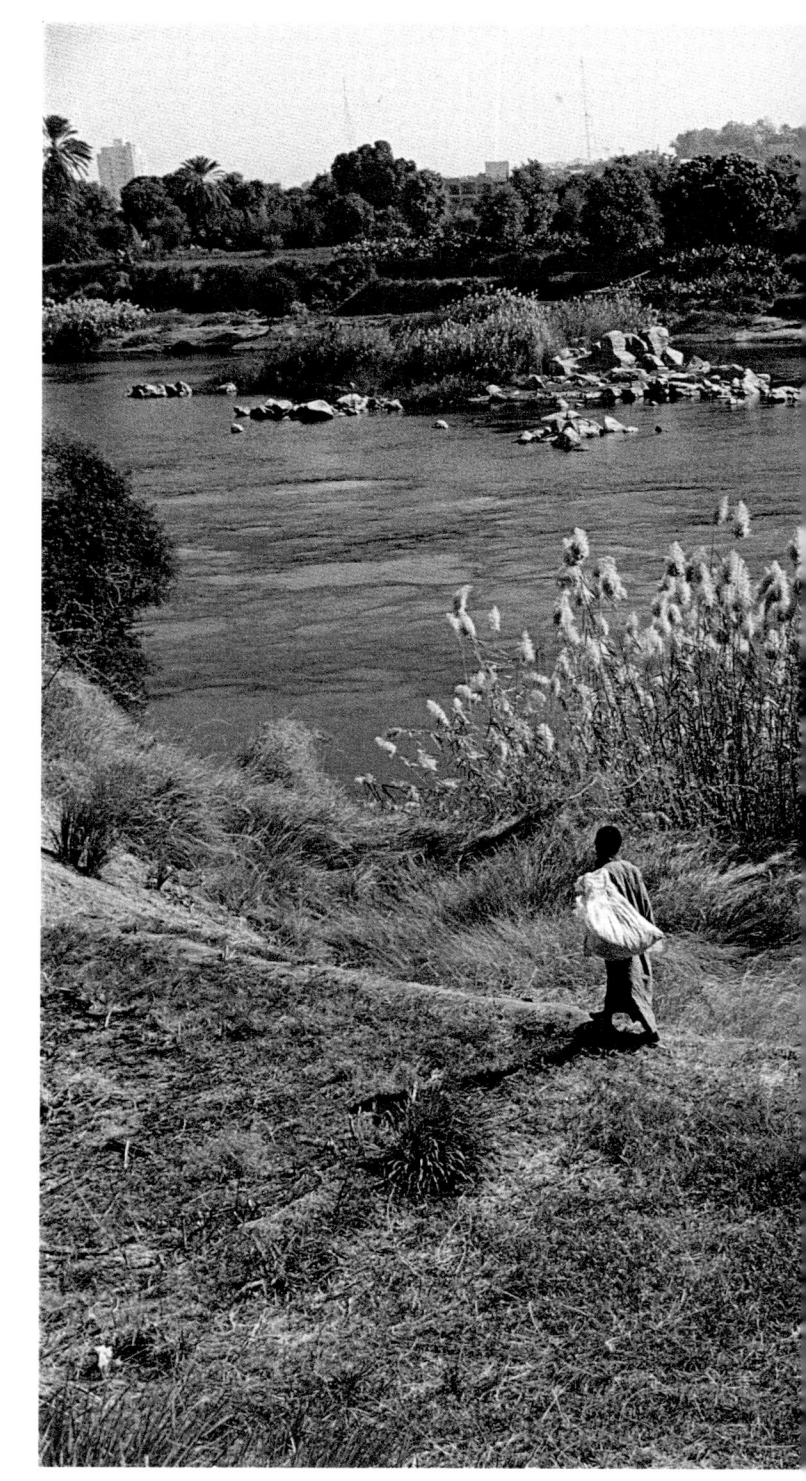

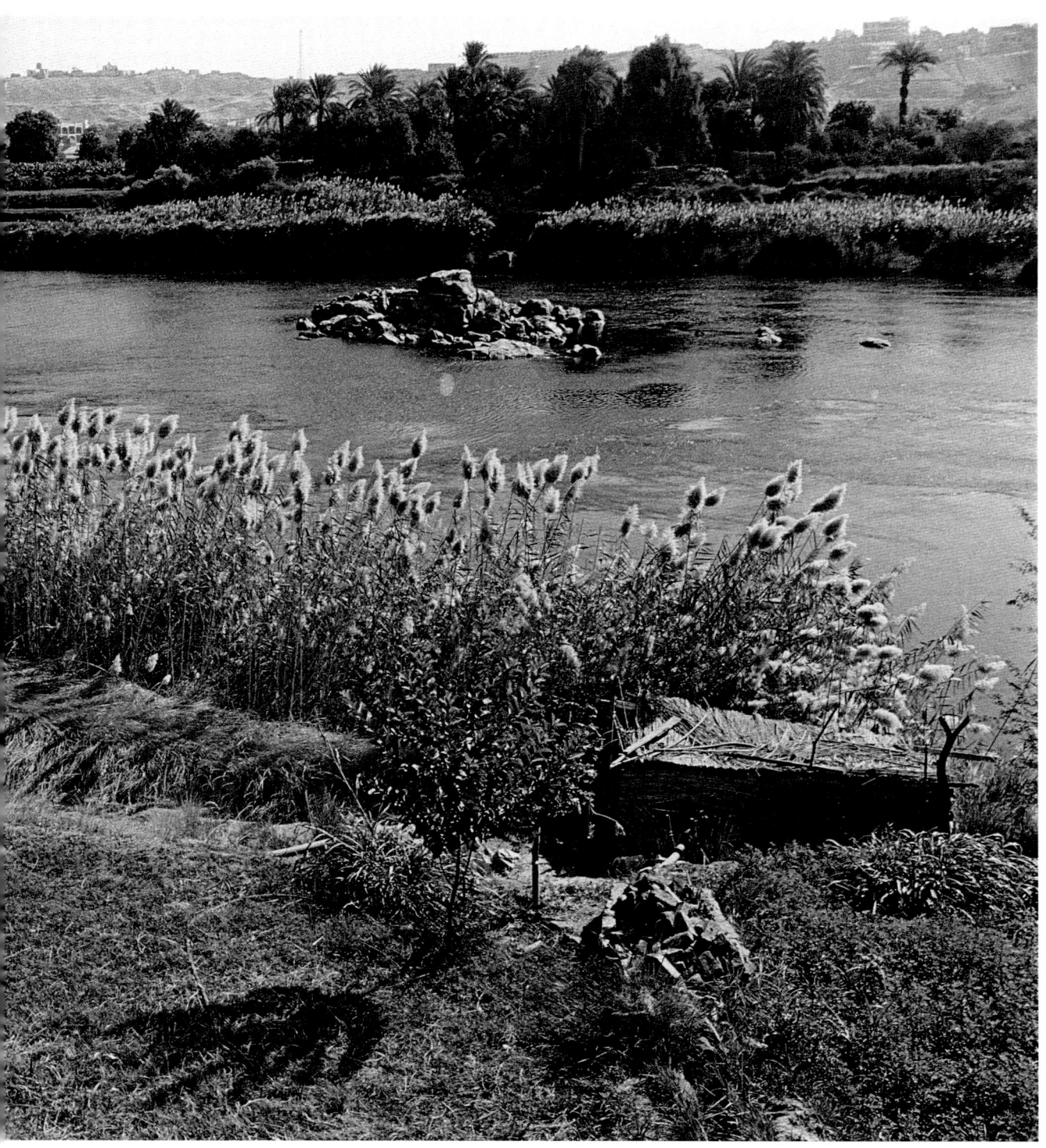

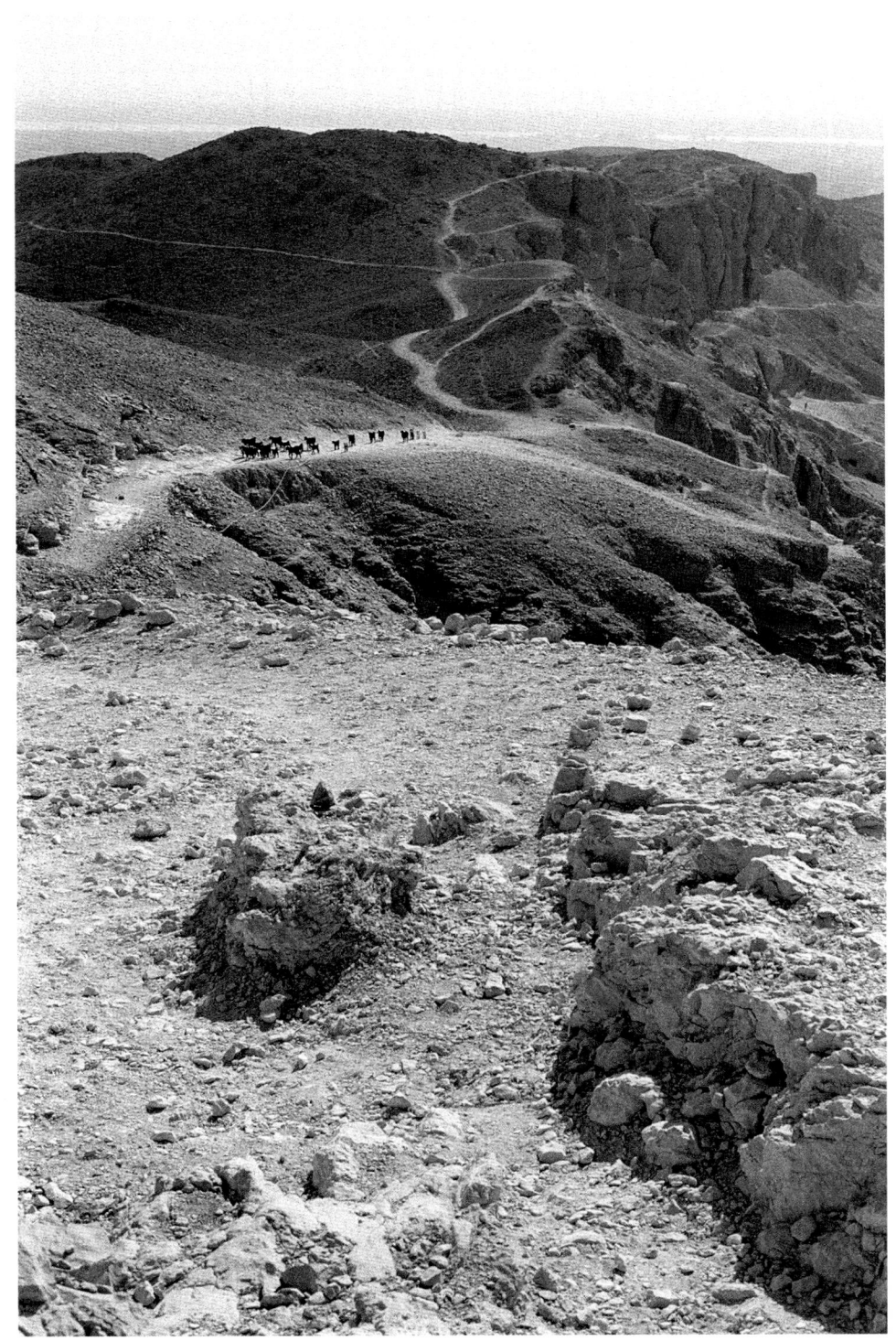

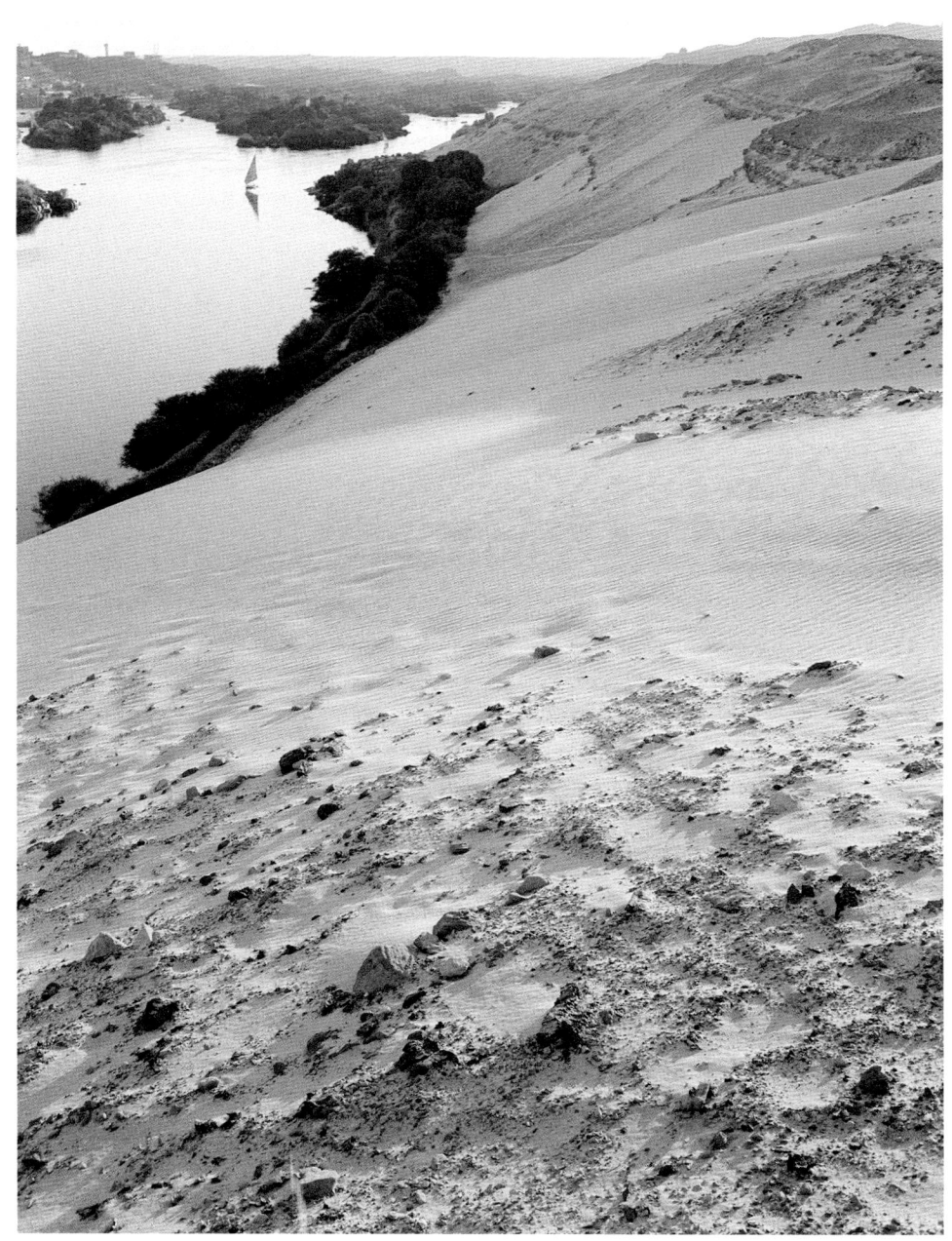

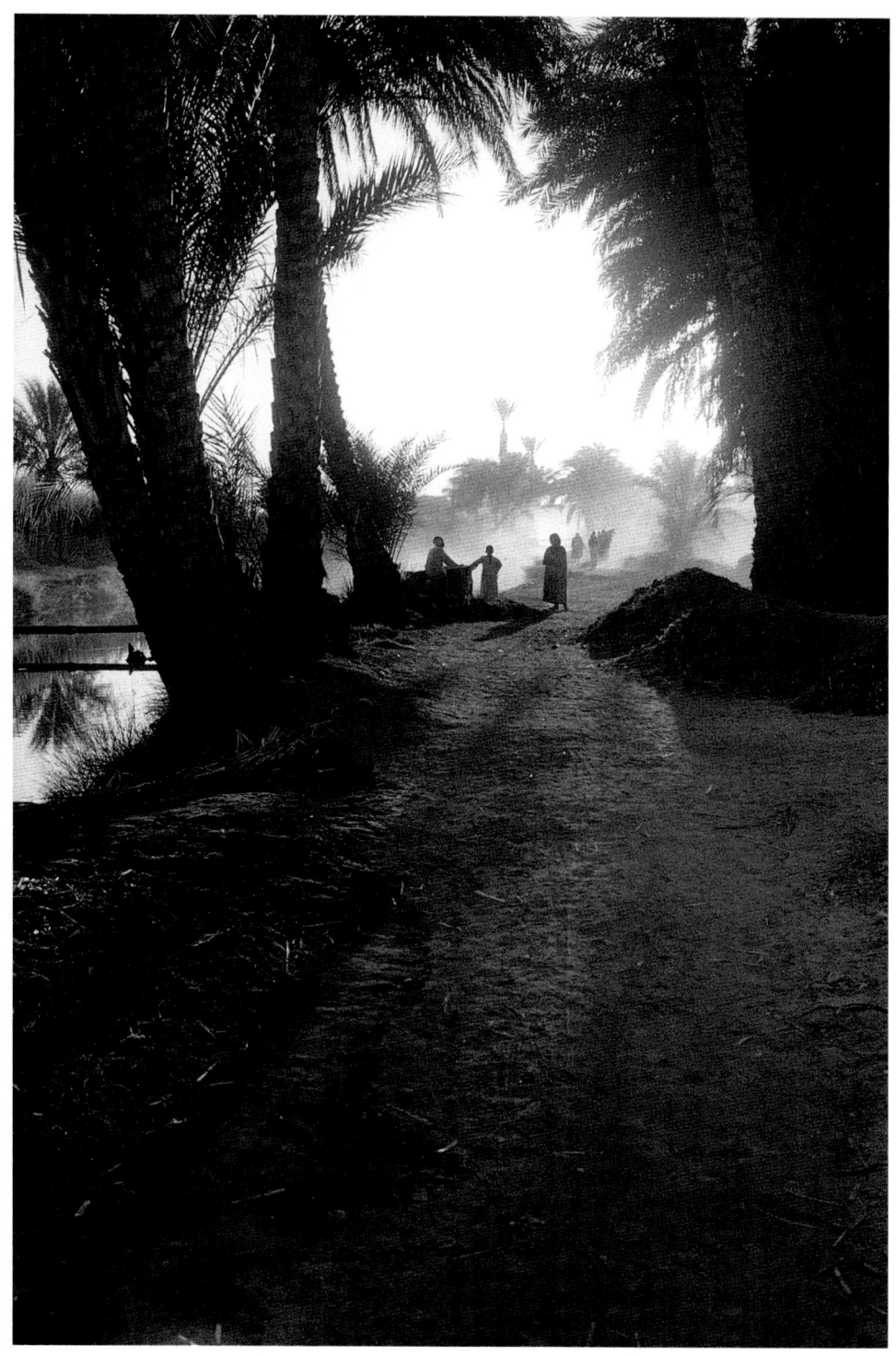

The Photographs

Page		Page		Page	
i	Luxor Temple, 1988	55	Cairo, 1990	101	Cairo, 1990
ii	Cairo, 1990	56	Aswan, 2008	103	The Nile, 2000
iv	Giza, 1990	57	Aswan, 2008	104	Gurna, 1995
13	Luxor, 1998	58	Elephantine Island, 2008	105	The Nile, 1996
14	Aswan, 2008	59	Aswan, 2002	106	Alexandria, 2004
15	Luxor Temple, 1998	60–61	Alexandria, 2004	107	Fayoum, 2004
16	Alexandria, 2004	62	Cairo, 2000	108	Alexandria, 2004
17	Cairo Museum, 2004	63	Alexandria, 2004	109	Luxor, 1995
18	Giza, 1996	64	Elephantine Island, 2004	110	Alexandria, 2004
19	Aswan, 2009	65	Gharb Aswan, 2004	111	Karnak Temple, 2004
20	Karnak Temple, 2004	66	Elephantine Island, 2008	112–13	The Nile, 2000
21	Giza, 1988	67	Cairo, 2004	114	Luxor, 2004
22–23	Aswan, 2009	69	Cairo Museum, 2004	115	Madinat Habu, 2004
24	Gharb Aswan, 2003	70	Sehel Island, 1998	117	Aswan, 2003
25	Gharb Aswan, 2003	71	Karnak Temple, 2004	118	Luxor, 2004
26	Elephantine Island, 2002	72	Alexandria, 2004	119	Luxor, 2004
27	Elephantine Island, 1996	73	Elephantine Island, 2008	120	Gharb Aswan, 2008
28	Fayoum, 2004	74	Aswan, 2004	121	Gharb Aswan, 2003
29	Village near Aswan, 2008	75	Sehel Island, 2002	122	Alexandria, 2004
30	Luxor, 2004	76	Luxor, 2004	123	Madinat Habu, 1996
31	Kom Ombo, 1988	77	The Nile, 2003	124	Cairo, 2004
32	Fayoum, 1990	78–79	Luxor, 1996	125	Alexandria, 2004
33	Alexandria, 2004	80	Cairo, 2004	126	Alexandria, 2004
34–35	Elephantine Island, 2002	81	Aswan, 1996	127	Gharb Aswan, 2004
36	Gurna, 1988	82	Sehel Island, 2000	128–29	The Nile, 2008
37	Alexandria, 2004	83	Aswan, 1999	130	Aswan, 2003
38	Elephantine Island, 1995	84	Sehel Island, 2002	131	Deir al-Bahari, 2004
39	Gharb Aswan, 2008	85	Kalabsha, 1999	132	Luxor, 1988
40	Cairo, 2004	87	Saqqara, 1990	133	Aswan, 2008
41	Gharb Aswan, 2008	88	Karnak Temple, 2004	134	Alexandria, 2004
42	Sehel Island, 2000	89	Alexandria, 2004	135	Aswan, 2004
43	Aswan, 1999	90	Aswan, 2004	136	Aswan, 2008
44	Luxor, 2004	91	Cairo, 2004	137	Gharb Aswan, 2008
45	Alexandria, 2004	92	Alexandria, 2004	138	Aswan, 2008
47	Aswan, 2000	93	Alexandria, 2004	139	Aswan, 2000
48	Kalabsha, 2008	94	Cairo, 1990	140–41	Aswan, 2000
49	Karnak Temple, 2004	95	Cairo, 1990	142	Luxor, 2004
50–51	Giza, 2004	96–97	Giza, 1988	143	Luxor, 2002
52	Aswan, 2008	98	Aswan, 2002	145	Luxor, 1998
53	Madinat Habu, 2004	99	Cairo, 2004		
54	Gharb Aswan, 2008	100	Sehel Island, 2003		

Xavier Roy

Xavier Roy was born in Bize in the southwest of France, the son of an artist mother and a father in advertising. He began his career in the musical publishing company Vogue. In 1968 he joined Midem Organisation (today Reed Midem), where he became general manager and then chief executive between 1989 and 2003. During his career he was made an Officer of the Ordre National du Mérite, a Knight of the Légion d'Honneur, and Commandeur des Arts et Lettres.

During these years he traveled widely around the world—to India, Egypt, Indonesia, Japan, the United States, Africa, South America—along the way developing a great passion for photography, his first camera a Nikkormat bought in Singapore in 1977. He also discovered the great masters of photography, such as Kertesz, Cartier-Bresson, Salgado, and Man Ray.

In 1985 he met Jean François Leroy, editor of *Photo Magazine*, who published his first photographs in a feature called "Photos aux 100 visas," and it was this publication that inspired Xavier to carry through his passion. In December 2003 he quits his professional career at Reed Midem to dedicate himself entirely to photography.

Exhibitions

2009 "The Other Saint-Tropez," Saint-Tropez
2008 "Viva o Brasil!," a touring exhibition in
–2009 the main cites of Brazil (Sao Paulo, Rio de Janeiro, Brasilia)
2008 "Détournements" (with sculptor Marie-Virginie Dru), Anne et Just Jaeckin Gallery, Paris (May); Ambassade du Tourisme, Saint-Tropez (July); photographs of Brazil and Madagascar
2006 "En Égypte," Forêt Verte Gallery, Paris—selected for the Month of the Photo
2006 "Enfances," UGGC Art Showroom, Paris
2005 "Cuba," Chambre Claire Gallery, Paris
2005 "L'eau: la Vie," Nathalie Duchêne Gallery, Saint-Tropez
2005 "Children," Palais des Festivals, Cannes
2004 "L'Âme Cubaine," Maison de l'Amérique Latine, Paris
2004 "Elsewhere," Broomstreet Gallery, New York
2003 Banville Showroom, Paris (with sculptor Armelle Chatriot)
2003 "Itinéraire des photographes voyageurs," Bordeaux (with 23 other photographers)
2002 "Elsewhere," Château de Suffren Gallery, Saint Tropez
2002 "Instant d'ailleurs," Musée de la Castre, Cannes

Publications

2009 *Viva o Brasil!*, Foreword by Sébastien Roy, Imprensa Oficial and Instituto Totem Cultural, Brazil. 85 photographs.
2009 *L'Autre Saint-Tropez*, Foreword by Dany Lartigue, Images en Manoeuvres, Marseilles. 75 photographs.
2007 *All Our Children,* Edel, Germany. 85 photographs.
2004 *L'Âme cubaine*, Foreword by Bernard Plossu, Flammarion, Paris. 90 photographs.
2001 *Instants d'Ailleurs*, Foreword by Bernard Plossu, catalog of 80 photographs in an exhibition at the Musée de la Castre, Cannes.

Plus numerous articles in the international photographic and general press.

Thanks

—to Neil Hewison, of the American University in Cairo Press, who sent me this mail on 21 September 2005: "Dear Xavier, Thank you—the pictures arrived safely, and we have enjoyed looking through them. They really are excellent photographs of Egypt—evocative, empathetic, and often humorous—and I hope we are able to publish a book of them." Today, after five years, this book is published! Thanks to you, Neil, thanks to your personal commitment and unshakeable trust in this project.

—to Gamal al-Ghitani, whose magnificent text adds enormous value, nobility, and spirit to my photographs.

—to my wife Sophie, who shares the same love as I do for Egypt and the Egyptians. She is my 'third eye,' and has made an enormous contribution to my photographic career.

—to Christophe Pingaud and Evelyne Demey, who saw the photographs and had a real 'coup de coeur.' They agreed immediately to partner the American University in Cairo Press and publish the book in French.

—to Daniel Regard (Les Artisans du Regard, Paris), who did a superb and talented job on the scanning of the images.

—to Andrea El-Akshar for her creativity: she has made a remarkable design for this book.

—to Maurice Coriat and Gabriel Bauret for their constant support and friendship.

—to all those who have contributed with their talent and professionalism to the realization of this book, in particular Catriona Macrae, Brigitte Beaujean, and Jean Christophe Dolmenech (Central Color Laboratory).

—and of course all the Egyptian people I met during my eleven sojourns in their magnificent country.

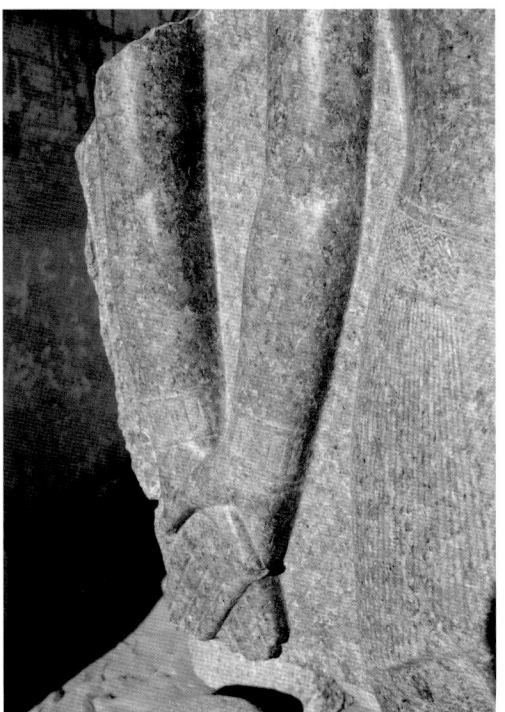

First Published in Great Britain in 2010 by
Haus Publishing Ltd
70 Cadogan Place
London SW1X 9AH
www.hauspublishing.com

This edition published by arrangement with
The American University in Cairo Press

Copyright © 2010 by Xavier Roy
Text copyright © 2010 by Gamal al-Ghitani

The moral right of the author has been asserted

A CIP catalogue record for this book
is available from the British Library

ISBN 978-1-906598-64-8

CONDITIONS OF SALE

All rights reserved. No part of this publication may be reproduced, stored in a retrieval system, or transmitted in any form or by any means, electronic, mechanical, photocopying, recording or otherwise, without the prior permission of the publisher.

This book is sold subject to the condition that it shall not, by way of trade or otherwise, be lent, re-sold, hired out or otherwise circulated without the publisher's prior consent in any form of binding or cover other than that in which it is published and without a similar condition including this condition being imposed on the subsequent purchase.

Designed by Andrea El-Akshar
Printed in China